A021852723

CW01402105

The labour aristocracy revisited

Takao Matsumura

The labour aristocracy revisited

The Victorian flint glass makers 1850–80

Manchester University Press

Published by
Manchester University Press
Oxford Road, Manchester M13 9PL, UK
and
51 Washington Street, Dover, N.H. 03820, USA

British Library cataloguing in publication data
Matsumura, Takao
    The labour aristocracy revisited
    The Victorian flint glass makers, 1850-1880
    1. Glass manufacture—Great Britain—History
    I. Title
    338.4'76661'0941   HD9623.G7

    ISBN 0-7190-0931-6

Library of Congress cataloging in publication data

Matsumura, Takao, 1942–
    The labour aristocracy revisited.
    Revision of thesis (Ph. D.)—Warwick University, 1976.
    Bibliography: p.173
    Includes index.
    1. Glass-workers—Great Britain—History—19th century.
    2. Trade-unions—Glass-workers—Great Britain—History—19th century.
    3. Skilled labor—Great Britain— History—19th century.
    I. Title.
    HD8039.G52G75 1983   331.7'6661'0941   83–7951
    ISBN 0-7190-0931-6

Printed and bound in Great Britain by
Biddles Ltd, Guildford and King's Lynn

Contents

List of tables

List of figures

Acknowledgements

This book is a revised and reconstructed version of my Warwick University Ph.D. thesis of 1976. I am indebted to more people than I am able to mention here. However, special thanks are due to the staff and students at the Centre for the Study of Social History, University of Warwick, in particular Professor Royden Harrison, who has supervised my research for four years. He read the manuscript thoroughly and gave me strict but warm-hearted criticism. Without his unfailing encouragement this work would not have been finished. I should also like to thank Dr Eric Taylor, who not only arranged for the loan of the *Flint Glass Makers Magazine,* but took me to the Black Country on a cold winter's day to help me realise that it was a real place with real people. Discussions with Professor Sidney Pollard, an external examiner of my thesis, Dr Tony Mason, Dr Geoffrey Crossick, Dr Eric Hopkins and Dr Frederick Kaijage were also invaluable and Richard Whipp and Jim Hagen read the manuscript.

The staffs of many libraries have been helpful. I would particularly like to thank those of Warwick University, the British Library, the Newspaper Library at Colindale, the British Library of Political and Economic Science, the Bishopsgate Institute and the Glass Manufacturers' Federation. I should also like to thank the staffs of the public libraries of Birmingham, Stourbridge and Brierley Hill. I was also helped by the staffs of the Public Record Office and the County Record Offices in Stafford and Worcester. Special thanks are due to Stevens & Williams Ltd of Stourbridge and Beatson Clark & Co. Ltd of Rotherham, who allowed me access to their records.

I also have a great debt to Japanese scholars. The late Professor Kinnosuke Otsuka, and Professors Chuhei Sugiyama and Chushichi Tsuzuki of Hitotsubashi University, Tokyo, suggested to me that a stay in England would be valuable and they have continuously encouraged my research. My colleagues, notably Professors Toshio Kurokawa, Kanae Iida, Masayoshi Chubachi and Katsumi Nakamura, at the Faculty of Economics in Keio University, Tokyo, showed great generosity by releasing me from teaching duties at the faculty for an exceptionally long period. I also received financial assistance from the Fukuzawa Fund of Keio University. Lastly, I am indebted to my wife, Rumiko, who throughout the writing of the book has shown patience and tolerance.

Introduction

This work attempts to provide a history of the flint glass makers in what was reputedly the classic age of the labour aristocracy. It tries to use that controversial concept to interpret the history of the glass makers while using the history of the glass makers to refine the concept itself. At any rate, the aim has been to set such a dialectic to work. In spite of the Webbs' attention to the flint glass makers and their union, little further research has been carried out, mainly because a major source, the *Flint Glass Makers Magazine*, has been missing. My research began with a rediscovery of a complete run of the magazine from its inception in 1851 to 1897.[1]

Pelling was correct in relating the concept of labour aristocracy to Marxist apologetics and polemics. Yet Marx hardly used the expression.[2] It was Engels who first articulated this concept. In the mid-1880s Engels was convinced that since 1848 'a permanent improvement can be recognised for two "protected" sections only of the working class'; (1) the factory workers protected by the Factory Acts and (2) the great trade unions of the engineers, the carpenters and joiners and the bricklayers. 'They form an aristocracy among the working class; they have succeeded in enforcing for themselves a relatively comfortable position, and they accept it as final.'[3] Engels clearly distinguished the labour aristocracy from 'the great mass of working people' but often confused the aristocracy with 'embourgeoisement'. The aristocracy was, for Engels, 'very nice people indeed nowadays to deal with, for any sensible capitalist in particular and for the whole capitalist class in general'.[4] Lenin referred to the labour aristocracy by drawing from British experience and related it to imperialism. The super-profits of monopolistic capital, which originated from capital exports to colonies, accounted for the existence of the labour aristocracy. 'The capitalists *can* devote a part (and not a small one, at that!) of these superprofits to bribe *their own* workers, to create something like an alliance (recall the celebrated "alliances" described by the Webbs of English trade unions and employers) between the workers of the given nation and their capitalists *against* the other countries.'[5] Yet Lenin never spelled out exactly what was the relationship between the labour aristocracy and imperialism or how this 'bribery' was supposed to work. For him the question as to how this 'little sop' was distributed among labour ministers, labour officials, workers organised in narrow craft unions, office employees and so on was 'a secondary question'.[6]

In this book the concept of the labour aristocracy is not employed in explaining away the non-occurrence of the proletarian revolution, but rather as an indispensable ingredient in the explanation of the dramatic change which overtook the institutional life and temper of British labour between the second and the third quarters of the nineteenth century. The world of labour in the age of the *Bee-Hive* was very different from what it had been in the age of the *Northern Star*. This change has to be accounted for. In recent years British labour historians have argued about the reality and usefulness of the concept of a labour aristocracy. To Eric Hobsbawm we owe what might be termed an 'economic anatomy'. In his pioneering study Hobsbawm established six criteria: (1) the level and regularity of a worker's earnings, (2) prospects of social security, (3) conditions of work, (4) relations with the social strata above and below, (5) general conditions of living, (6) prospects of future advance for the worker and his children.[7] He regarded the first as the most important. Then he turned his attention from the definitional problem to the size of this aristocracy. He thought it could be measured by wage rates and membership of trade unions, and came to the conclusion that about 10 per cent of the working class constituted the labour aristocracy in its classic period, 1840–90.[8] Trygve Tholfsen, who, implicitly challenging Hobsbawm's hard distinction between the labour aristocracy and the 'respectable working men', began a cultural delineation.[9] Royden Harrison developed Hobsbawm's argument by exploring with a new sophistication the stratum's political consciousness and behaviour. Whereas Hobsbawm concentrated his attention mainly upon the economic dimension, Harrison turned to complicated differences between the economic, social and political dimensions. What Harrison emphasised was the 'profound gulf between the "aristocracy" and the "plebeians", between the organised and the unorganised', although this did not prevent 'the spokesmen of the former stratum from presuming to speak on behalf of all the working classes. *Socially* and *industrially* the labour aristocracy took care to separate itself from the vast labouring majority, but *in politics* it sometimes found it convenient to pose as the authentic spokesman of the working classes as a whole.'[10] Thus Harrison led us away from the notion that the labour aristocracy was always and everywhere a retarding force, and contended that the aristocracy had its 'golden age' in the third quarter of the nineteenth century rather than in the longer period identified by Hobsbawm.

Valuable contributions to the debate have been made by R. Q. Gray, Geoffrey Crossick, John Foster and less centrally by Eric Hopkins and G. Stedman Jones,[11] by introducing a fresh sense of its sociological dimension, in which it is related not merely to the experience of particular trades, but to particular communities. 'The use of the term "aristocrats",' they insist, 'implies a social and cultural demarcation.'[12] Crossick has chosen the towns of Kentish London, Gray Edinburgh and Foster mainly Oldham. They laid stress on the life style of workers in particular communities, socio-spatial segregation, marriage patterns, leisure activities and so on, but in some respects they differed from each other. Foster adapted Lenin's theory of imperialism and the existence of the labour aristocracy retrospectively to the mid-nineteenth century, when 'one gets a massive switch to capital exports, a general increase in wage differentials and the rapid disintegration of a previously powerful working-class movement'.[13] He demonstrated that 'Oldham's bourgeoisie consciously *used* its industrial power ... to split the labour force and bribe its upper layers into political acquiescence'.[14] Gray denied Foster's conscious process of 'social control' and stressed the spontaneous process of 'hegemony'. Preoccupied with Gramsci's theory of 'hegemony', Gray stressed the necessity of examining 'the ensemble of organisms commonly called "private",[15] voluntary organisations, the provision of facilities for leisure, thrift and adult education'. The ruling class was able to limit working-class struggle by means of a socio-cultural hegemony, exerted partly through 'the ensemble'. For Gray's argument 'the links between economic position and ideological structures are central . . . The formation of a labour aristocracy made possible particular forms of ideological hegemony, which set limits on the articulation of working-class consciousness.'[16] Crossick's attempt at integrating both 'economic' and social dimensions is an attempt to overcome, on the one hand, 'Foster's rigid economic determinism' and, on the other, Tholfsen's work, which is 'fundamentally idealist in its analysis of ideology and consciousness'.[17] Traditionally historians have thought that the skilled artisans in the mid-Victorian period accepted middle-class ideology such as 'respectability' or 'independence'. But what Crossick made clear was that the ideology of the labour aristocracy should not be identified with that of the middle class: they were not indoctrinated with, or persuaded to accept, middle-class values and ideals. Both Gray and Crossick criticised Hobsbawm's method as 'economic determinism'. It is undeniable that their analysis of social or cultural aspects in the context of the local community is deeply linked with the various attempts to revise fundamental aspects of Marxism in the last few years. All these researches were locally focused and consequently sharpened the issues identified in the national surveys attempted by Hobsbawm and Harrison.

Of course, the development of the study of labour aristocracy has been challenged. According to Henry Pelling, the concept 'does more harm than good to historical truth'.[18] He contended that 'the term "labour aristocracy" really derives its significance from its use by Marxist writers in their efforts to reconcile the observable phenomena of Victorian and Edwardian life with the Marxist theory of economic development'.[19] At the same time, however, he insisted that 'the Marxist historians have completely got the wrong end of the stick: militancy was much more likely to be found among the better-off than among the poorer workers'.[20] Pelling's logic is perplexing. He insists that the concept of the labour aristocracy is meaningless, and then adds that the better-off were more radical than the rest of the working class.[21] He doubted whether such a concept could help in accounting for a 'change' before and after the mid-century.

A. E. Musson denied that there was a 'change' which needed to be explained.[22] Patrick Joyce and others discovered that it simply did not 'turn up' in their industries or places. Joyce wrote that 'the application of the "labour aristocracy" notion to the factory worker does not seem especially productive'.[23] He insists that 'a concentration on what is taken to be an elite in the working class not only diverts attention from the majority, but fails also to discern that what working people had in common is more important for an understanding of class relationships than that which is held to have divided them in work and in the life beyond work '.[24]

My research employs the concept of a labour aristocracy. The aristocracy is the upper stratum of the working class and its members distinguish themselves as a superior group from other working men both at work and in the wider community. Any denial of the reality of the labour aristocracy as a point of mid-Victorian social awareness must present an alternative picture which accommodates the contemporary 'common place'[25] within a more adequate account of the working class. The content and size of the aristocracy must have varied from trade to trade and from region to region. If Joyce is right about its irrelevance for his textile workers in the North, it is equally indispensable for the flint glass makers.

My research is an occupational study. In spite of fashionable cultural/social analysis it should be stressed that the basic condition for the existence of the labour aristocracy was at the point of production. In this sense I begin with neither Lenin's nor Gramsci's theory, but go back to Marx's analysis of the labour process, particularly of the division of labour. It was in 'the economic' dimension that Hobsbawm's pioneering contribution was most marked, but since he used the level and regularity of a worker's earnings as the 'main criterion' of his six, the other five remained almost untouched. My research attempts to enlarge Hobsbawm's 'economic' consideration in concrete ways. As John Field has pointed out, the debate about the labour aristocracy has been conducted 'without any discussion of exactly *what* constitutes the "economic"'.[26] In my work the 'economic' dimension is supposed to have three meanings.

First, 'the economic' relates to the industrial structure and market position of the products. Certainly Victorian economic prosperity between around 1850 and the mid-1870s provided a necessary condition for the formation of a labour aristocracy. In glass-making a 'golden age' started around mid-century, symbolically with the Crystal Palace in the Great Exhibition of 1851, and ended with the onset of depression in the early 1870s. The formation of the dual structure in the flint-glass market (blown glass and pressed glass) after 1850 was of vital importance for the periodisation of the labour aristocracy. Second, the analysis of the 'economic' must be extended to the production process at factory or workshop level, because the stratification of working men was formed within the labour process. Particularly important was the division of labour within the work groups, which created a hierarchy corresponding to specific skills. The superior workers in the hierarchy discriminated against the less skilled and thus emerged as labour aristocrats. Here is the key to the problem of why the labour aristocracy showed political sympathy with the working class as a whole but not with kindred workers. In this context 'skill' is definitely important. More than that, wage rates, methods of wage payment, hours of work, the weekly working cycle, the environment in the factory, promotion of workers from lower to higher status, all these factors constituted the 'economic'. Third, the labour aristocracy should be considered not only in terms of wage differentials between the skilled and the unskilled but in terms of the life cycle of individual workers. A young worker who was apprenticed might belong to the 'reserve army' of labour aristocrats but not to the labour aristocracy in a literal sense. With promotion he might enter the territory of the labour aristocracy after passing beyond a certain wage level. Although wage curves over a lifetime differed from trade to trade, it is possible to supply a wage curve for the average glass-makers. The labour aristocracy should be understood also in terms of the hereditary transmission of skills from father to son. A dynamic analysis in this sense provides a way forward.

This work dwells on such an enlarged 'economic' dimension of the labour aristocracy because of the fact that no previous work has adequately explored it. At the same time, however, the work also embodies a social/community analysis, because the process of stratification in social relationships in the local community is indispensable for an understanding of the social dimension of the labour aristocracy. As a local community special attention is paid to a major flint glass-producing area, Stourbridge.[27] Presumably both existence and behaviour in big cities like Gray's Edinburgh and Crossick's Kentish London differed from those in small towns where specific industries were concentrated. It can be imagined that in a small town like Stourbridge a superiority in the 'economic' sphere related more directly to social stratification in the district than would be the case in big towns. Yet the ambivalence in the attitudes of glass makers as between the trade and the local community existed. This ambivalence is explored.

The labour aristocrats' position both at work and in the community was secured and strengthened by their trade union. Accordingly the structure and policies of the union require close study. Apprentice restriction, promotion restriction, friendly benefits, emigration, co-operation, and the government and financial system of the union must be analysed so as to understand how the prestigious position of skilled workers at the point of production was secured. In the local community a problem of to what extent the union took the initiative in local cultural activities such as festivals and the local movement for parliamentary reform is also examined. The study of the flint glass makers union leads us to re-examine the usefulness and reality of 'New Model' unionism. Since the early 1960s a critique of the Webbs' methodology and, more specifically, a denial of their 'the New Spirit and the New Model' as 'a piece of historical fiction' or 'the greatest distortion by the Webbs' became fashionable.[28] Nonetheless, it is a mistake to neglect the significance of the establishment of the *national* union around mid-century. In the study of flint glass makers a 'New Model' union theory is indispensable, although it must be revised in some respects. Moreover, an attempt is made to solve a problem presented by the Webbs' account of mid-Victorian trade unionism: if the flint glass makers' union was such a leading example of the 'New Spirit and the New Model', how did it come about that it identified itself with the *Bee-Hive* and George Potter? Not all the labour aristocrats supported the Junta. It is too easy to think that the mid-Victorian labour aristocracy abandoned the strike weapon and entered into a happy mutual relationship with their employers. The flint glass makers' union never abandoned the strike weapon, despite the Webbs' indication that they did. Of course, industrial relations and militancy varied from time to time and from region to region but the flint glass makers' strike of 1858–59 is worthy of investigation. My research attempts to connect in concrete ways the 'economic', social and political dimension, or the trade and the local community, of the labour aristocracy, by means of the analysis of a trade union. Therefore this book begins with an analysis of the 'economic' at the point of production (chapters one, two and three), and then examines the trade union (chapters four and five), and finally passes to the local community (chapter six).

Notes

1 When the Webbs wrote *The History of Trade Unionism* in 1894 the *Flint Glass Makers Magazine* was already 'not preserved in any Public Library' so that they were indebted to Mr Haddleton, a flint glass maker and the seventh secretary of the Birmingham Trades Council from 1885 to 1895, who possessed a complete set (S. and B. Webb, *History of Trade Unionism*, London, 1894 edition, p. 179, n. 3, and 1920 edition p. 197, n. 3—hereafter the 1920 edition will be cited—and J. Corbett, *The Birmingham Trades Council, 1860–1966*, London, 1966, p. 186). Sidney took 256 pages of notes (Webb Trade Union Collection, Section A, vol. XLIII, 1; British Library of Political and Economic Science, London). The Webbs assessed the *Magazine* as 'the best' of trade publications and 'the only one which has enjoyed a continuous existence (from the mid-nineteenth century) down to the present day' (Webb, *History of Trade Unionism*, p. 197). Not only the Webbs but other contemporaries valued the *Magazine* highly. For instance, the *Birmingham Mercury* noted that 'social, commercial, and educational questions are discussed in well-reasoned articles, which show that there is an amount of intelligence in the operative portion of the Glass-making community highly creditable to them' (10 April 1852). When D. N. Sandilands researched the Midland flint glass makers in the late 1920s he was still able to use this complete set 'through the kindness of the officers of the Birmingham District of the Flint Glass Makers Society' (D. N. Sandilands, 'The History of the Midland Glass Industry, with Special Reference to the Flint Glass Section', M. Com. thesis, University of Birmingham, 1929, foreword). Thereafter the *Magazine* was 'lost'. In 1962 an editorial in the *Bulletin of the Society for the Study of Labour History* asked the members 'what has become of the Flint Glass Maker's Magazine ... Let us hope that our members in Birmingham can discover its whereabouts' (*Bulletin*, No. III, autumn 1961, p. 1). The discovery was

made by Dr Eric Taylor in 1972 and my research owes much to the *Magazine*, now in the possession of Mr Price, a Stourbridge flint glass maker.

2 One of Marx's few uses of the term is found in his *Capital:* ' . . . I may be allowed to show, by one example, how industrial revulsions affect even the best-paid, the aristocracy, of the working-class' (K. Marx, *Capital*, vol. I, English edition, London, 1889, p. 685).

3 F. Engels, preface to the English edition of 1892; *The Condition of the Working Class in England*, 1845, trans. and ed. W. O. Henderson and W. H. Chaloner, 2nd edition, Oxford, 1971, p. 368.

4 *Ibid.*

5 V. I. Lenin, *Imperialism and the Split in Socialism*, 1916; *Collected Works*, Moscow, 1964, vol. XXIII, p. 114: quoted in E. J. Hobsbawm, 'Lenin and the "aristocracy of labour"', in *Revolutionaries. Contemporary Essays*, London, 1973, p. 125.

6 *Ibid.*, p. 115.

7 E. J. Hobsbawm, 'The labour aristocracy in nineteenth-century Britain', in *Labouring Men. Studies in the History of Labour*, London, 1964, p. 237.

8 *Ibid.*, p. 279. The result of Hobsbawm's calculation from Dudley Baxter's data was that about 11% of the working class, earning more than 28s a week, belonged to the labour aristocracy in the 1860s. (Dudley Baxter regarded men earning more than 28s a week as 'highly skilled workers' and he divided this section into two, subsection I earning 35s a week and subsection II earning 28s to 30s: *The National Income*, London, 1868, p. 89, appendix IV. But G. D. H. Cole revised Baxter's figures and concluded that 14·4% out of 7,784,000 men, women and juveniles were 'highly skilled': *Studies in Class Structure*, London, 1955, p. 57.) Next, using the Webbs' trade union membership figures indicating that 20% of the working class was organised in trade unions in 1892, relying on 'more or less plausible guesses', Hobsbawm halved this to allow for organised non-aristocratic elements. His calculation was sufficiently ambiguous to allow for objections. The fixing of the demarcation line at 28s to distinguish the labour aristocracy from the rest of the working class is also debatable. If a dividing line is required, it must be set up separately in specific occupations, in specific regions and moreover in specific periods.

9 T. R. Tholfsen, *Working Class Radicalism in Mid-Victorian England*, London, 1977, particularly chapter I.

10 R. Harrison, *Before the Socialists. Studies in Labour and Politics, 1861–1881*, London, 1965, p. 32. My emphasis.

11 R. Q. Gray, 'Class Structure and the Class Formation of Skilled Workers in Edinburgh, *c.* 1850–*c.* 1900', Ph.D. thesis, University of Edinburgh, 1971, and *id.*, *The Labour Aristocracy in Victorian Edinburgh*, Oxford, 1976. G. Crossick, 'Social Structure and Working-class Behaviour: Kentish London, 1840–1880', Ph.D. thesis, London University, 1976, and *id.*, *An Artisan Elite in Victorian*

Society. Kentish London, 1840–1880, London, 1978. J. Foster, *Class Struggle and the Industrial Revolution. Early Industrial Capitalism in three English Towns*, London, 1974. E. Hopkins, 'The Working Classes of Stourbridge and District, 1815–1914', Ph.D. thesis, London University, 1972. G. Stedman Jones, *Outcast London. A Study in the Relationship between Classes in Victorian Society*, Oxford, 1971.

12 Gray, 'Class Structure and the Class Formation of Skilled Workers', Ph.D. thesis, *op. cit.*, p. 31.

13 Foster, *Class Struggle and the Industrial Revolution*, p. 204.

14 *Ibid.*

15 A. Gramsci, *Selections from the Prison Notebooks*, ed. and trans. Q. Hoare and G. Nowell Smith, 1971, p. 12; quoted in Gray, *The Labour Aristocracy*, p. 5.

16 Gray, *op. cit.*, pp. 4–5.

17 Crossick, *An Artisan Elite*, pp. 14–15.

18 H. Pelling, 'The concept of the labour aristocracy', in *Popular Politics and Society in Late Victorian Britain*, London, 1968, p. 61.

19 *Ibid.*, p. 37.

20 *Ibid.*, p. 61.

21 See Hobsbawm's review of Pelling's book, in *Bulletin of the Society for the Study of Labour History*, No. XVIII, spring 1969, p. 52, and Harrison's review of Pelling's book, in *Victorian Studies*, XIII, 1970, p. 364.

22 A. E. Musson wrote that 'a "labour aristocracy" was not, as Hobsbawm and R. Harrison have argued, a new feature of trade unionism in the third quarter of the nineteenth century . . . Trade societies had almost always been composed of "labour aristocrats" – either of the old elite of skilled handicraftsmen or of the new elite of engineers, cotton spinners, etc. – and they had always been strongly sectional' (A.E. Musson, *British Trade Unions, 1800–1875*, London, 1972, pp. 50–1). See also *id.*, 'The Webbs and their phasing of trade-union development between the 1830s and the 1860s', in *Bulletin of the Society for the Study of Labour History*, No. IV, spring 1962, pp. 6–8, and *id.*, *Trade Union and Social History*, London, 1974, chapter I.

23 P. Joyce, *Work, Society and Politics. The culture of the factory in later Victorian England*, Brighton, 1980, p. xiv.

24 *Ibid.*

25 R. Harrison pointed out that 'the concept of a labour aristocracy is not an invention or discovery of Marx and Engels, but almost a commonplace of mid-Victorian socio-economic literature' (*Before the Socialists*, p. 5). When Ernest Jones, a Chartist leader, criticised the struggle of the Amalgamated Society of Engineers (hereinafter referred to as the A.S.E.) in that the union requested the abolition of overtime and piecework for the sake of the skilled mechanics, he wrote, 'THE ARISTOCRACY OF LABOUR MUST BE BROKEN DOWN the same as other aristocracies. If *you don't*, when you have

established democracy, *these men will carry the Reaction . . .'* (*Notes to the People*, vol. II, p. 862, February 1852; reprinted in J. Saville, *Ernest Jones: Chartist*, London, 1952, p. 194).

26 John Field, 'British historians and the concept of the labour aristocracy', *Radical History Review*, XIX, winter 1978–79, p. 78.

27 My research paralleled Hopkins's analysis of the Stourbridge working class (Hopkins, 'The Working Classes of Stourbridge and District, 1815–1914', Ph.D. thesis, *op. cit.*). He made it clear that in Stourbridge there were two different groups of working-class people (glass makers *v.* nailers) in terms of work situation (factory *v.* domestic), wage levels, life style, and segregated residence. My research mainly compares glass makers with those in other areas.

28 V. L. Allen, 'Abstract of a "methodological criticism of the Webbs as trade union historians"', *Bulletin of the Society for the Study of Labour History*, No. IV, spring 1962, p. 5, and *id.*, 'Valuations and historical interpretation', *British Journal of Sociology*, XIV, 1963.

Chapter one

The flint glass trade and the flint glass makers

I *The development of glass-making before 1850*

Glasses belong to a group of supercooled liquids which have passed into a rigid state without undergoing any noticeable structural change. Glass is a congealed solution of a number of substances, of which silica and alkali are invariables. The temperature at which fusion takes place is governed by the amount of alkali present, since this acts as flux which promotes the melting of the remaining ingredients. Although all glasses have the common property of being amorphous and not crystalline, where lead is used as an additional flux a crystalline structure may develop. The principal source of silica is sand, although certain kinds of rock may be used. For the finest glass a sand which is virtually free from iron is essential. Historically alkalis were derived either from wood ash or from burning seaweed. The former yielded potash glass; the latter, soda glass. Soda glass remains in a plastic state over a wider temperature range and is therefore easier to work.

The ways in which glass has been formed, cut and decorated are almost infinite in their variety, and it is not part of this work to attempt to describe them. Yet these few sentences serve to indicate the essential factors which govern the location of the industry: the presence or availability of the basic materials (including adequate supplies of suitable fuels); the technical understanding and skill of the producers; the presence and accessibility of markets. The history of glass production is told in the interplay between these factors, for even 'raw materials' is a category which changes its significance in the light of the other two. Thus it will be shown how the prohibition of the use of timber placed a premium upon a kind of clay for the making of pots, a kind of clay in which the Stourbridge region was peculiarly rich.

The glass industry was divided into five branches, according to the excise duty regulations: flint, crown, plate, broad and bottle. Flint glass was a general term for colourless glass such as was used for tumblers, goblets and table wares. The origin of flint glass came from the prohibition of the use of timber as fuel for glass-making furnaces ordered by the government in 1615.[1] With the introduction of coal, closed pots were substituted for open pots so as to prevent the smoke from spoiling the quality and the purity of the glass exposed to it. The closed pots, however, led to a greater difficulty in melting the glasses, so that lead was used as a powerful flux; it also imparted a lustre and brilliance unknown before. Since blown flint glass contained a substantial proportion of lead, it was called 'lead crystal'.

The transition from charcoal to coal effected a geographical redistribution of the glass trade. It rapidly disappeared from Surrey and Sussex,[2] where it had flourished using wood as fuel. In addition to London, two major centres of manufacture emerged, Newcastle and Stourbridge. In 1616 Robert Mansell moved from London to Newcastle,[3] and in 1612 Paul Tyzack and other Lorrainers moved to Stourbridge.[4] Apart from sufficient coal supplies in both areas, the advantages for glass-making were water carriage in Newcastle and fine clay in Stourbridge. The glass, packed in cases, was sent from Newcastle to London by collier and the returning barges called in at Kings Lynn to bring superior sand for glass-making. The clay underlying the coal in the mines of the Stour valley was the best for pot-making,[5] 'No other substance being known which will stand the tremendous heat to which these articles are subjected.'[6] The clay was employed not only in Stourbridge but in many other glass-producing districts in England. In later years it was also exported to America, France and Germany.[7]

At the end of the seventeenth century the glass industry was concentrated in London, Stourbridge, Bristol and Newcastle. Bristol had joined the group from the mid-century,[8] having many advantages such as near-by Kingswood coalfields, an efficient port and a demand for glass bottles from local brewers and cider makers. Besides these areas there were a number of factories in isolated districts such as Swansea, Nottingham, Yarmouth, Kings Lynn and the Isle of Wight. But during the eighteenth century regional concentration and specialisation occurred. Between 1696 and 1784 the number of glass factories in the West Midlands grew, and the area increased its share of total glass manufacture in England and Wales from 22·3% to 25·0%. London was reduced to second place, its share falling from 29·7% to 20·0%, whereas Newcastle increased its share from 11·7% to 15·0%.[9] Bristol fell back from 17·0% to 15·0%. Throughout the eighteenth century the glass industry in the Newcastle area flourished, specialising in crown glass production. By the end of the century 'not iron but glass was the richest branch of trade at Newcastle next to coal'.[10] By then the Stourbridge industry had moved from broad glass and con- centrated much more on flint and bottle glass-making. Meanwhile Bristol was in decline, owing to the failure of the Kingswood coalfields to supply glass manufacturers with enough coal. But the industry did appear at Nailsea, eight miles to the south-west.

By the mid-nineteenth century the glass industry's geographi- cal redistribution was complete. In the Newcastle area after about 1830 it went into a gradual decline, mainly because the advantage of water carriage was diminishing. Raw materials for glass-making had been brought back as ballast by the returning colliers from Holland and the Continent. The development of iron ships eventually led to the use of water ballast and the curtailment of these raw materials for the glass industry.[11] After 1830 crown glass was drastically affected by the French and German method of producing sheet glass, because sheet glass supplied the desideratum of larger panes at low prices without knobs or bullseyes, which had been produced in the centre of crown glass and limited the size of the window panes. The heavier duty on crown glass, amounting to nearly 300% on its original value at one time, accelerated the replacement.[12] In the mid-1850s only one crown glass factory was left[13] and by the early 1860s all crown glass factories on Tyneside had closed. In contrast to the decay of crown glass, sheet glass began to be produced in Cookson's Works in 1837 with the introduction of French glass workers familiar with the process[14] and thereafter flourished. In the 1840s James Hartley of Sunderland invented 'rolled plate' glass, and this new technology forced the abandon- ment of the age-long process of blowing plate glass. With the increased building of factories, railway stations and so on, this type of glass was in great demand, because it was strong, cheap, and translucent, and particularly suitable for skylights and glass roofing. The Newcastle manufacturers were in competition with St Helens, where the Lancashire coalfield and local sand gave the local plate glass industry the advantage. In the early nineteenth century, by attracting a number of skilled glass makers from Bristol, St Helens developed a prominent position in flat glass-making and became the second excise duty payer after Newcastle. Pilkington was the biggest establishment among the St Helens firms.[15] In neither Newcastle nor Lancashire did flint glass flourish in the first half of the century. In the Newcastle area there were only five flint glass houses in the 1830s,[16] and in Lancashire there were only a small number of flint glass houses in Bolton, St Helens, Warrington and Manchester.

By the middle of the century, flint glass making had concentrated overwhelmingly in Stourbridge and Birmingham. Birmingham was somewhat late in its development of the glass trade. It began with small enterprises, like toy manufacture, button making and glass cutting in the late eighteenth century.[17] At the turn of the century a number of firms arose and soon became large producers.[18] In the early 1830s the five Birmingham factories produced more glass than the eleven Stourbridge firms put together.[19] F. & C. Osler & Co.[20] and Lloyd & Summerfield were the representative flint glass factories in the city. The Birmingham flint glass manufacturers were competing strongly with those of Stourbridge, although Stourbridge was more specialised. In Birmingham, besides nineteen 'glass manufacturers' and five chandelier and lustre manufacturers there were twenty glass-button manufacturers and twenty glass toy manufacturers in 1851.[21] In Stourbridge, out of eleven glass houses, nine were making flint glass and two were making bottle glass in 1850.[22]

London became relatively unimportant for the glass industry in the nineteenth century and most of the glass houses came to concentrate their business not in production but in selling and decoration. At the lowest ebb of the London glass trade two flint glass firms, the Whitefriars Works and the Falcon Works, continued to flourish by finding skilful artisans and talented designers or by introducing new techniques. In Scotland the famous Holyrood Glass Works was started in Edinburgh at the beginning of the nineteenth century and maintained a high reputation throughout. To compete with Stourbridge flint glass, uniqueness of product was essential to glass-making in other areas. In Yorkshire the mushroom growth of bottle glass houses began in the mid-nineteenth century.[23] The Yorkshire bottle houses were known to be establishments founded by well-off workers.[24]

In Ireland the glass industry took a different course. Coal was obtained chiefly from South Wales and clay from Stourbridge.[25] Penrose, who established the first glass house at Waterford in 1783, imported skilled workmen from Stourbridge.[26] The firm had a world-wide reputation and many other glass factories followed it. By the mid-nineteenth century most of them had disappeared, mainly because a heavy export tax was imposed in 1825 and the market was lost outside Ireland. The Waterford glass firm closed in 1851, when many of the workers went to Belfast, where the industry struggled on until 1870.[27] In 1825 there were eleven glass houses in Ireland, while in 1852 there were only three left, two in Dublin for flint glass and bottles, and one in Belfast.[28]

II *The third quarter of the nineteenth century*

Three major changes occurred around the mid-nineteenth century. They related to the general prosperity of the trade, market position and workers' organisation. These three factors were interrelated. Together they provided the necessary conditions for the achievement by flint glass makers of full labour aristocratic status.

First, the flint glass trade, together with the other branches of the glass industry, began to experience a golden age of prosperity which continued until the late 1870s. The final repeal of the excise duty on glass in 1845 was certainly a pre-condition of the rapid expansion of production. The great impediment to the development of glass manufacture in Britain had been the heavy duty which was first imposed in 1695. It was repealed soon after, in 1698, but reimposed by an Act of 1745.[29] The *Penny Magazine* wrote of this 'obnoxious' duty in 1844 that:

So close and binding are the restrictions, that a manufacturer can hardly make any experiments on a large scale, nor can he introduce any improvements except in a few minor details... Every furnace, pots, oven and warehouse must be registered; every 'charge', or filling, must be under the control of the officers; every drawing out from the annealing oven must be at prescribed hours... From the making of the pots themselves, to the packing up of the glass for sale, everything is done after a certain manner, which is determined by Act of Parliament.[30]

But if repeal of the duty was a prerequisite of prosperity a major factor was the Great Exhibition of 1851. The contract for the Crystal Palace stimulated the production of rolled plate glass,[31] and the exhibits of eighteen flint glass manufacturers were 'truly extraordinary'.[32] Osler's factory exhibited a chandelier. Elihu Burritt wrote in 1868 that 'if the vote were taken of the million of different countries who saw what that first Crystal Palace contained, as to the most impressive, attractive, and best remembered object, a majority would say that it was Osler's Crystal Fountain.'[33] It marked the beginning of the golden age of flint glass making.

In the second half of the 1850s the development of flint glass was retarded, owing to recession in 1855 and then the flint glass makers' long strike and lock-out of 1858–59. In the first half of the next decade these hindrances were over and flint glass flourished. As a result, in the third quarter of the century, exports approximately doubled from £718,000 in 1850–54 to £1,511,000 in 1870–74.[34] In 1873 they reached the highest peak for the period, at £359,000 a year. But the latter 1870s saw a decline in exports, owing to the depression which affected flint glass in 1877. From 1880 to 1884 exports rose again, though by small margins, but in 1885 they fell once more. In the third quarter, on the other hand, exports of 'all glass' increased by 240% and exports of flint glass shared between 30% and 40% of those of 'all glass'.

As a matter of course such developments increased employment. Between 1851 and 1881 national employment in glass manufacturing more than doubled, from 10,238 to 23,295.[35] Each decade during the period showed a continuous increase, but the rise between 1871 and 1881 (9·4%) was the smallest of any decade in the nineteenth century.[36] Between 1851 and 1881 increased employment in the glass trade was recorded for all regions, but there were marked variations in the proportions of the national total. As table 1:1 shows, the West Midlands' share decreased from 28·9% to 21·4%, although it was still one of the leading regions for glass-making over the period. The Newcastle area also continued to decline from 20·0% to 13·8% in the same period. Both London and Bristol shared the same fate. On the other hand, both Lancashire and Yorkshire showed a remarkable increase, particularly Lancashire, which came to have the largest share of all regions in 1871, and had about a quarter of all employment in 1881. Scotland showed some revival in the 1850s and the 1860s but declined in the 1870s.

TABLE 1:1 Regional distribution of employment in the whole glass industry and in the flint glass industry between 1851 and 1881 (%)

Region	1851		1861		1871		1881	
	All glass	Flint glass (1852)	All glass	Flint glass	All glass	Flint glass	All glass	Flint glass
West Midlands	28·9	39·6	27·0	41·3	21·0	39·2	21·4	40·9
Newcastle area	20·0	19·4	18·8	7·5	17·4	4·3	13·8	5·2
Bristol area	2·6	0·7	1·8	0·5	1·9	0·2	1·1	0·2
London	16·2	8·1	12·9	2·6	14·6	3·0	12·7	3·3
Lancashire	17·8	20·8	20·5	22·1	21·8	30·3	25·7	26·3
Yorkshire	7·2	11·9	10·2	14·3	12·0	13·4	16·7	14·6
Scotland	5·8	9·5	7·3	11·7	9·1	9·6	6·7	9·5
Remainder	1·5	0·0	1·5	0·0	2·2	0·0	1·9	0·0
Totals	100·0	100·0	100·0	100·0	100·0	100·0	100·0	100·0

Source. 'All glass' workers are calculated from the printed census tables of 1851, 1861, 1871 and 1881, by C. B. Brown, 'Changes in the Location of the British Glass Industry since about 1833', Ph.D. thesis, op. cit., pp. 77, 84, 90. Flint glass makers are calculated from the members of the Districts in the F.G.M.F.S. of 1852, 1861, 1871 and 1881 obtainable from the Quarterly Report, in *Flint Glass Makers Magazine*. Flint glass makers in Ireland are excluded.

Changes in the regional weight of plate glass-making can explain these variations. In 1858 a syndicate took over almost all plate glass manufacture in England.[37] By the mid–1860s production had come to be monopolised by Chance Bros of Birmingham, Pilkington's of St Helens, and Hartley's of South Shields. However, particularly after 1870 flat glass-making in the North-east declined as a direct consequence of competition from Pilkington and Chance. The decline in Newcastle's relative share was chiefly due to the decline of flat glass-making in the area. Only Pilkington continued to develop and largely contributed to the continuance of Lancashire as the country's leading employer. The increase in employment of Yorkshire over the period was due to the mushroom growth of small-scale bottle glass houses in the county after mid-century.

So far as the flint glass trade was concerned, the pattern of regional distribution which had emerged by the mid-nineteenth century was strengthened and consolidated in the third quarter when the West Midlands, particularly Stourbridge, became more significant as the centre of flint glass-making. Some 40% of national flint glass makers were concentrated in the West Midlands and its 40% share remained constant over the period. In Newcastle (blown) flint glass makers were a smaller proportion, only 9·4% in 1851, and the region's share declined over the period to 5·2% in 1881. The same tendency occurred in London and, on a much smaller scale, in Bristol. On the other hand, both in Lancashire and in Yorkshire there were relatively high proportions of flint glass makers, respectively 20·8% and 11·9% in 1852. In addition, the shares of both areas tended to increase over the period. The rapid development of the flint glass industry in Manchester is mainly responsible for the increase of the proportion in Lancashire, from 20·8% in 1851 to 30·3% in 1871. But Lancashire's share fell to 26·3% in 1881 as depression affected the Manchester flint glass trade more severely than anywhere else. The situation in Scotland was unique. Its share of flint glass makers was not large, but it was stable, consistently some 10% over the whole period.

It is important to see that glass workers were geographically segregated according to the kind of glass produced. It is meaningless to talk of glass workers as a whole. In their consciousness there were sharp distinctions between types of product. Flint glass makers were proud of their products, which differed from other kinds of glassware, and they looked down upon other glass workers. The *F.G.M.M.* stated in 1851 that 'The Crown Glass Makers, the German Sheet Blower, and the Bottle Maker are all confined to one article each and all of them are the same thing over again, there is no variety: every day's work is but a repetition of the former days always the same no changing of patterns.'[38]

In the course of the golden age, in the 1860s, foreign glass slowly but gradually began to encroach upon the English trade.[39] Belgian tumblers and wineglasses began to displace those of British origin both in home and foreign markets, while the Germans also became dangerous rivals. In the late 1860s some glass manufacturers and glass makers began to feel the threat of foreign competition. Before the Royal Commission on Trade Unions in 1868, George Lloyd, chairman of the Midland Flint Glass Manufacturers' Association, remarked that 'profits have diminished, but I would not represent it as altogether due to the price of labour or the scarcity of labour, because foreign competition is an element'.[40] W. T. Swene, a Birmingham flint glass maker, reported to the Society of Arts of Birmingham, after returning from the Paris exhibition in 1867, that 'there can be no doubt that the extent of the competition existing between the Continental and our own manufacturers, will be found to show a decided advance in favour of the former'.[41] Most manufacturers and glass makers had earlier believed that the quality of English flint glass would prevent foreign glass from encroaching upon the English trade. As a manufacturer, James Couper, of the City Flint Glass Works in Glasgow, remarked in April 1878, 'A number of years ago, when foreign glass was imported, both employers and employed thought it could not affect us, the metal being very inferior and shapes bad, but now many articles imported not only compare favourably with ours in metal and shape, but being lower in price, materially injure the sale of home-made goods.'[42] The devices to combat foreign competition came too late. The *F.G.M.M.* wrote in February 1877:

A years ago, employers thought they were safe against the aggression of foreigners, by the latter not being able to compete with them for colour or brilliancy of metal in their best flint glass, but this difficulty has been overcome; and employers admit that, in many instances the quality of foreign glass is equal to their own.[43]

The state of the trade worsened to the extent that the *Brierley Hill Advertiser* reported in 1879 that 'foreign decanters are being largely sold in the Midlands, completely finished, at a price which is little if any more than the cost of cutting would amount to in an English shop'.[44] In 1880 the Factory Inspector reported that the flint glass trade 'has been suffering much from the effects of foreign competition. Great efforts are being made to retain our position.'[45] The golden age of flint glass-making had come to an end.

The second change that took place around mid-century concerned the market position of flint glass products. The advent of pressed glass transformed a single market into a dual one. Pressed glass was an American invention of the 1820s[46] and it was soon being used in England. Although most of the early pressed glass was made in the West Midlands,[47] it had found its way to the Newcastle area by the middle of the century. It is likely that in the West Midlands, where skilled glass makers were concentrated by that time, glass manufacturers found it difficult to continue pressed glass production. A big strike in a Birmingham flint glass factory in 1848 well illustrates the difficulty.[48] Pressed glass contained little or no lead and required less skill in its production than blown glass. Whereas in blown glass-making the melted metal was shaped by the pressure of the glass maker's breath, in pressed glass it was done by a metallic plunger which meant that it was produced quite cheaply, but at the cost of brilliance. The designs were simple and well adapted for mechanical reproduction, so that productivity was incomparably higher than that in blown flint glass-making. Whereas 160 common wineglasses were produced by blowing in six hours, 1,100 to 1,200 tumblers could be pressed in seven.[49] In the early 1860s 'one firm formerly produced annually 350,000 lbs. weight of blown flint glass, now made of pressed glass about 3,500,000 lbs. weight'.[50] Since, to the eye, pressed glass was almost the same as the blown flint glass, it could rapidly expand its market as the railway network grew. Newcastle pressed glass was no longer a local matter. Blown flint glass makers had to acknowledge pressed glass makers as their competitors even while insisting that they were their inferiors. In pressed glass-making the lower level of skill required only five years' apprenticeship[51]—two years less than for blown flint glass makers.

In the third quarter of the century pressed glass manufacturers expanded rapidly. In 1865 the Ellison Flint Glass Works of Gateshead was the home of 'the largest manufacturers of pressed flint-glass in the kingdom',[52] with 450 men. By the early 1880s it had developed to 'the largest pressed glass manufactory in the world',[53] employing 700 – 1,000 men. Geo. Davidson & Co., founded in 1868, also expanded pressed glass production in

Gateshead,[54] which became a centre of that branch. The production of pressed glass making came to be a more extensive and more integrated process than that of blown glass-making. In the Ellison Flint Glass Works in the late 1880s 'the whole of the iron work for the making of "Presses" is done on the premises, from the handling of the pig-iron to the completion of the elaborate iron mould'.[55] One of the contributory factors to the great success of the Ellison Works was that pressed glass production 'to a great extent renders the manufacturers of it independent of the skilled glass blowers, by whose combinations manufacturers of the blown glass are much fettered'.[56]

In contrast to pressed glass factories, blown flint glass houses were relatively small. Indicators of the exact number of flint glass makers employed (not the number of organised glass makers) are difficult to obtain. Printed census tables show the number of glass workers, but do not classify them into flint glass makers, glass cutters and so on. The *Birmingham Mercury* of 1851 estimated that the total number of flint glass makers in the United Kingdom was about 1,000, and 'between 200 and 300 glass makers and the same number of glass cutters or grinders were employed in Birmingham'.[57] The *Morning Chronicle* estimated in 1850 that 'the flint glass manufacture of Birmingham gives employment to about 210 glass makers or blowers, and to about the same number of glass cutters or grinders'.[58] Around 1850 there were ten flint glass factories in Birmingham, so that the average size of a factory is estimated to be between forty and sixty, supposing that the glass-making section and cutting section were on the same premises. The national survey undertaken by the F.G.M.F.S. in 1857 suggests that in twelve areas 1,244 flint glass makers were employed in forty-two factories.[59]

So the national average size of the flint glass-making sector was about thirty employees per factory. In Stourbridge 311 flint glass makers were employed in eleven factories, an average of about twenty-eight people per factory; in Birmingham, 305 glass makers in ten factories, an average size of thirty-five persons. According to the census enumerators' books of 1861 there were 389 flint glass makers, 432 glass cutters and twenty-seven glass engravers in Stourbridge. Beside them there were 164 other glass workers such as teasers and packers.[60] Since there were eleven glass factories in the district, the average size would have been about thirty-five for the glass-making section and about forty for the cutting section. The number of glass makers in the six factories in the area is shown in table 1:2. Thus it is clear that the blown flint glass factory was far from the large-scale modern factory in size. The small-scale character of production had a bearing on the old artisan consciousness of flint glass makers.

TABLE 1:2 Number of glass workers in the six factories
in Stourbridge in 1861

Manufacturer	Men	Boys	Women	Total
William Walker	74	24		98
John Davis	69	16	9	94
William Richardson	70	16	6	92
John Renald	51	25		76
Frederic Stuart	50	13	9	72
Edward Webb	30	8		38

Note. The enumerators' books have no column for the number of employees, but the figures shown above are written in the outside columns of each manufacturer by the enumerators.
Source. Census Enumerators' Books of 1861, Stourbridge.

Flint glass makers were possessed not only of artisan consciousness but of artistic pretensions. The *F.G.M.M.* wrote in 1858 that 'the members of our society may count themselves among those who have the honour of contributing daily to the luxuries of the tables of the nobility of the land, including Her Majesty the Queen. Seeing, then, that we labour at a beautiful art, is it not our duty and privilege to excel in the same — to be ambitious for our own credit and attainments, and to study taste, richness and beauty?'[61] They were proud of their luxury products, which were bought mainly by the upper and middle class. The production of pressed glass for working-class consumption injured the blown glass makers' pride. Samuel Neville, a partner in the Ellison Works, became a prime target in the early 1850s. Blown glass makers thought that under the 'Nevillonian system', as it was called, 'the beautiful trade of Glassmaking shall be brought as low as nail making'.[62]

The third change taking place in mid-century was the emergence of the flint glass makers' trade union. It would be absurd to investigate the question of the labour aristocracy without taking their trade union into consideration. It is true that the relative affluence of flint glass makers formed and sustained their union, but at the same time the activities of the union secured and strengthened their privileged position. These interrelated processes must be considered.

Flint glass makers organised the 'powerful' United Flint Glass Makers' Society in 1844 and reorganised it in 1849. The newly organised society emerged as a 'New Model' union.[63] In 1852 it had 1,017 members in twenty Districts, covering England (sixteen Districts), Scotland (two Districts) and Ireland (two Districts). It was literally a national union. Membership continued to increase each year until 1877, except for a slight fall in 1855, 1861 and 1868. There were 912 members in 1855, 1,300 in 1860, 1,612 in 1865, 1,762 in 1870 and 1,994 in 1875. In 1877 it reached 2,088, but after that it began to fall, reaching 1,937 by 1881. The decline was largely the result of the trade depression. We can say that compared with other unions, such as the Engineers, Carpenters and Joiners, Stonemasons, Ironfounders and Boilermakers, the increase of membership of the F.G.M.F.S. in the third quarter of the century was relatively small, and in 1880 the scale of the society remained small. The structure and policies of the union will be described in detail later, but it is here necessary to indicate that the union prevented or retarded technical innovation in the flint glass production process.

The introduction of more efficient furnaces was opposed bitterly. In 1851 R. M. Deeley, a partner in the Dial Glass House of Stourbridge, obtained a patent for a new furnace which would enable cheap slack to be used. The innovation was important, because the increasing price of coal in the district, due largely to the development of the iron industry, was a drawback for the glass trade. 'But our Workmen at that time joined a "Trades Union",' Deeley recalled, 'and objected to work the patent furnaces, and actually stopped working rather than do so. We were then driven to get men from wherever we could, Yorkshire, Bristol etc.'[64]

The year 1861 was of some importance on account of the Siemens patent furnace, adopted in the Birmingham flint glass trade. In 1861 the brothers Siemens took out a patent for a gas-fired regenerative furnace suitable for glass-making. Since the heat from the gas was intense, easily regulated and relatively uniform, the temperature of the furnace could be raised quickly for melting and refining the glass and then lowered for working it. Lloyd & Summerfield introduced the Siemens furnace at their works at Spring Hill when George Lloyd became 'the first person that introduced it into this country'.[65] Chance Bros adopted it the following year at Spon Lane, and F. & S. Osler followed a little later.[66] George Lloyd remarked of the furnace before the Royal Commission on Trade Unions in 1869 that 'I met with the very greatest opposition from my own men in carrying it out, so much so, that if I had not had rather more obstinacy in persisting in what I supposed to be right than they had in the opposite direction, I must have put it out and abandoned it.'[67] The introduction of the furnace led the men to believe that it would produce more 'metal' and force them to produce more glass of lower quality at the expense of their skill. In fact the opposition, as Lloyd complained, came not from the furnacemen but 'from the glass blowers who have nothing to do with the management of the furnace'.[68]

The Siemens melting tank, invented in 1870 and improved in 1872, displaced the fireclay pots previously used to hold the 'metal'. It had a much greater capacity and lasted far longer. More important, it was expected to achieve continuous production. This was not introduced into the flint glass houses, because flint glass makers were afraid that it would change their traditional work cycle and working pattern. This presents a striking contrast with other kinds of glass makers. Pilkington's were quick to employ the Siemens' new discovery of 1872. Having built one successful tank in 1873, they began to substitute tanks for pots at a rapid rate and by August 1876 there were nine tank furnaces in operation. The installation of continuous tank furnaces on this scale resulted in a considerable increase in sheet glass and rolled plate glass production.[69] The introduction of the new tank furnace resulted in a drastic change of working shifts. So long as pot furnaces were used, the men had to work altogether four ten-hour shifts a week, followed in each case by twenty-four hours off while the pots were being recharged. With the coming of tanks during the 1870s, work could continue uninterruptedly throughout the week and the week rest was shortened; they had to work on Saturdays, which previously had been free. Under the new system three eight-hour shifts a day for six days a week were fixed.

Accordingly they worked longer hours altogether — forty-eight instead of about forty. The new arrangements do not seem to have been unfavourably received by the glass makers.[70]

The Siemens melting tank was also introduced into bottle glass production, leading to changes in the traditional working shifts. Kilner Bros at Thornhill Lees constructed the first such furnace in the West Riding in 1873. Instead of the working day consisting of a period of founding followed by a journey, it could now consist of two shifts involving both founders and glass makers. The two-shift system, each shift lasting nine and half hours, was introduced during the 1870s in nearly every factory which employed a gas melting furnace. An attempt to go further by establishing a three-shift system in a Barnsley factory met with militant resistance, in which the men were supported by the Yorkshire Bottle Makers' Union. The conflict over the three-shift system was an underlying issue in the famous lockout of bottle glass makers in 1893.[71] In contrast to bottle, sheet, and plate glass makers, flint glass makers continued to use the pot furnace, despite the troublesome 'pot setting'.[72] The different degrees to which the melting furnace spread among the different branches of the industry well illustrates how deeply the diffusion of the new innovation was regulated by the strength of the respective unions and the consciousness of the members.

The golden age of the flint glass trade, the formation of a clear dual market between blown and pressed flint glass, and the preservation of traditional skill through a newly formed trade union — all these factors emerged around the mid-century, and all were necessary conditions in which flint glass makers might appear as *classic* labour aristocrats, and not in the second but in the third quarter of the century. The next step is to investigate, under these conditions, how the labour aristocracy was actually created in flint glass-making. For this purpose we must concentrate on the labour process and go deeper into the workshop.

Notes

1 A decree, the *Proclamation touching Glass* issued by James I on 23 May 1615; A. Hartshorne, *Old English Glasses*, London and New York, 1897, p. 413.
2 W. E. S. Turner, 'The British glass industry: its development and outlook', *Journal of the Society of Glass Technology*, VI, 1922,

p. 114. The first written grant in glass-making appeared in 1226 in the Wealden village of Chiddingfold (H. J. Powell, *Glass-making in England*, Cambridge, 1923, p. 11). See also G. H. Kenyon, *The Glass Industry of the Weald*, Leicester, 1967, and E. S. Godfrey, *The Development of English Glassmaking, 1560–1640*, Oxford, 1976.

3 Robert Mansell established his firm on the Ouseburn in Newcastle and in 1618 he obtained a patent for making glass with coal (*V.C.H.*, Durham, vol. II, 1907, p. 309, and J. Clephan, 'Manufacture of glass in England: rise of the art on the Tyne', *Archaelogia Aeliana*, new ser., VIII, 1880, pp. 180–226).

4 D. R. Guttery, *From Broad-glass to Cut Crystal. A History of the Stourbridge Glass Industry*, London, 1956, p. 5. For information about the origin of the Stourbridge glass industry see D. N. Sandilands, 'The early history of glass-making in the Stourbridge district', *Journal of the Society of Glass Technology*, XV, 1931, pp. 219–27, and *Brierley Hill Advertiser*, 20 July 1867.

5 The first concession awarded for digging clay for glass pots in Stourbridge is dated 1566 (G. Harrison, 'Stourbridge fireclay', in S. Timmins (ed.), *Birmingham and the Midland Hardware District*, London, 1866, p. 133). The clay was about 150 ft below the surface, and 45 ft below the coal, to the extent of nearly 200 acres, but the best sort was only found upon about forty-eight acres (R. Simms, *Contributions towards a History of Glass Making and Glass Makers in Staffordshire*, Wolverhampton, 1894, p. 10).

6 *Brierley Hill Advertiser*, 18 May 1867.

7 *V.C.H.*, Worcester, vol. II, 1906, p. 281.

8 In Bristol glass was first made by Edwin Dagma in 1665. See F. Buckley, 'The early glasshouses of Bristol', *Journal of the Society of Glass Technology*, IX, 1925, pp. 36–61.

9 The figures in 1696 are taken from John Houghton, *A Collection for Improvement of Husbandry and Trade*, 1692, and those in 1784 are taken from *Bailey's Directory* of 1784, vols. I–IV. The percentages are calculated by C. M. Brown, 'Changes in the Location of the British Glass Industry since about 1833', Ph.D. thesis, University of London, 1970, pp. 44, 51.

10 Rev. John Vaillie, *An Impartial History of the Town and County of Newcastle upon Tyne and its Vicinity*, 1801, quoted by S. Middlebrook, *Newcastle upon Tyne. Its Growth and Achievement*, Newcastle, 1950, p. 141.

11 U. Ridley, 'The History of Glass Making on the Tyne and Wear', p. 5.

12 G. B. Hodgson, *The Borough of South Shields*, Newcastle, 1903, p. 362.

13 That was R. W. Swinburne & Co. (T. Salmon, *South Shields. Past, Present, and Future*, South Shields, 1856, p. 21). Swinburne wrote in 1864 that 'in the birthplace of the art in England, there is now not a foot of window glass manufactured' (R. W. Swinburne, 'The manufacture of glass', in W. Armstrong et al. (ed.), *The Industrial Resources of the District of the Three Northern Rivers*, 2nd ed, London, 1864, p. 199).

14 Hodgson, *The Borough of South Shields*, p. 362, and *Penny Magazine*, XIII, June 1844, p. 256.
15 For the history of Pilkington's, see T. C. Barker, *The Glassmakers. Pilkington: the Rise of an International Company, 1826–1976*, London, 1977.
16 Powell, *Glass-Making*, p. 96.
17 Timmins (ed.), *Birmingham and the Midland Hardware District*, p. 527; Powell, *Glass-making*, p. 104, and *V.C.H.*, Warwick, vol. II, 1908, p. 244. G.C. Allen wrote that 'as far as table-ware is concerned, the industry (in Birmingham) appears to have spread from Stourbridge about 1750', (*The Industrial Development of Birmingham and the Black Country, 1860–1927*, London, 1929, p. 19).
18 R. K. Dent wrote that 'previous to Mr. Hawker's first attempt to manufacture glass in Birmingham in 1785, the Midland counties were supplied from Stourbridge, but before the end of the century, Birmingham glass was competing strongly with that of Stourbridge and other neighbouring towns, and its manufacture was rapidly becoming an important local industry' (*Old and New Birmingham*, Birmingham, 1879, p. 342).
19 W. H. B. Court, *The Rise of the Midland Industries, 1600–1838*, London, 1938, p. 224.
20 Osler's factory is described in detail in 'British industries. III, Glass', *Tinsley's Magazine*, August 1889, pp. 343–53, and *Birmingham and General Advertiser*, 24 August 1848.
21 *Birmingham Mercury*, 17 May 1851.
22 *Brierley Hill Advertiser*, 13 July 1867. For the Stourbridge glass industry see Guttery, *From Broad-glass to Cut Crystal*, H. J. Haden, *The Stourbridge Glass Industry in the 19th Century*, Black Country Society, 1971, and H. W. Woodward, 'The glass industry of the Stourbridge district', *West Midland Studies*, VIII, 1976, pp. 36–42.
23 For the history of the glass bottle industry in Yorkshire see David Brundage, 'The Glass Bottle Makers of Yorkshire and the Lock-out of 1893', M.A. thesis, University of Warwick, 1976, chapter I.
24 Hobsbawm, 'The labour aristocracy in nineteenth-century Britain', p. 296.
25 M. S. D. Westropp, *Irish Glass*, London, 1920, pp. 171, 176.
26 D. A. Chart, *An Economic History of Ireland*, Dublin, 1920, p. 86. D. N. Sandilands pointed out that in 1785 a Stourbridge glass maker, Hill, emigrated to Ireland with 'the best set of workmen that he could get in the County of Worcester' ('The early history of glass making in the Stourbridge District', p. 227).
27 E. M. Elville, *English and Irish Cut Glass, 1750–1950*, London, 1953, p. 62.
28 Westropp, *Irish Glass*, p. 142.
29 For the excise duty on glass see Powell, *Glass-making*, chapter XII, pp. 153–7, and D. N. Sandilands, 'The last fifty years of the excise duty on glass', *Journal of the Society of Glass Technology*, XV, 1931, pp. 231–45.

30 'A day at a glass factory', *Penny Magazine*, XIII, June 1844, p. 256.
31 Plate glass for the Crystal Palace was produced jointly by Hartley's, Chance's and Pilkington's.
32 *Birmingham Mercury*, 17 May 1851.
33 E. Burritt, *Walks in the Black Country and its Green Border-land*, London, 1868, p. 118. See also J. Ward, *The World in its Workshops*, London, 1851, p. 132.
34 Calculated from the data in Turner, 'The British glass industry', p. 133.
35 Printed census tables of 1851 and 1881.
36 Brown, 'Changes in the Location', Ph.D. thesis, *op. cit.*, p. 90.
37 Hodgson, *The Borough of South Shields*, p. 364 and *V.C.H.*, Durham, vol. II, 1907, p. 310.
38 *Flint Glass Makers Magazine*, I, p. 178.
39 After 1868 the ratio between exports and imports of 'all glass' (in money terms) went down below 1·00. The average ratio in each decade was 4·86 (scaled up) in the 1850s, 1·42 in the 1860s, 0·68 in the 1870s and 0·61 in the 1880s (calculated from the data in Turner, 'The British glass industry', p. 133).
40 *Royal Commission on Trade Unions*, 10th Report, 1867–68 (P.P. XXXIX), p. 21, q. 18346.
41 *Reports of Artisans, selected by a Committee appointed by the Council of the Society of Arts to visit the Paris Universal Exhibition, 1867*, London, 1867, p. 144.
42 *Capital and Labour*, 3 April 1878.
43 *Flint Glass Makers Magazine*, VIII, p. 935.
44 *Brierley Hill Advertiser*, 22 March 1879.
45 *Factory Inspectors' Report, ending October 31 1880*, 1881 (P.P. XXIII), p. 6.
46 G. S. and H. MacKearin, *American Glass*, New York, 1941, p. 334, and L. W. Watkins, *American Glass and Glass Making*, London, 1950, p. 65. The first patent was taken out by J. P. Bakewell & Co., Pittsburgh, on 9 September 1825 (MacKearin, *op. cit.*, p. 334).
47 In 1832 the Richardsons' factory at Stourbridge introduced a machine for 'pressing' flint glass into England. Before long it was followed by Rice Harris, Bacchus & Green of Birmingham, Thomas Hawkes of Dudley and Sheeley & Davis of Stourbridge. At the Birmingham exhibition in 1849 Rice Harris, Bacchus and Lloyd & Summerfield displayed pressed glass (H. G. Wakefield, *Nineteenth Century British Glass*, London, 1961, p. 59). At the Great Exhibition Rice Harris was the only firm to display pressed glass (Powell, *Glass-making*, pp. 160–1).
48 About this strike see below, p. 87–8.
49 The number of pressed glasses is taken from an article on 'The Sowerby art glass in Gateshead', *Newcastle Daily Chronicle*, 21 October 1882.
50 Swinburne, 'The Manufacture of Glass', p. 201.
51 *Rules and Regulations of the Pressed Glass Makers' Friendly Society*

of the North of England, 17 February 1872 (Webb Trade Union Collection, Section C, vol. 42, XVI), provision XXXVII.

52 *Children's Employment Commission*, 4th Report, 1865 (P.P. XX), p. 182, q. 19, and J. B. Lauderdale, *'History of Sowerby's Ellison Glass Works, Limited'* (T), P. 1.

53 *Newcastle Chronicle*, 21 October 1882.

54 *Newcastle and District. An Epitome of Results and Manual of Commerce*, Newcastle, 1889, p. 169, and L. Fraser, *Pressed Glass. A Short History of Geo. Davidson & Co. Ltd., 1867–1948*, Newcastle, 1948, p. 1.

55 *Newcastle and District, op. cit.*, p. 164.

56 *Children's Employment Commission*, 4th Report, 1865, p. 182, q. 19.

57 *Birmingham Mercury*, 17 May 1851.

58 *Morning Chronicle*, 23 December 1850.

59 Calculated from the *Returns of National Survey* undertaken by the F.G.M.F.S. in 1857, in *Flint Glass Makers Magazine*, III, p. 248. Twelve out of twenty-three Districts in the F.G.M.F.S. reported both the number of glass factories and flint glass makers employed. The number in the survey was not limited to the organised members of the society, but did not include the takers-in.

60 For details, see table 6:1. See also E. Hopkins, 'Changes in the scale of the industrial unit in Stourbridge & district, 1815–1914', *West Midland Studies*, VIII, 1976, p. 32.

61 *Flint Glass Makers Magazine*, III, p. 293.

62 *Ibid.*, I, p. 225.

63 About a 'New Model' union see below, pp. 81–2.

64 Richard Mountford Deeley, 'Reminiscences', Ms, Birmingham Reference Library, p. 45.

65 *Royal Commission on Trade Unions*, 10th Report, 1867–68, p. 26, q. 18493.

66 Timmins (ed.), *Birmingham and the Midland Hardware District*, p. 531, and *V.C.H.*, Warwick, vol. II, 1908, p. 247.

67 *Royal Commission on Trade Unions*, 10th Report, 1867–68, p. 24, q. 18408.

68 *Ibid.*, p. 24, q. 18417.

69 Barker, *The Glassmakers*, pp. 133–6.

70 *Ibid.*, pp. 176–7.

71 Brundage, 'The Glass Bottle Makers of Yorkshire', M.A. thesis, *op. cit.*

72 Pot-setting, a hard, hot and arduous task, was performed not by teasers but by glass makers. There was no uniformity in payment. In some Districts it was paid per pot, and in other Districts per head. In some Districts it was paid not in cash but in ale. But by 1876 in most Districts the uniform level of payment for pot-setting was established as a result of the union's struggle. (*Flint Glass Makers Magazine*, VIII, pp. 546–62.)

Chapter two

The work situation

I *The production process and working cycle*

The manufacture, drying and baking of the melting pots was the first important process in flint glass-making, since the preservation and the proper melting of ingredients were essential to the subsequent work on the glass. David Bremner wrote in 1869 that 'the pots are the source of the glass-makers' great anxiety, for, notwithstanding the utmost care in making and annealing them, some give way after being in use only for a week or two; others endure for three or four months; but few reach the age of a year. It occasionally happens that a pot splits when full of "metal", as the fused glass is called, and then the accident entails a serious loss.'[1] Many glass manufacturers made their own pots.[2] In making pots the greatest care and delicacy of handling were required. Stourbridge clay was used exclusively. The clay was crushed into a fine powder, and mixed with a quantity of burnt clay. After that it was mixed with water and well kneaded and tempered by the feet of the workmen. Then it had to lie from five or six weeks to three months till it had acquired the requisite adhesion.[3] The pots were then built gradually by the workman's fingers. The longer they could be left before they were used, the better. Consequently it was important to keep a considerable number on hand. A visitor to the Pellatt Glass Works in London was 'struck with the singular appearance of a large dark room, the floor of which was studded with nearly a hundred of these dome-shaped vessels . . . The pots are left in this room for several months.'[4] Before being set in the furnace they were annealed in a small furnace called a 'Pot arch' for four or five days.[5]

The melting of ingredients was also an important process. Bad metal was one of the main concerns of glass makers. William Gillinder, a Birmingham flint glass maker and the first Central

Secretary of the F.G.M.F.S. from 1851 to 1854, wrote that 'no matter how clever or practical a man may be in making metal, if he does not have the best of material, he will never produce a first-rate glass, which should have the rich white lustre of silver and colourlessness of water'.[6] The constituents of flint glass were one part of carbonate of potash, two parts lead of litharge, three parts sand washed and burned, plus saltpetre oxide of manganese. The flint formerly employed, which gave the glass its name, had long been superseded by sand from Lynn in Norfolk, Alum Bay in the Isle of Wight and elsewhere. The French sand from Fontainebleau was, however, found to be the best for the purpose and came to be used almost exclusively. The potash came from Smethwick and the manganese from chemical works in Liverpool, Glasgow and London. The proportions in which each ingredient was used varied at different times and in different localities, and even in different glassworks in the same district. As Ure mentioned, 'every different flint-house has a peculiar proportion of glass materials'.[7] In particular the proportion of lead, the most expensive constituent, was kept secret. Harriet Martineau visited a flint glass factory in Birmingham in 1852 and found that 'red lead is added, to give density to the glass; but in what proportions we did not inquire here, having learned elsewhere that that is the one question which a stranger ought not to ask. It is the grand secret of most glasshouses.'[8]

The glass houses were usually built in the form of a cone, sixty to a hundred feet high, and fifty to eighty feet in diameter at the base.[9] The furnace was constructed in the centre. Generally the pots were charged every Saturday morning. Each contained about eighteen hundredweight of glass, the ingredients being added gradually as the fusion proceeded, twelve to fifteen hours being required to complete the charging. But the glass was not ready for working early the next Monday or Tuesday morning, because, though the ingredients became molten, the metal was not in a fit state for working owing to the presence of air bubbles. The bubbles could be excluded only by stoking the furnace to its utmost intensity for thirty to forty hours, the mouths of the pots being sealed during that time.[10] On Monday or Tuesday morning a sufficient weight of melted glass was gathered or coiled on the heated end of the hollow iron blowpipe, varying in length from five to six feet, and in external diameter from three-quarters of an inch to two inches, according to the weight of glass it was intended to gather. The right weight was determined by the nicety of the gatherer's touch. Thus the most skilful work began.

Flint glass makers worked in groups of four known as a 'chair', consisting of a workman (sometimes called the 'gaffer'), a servitor, a footmaker, and a taker-in.[11] Chairs were placed round the furnace and each chair had, on an average, two pots, but varied with the size of the pots and the nature of the work.[12] The names of the hierarchy were derived from the processes employed in making a wineglass. A workman, sitting before the furnace on a peculiar kind of chair fitted with a rail on each side, executed the most difficult parts of the work. The rails were perfectly parallel, but sloped slightly downwards from back to front. On the rails the workman rested the blowing iron, and rolled it to and fro. 'The lump of glass projects over the right arm and is revolved as the blowing iron or puntil is rolled backwards and forwards, so that by the aid of very simple tools the necessary shaping can be performed.'[13]

The servitor, a chief assistant, extracted the glass from the melting pots and shaped it roughly for the workman. The footmaker, a second assistant, helped the servitor not only by fashioning the feet and stands of wineglasses and goblets but by doing other miscellaneous tasks. Hence the *Flint Glass Makers Magazine* wrote in the 1860s that 'rapidly as tumblers or windglasses can be turned out by the joint exertions of the three men—It is just possible for them to produce a hundred and sixty of the commonest wine-glasses, or about eighty of the best kind, in six hours—it would be difficult for any one man to work unaided'.[14] The taker-in or boys looked after the blowing irons, carried vessels to be annealed, held the 'battledore' and ran errands. The stratification of glass makers within chairs, as we shall see later, had a vital importance for the formation of the labour aristocracy.

The weekly work cycle was irregular. Because of the time taken to make the 'metal' the glass makers generally worked four days or four and a half. There were regional variations in the commencement of the working week. W. H. Packwood, a flint glass maker in Stourbridge, remarked in 1875 that:

The custom varies in the commencement of the work in the different districts; some districts are in the habit of commencing work on Mondays, and in other districts according to the custom they commence on the Tuesday; in Stourbridge we commence regularly working throughout the whole of the district on Tuesday.[15]

It is plausible to suggest that the Stourbridge glassworks began their week's work on Tuesday because of the prevalence of 'St Monday' among some working people in the Black Country.[16] The chairman of the manufacturers' association complained in 1875 that 'as a rule we do not work on Monday because a great many of the workmen will have the Monday, whether we give it them or not, so we commence on Tuesday in order that what are termed the chairs may not be broken'.[17] In 1875 J. Derbyshire, a Manchester flint glass manufacturer, in evidence before the Factory and Workshops Acts Commission, when asked if it was essential that flint glass makers took Friday, Saturday, and Sunday as holidays, replied, 'In Lancashire it is, in the north of England and the Newcastle district it is not so usual.'[18]

To avoid stopping the furnace the relay system of six-hour shifts, two shifts a day, was adopted in the larger flint glass works. 'When proceedings once begin,' the *Flint Glass Makers Magazine* wrote, 'there is not intermission until the following Friday night, unless indeed the quantity of glass prepared should run short before then.'[19] A first batch of workmen, a 'chair', began work at six or seven in the morning. They worked for six hours until noon or one o'clock. This was called a 'turn'. Another 'chair' then relieved the first and worked from noon or one till six or seven in the evening. This was the second 'turn'. The first set relieved again at 6.00 or 7.00 p.m. and worked for six hours until midnight or 1.00 a.m., when they were once more relieved by the second relay. Therefore a glass maker worked twelve hours a day.[20] In flint glass-making this had been the traditional routine for several centuries. 'The almost incredible split shift' could be found in Stourbridge as early as 1624.[21] The arrangement of six-hour shifts was said to have originated in 'the inability of the men, owing to the heat, to continue the work for a period of twelve hours'.[22]

Four days' work in flint glass-making meant forty-eight hours, and likewise four and a half days' work meant fifty-four hours. In Stourbridge in 1875 the working hours per week ranged between forty-eight and fifty-six and in Birmingham between fifty and fifty-four.[23] When compared with working hours of between fifty-six and sixty-one in other industries at mid-century,[24] it is clear that flint glass makers had an exceptionally short working week. They seldom worked at the weekend, which was therefore 'available for leisure by the glass makers, deducting a portion required for sleep, after the end of the working week'.[25] Over the weekend the metal mixer prepared the metal.

In pressed glass-making 'chairs' of glass makers consisted of six people[26] working in relays in the same way, but the turn was eight hours instead of six. The first turn began at 5.00 or 6.00 a.m. on Monday, the second at 1.00 or 2.00 p.m.; the first came on again at 9.00 or 10.00 p.m. and worked until 5.00 or 6.00 a.m., and so on, the turns changing weekly so as to divide the night work.[27] There was also a break of about two turns in the middle of the week to refill the pots. They 'cease work for that week not later than six o'clock on Saturday morning'.[28] Only Saturday and Sunday were holidays. The F.G.M.F.S. continued to oppose this system of working.

Among the 'cribs' employing very small numbers of hands where the furnaces and pots were small, a third pattern of working hours prevailed, that of twelve-hour relays.[29] In most cases there were day and night relays, which changed weekly, but in some very small places the men worked by day only, the pots being filled and the metal melted during the night. Blown flint glass makers rejected this pattern of working hours as well, because working in this way produced glass of low quality. 'Cribs men' often worked five or six days a week, but a commissioner was able to find cases of seven-day working, stopping at 7.00 a.m. on Sunday and beginning at 7.00 p.m. on the same day.[30] Even while the excise duty was payable, before 1845, such 'cribs' existed in out-of-the way places so as to evade payment, but an immediate effect of the repeal of the duties was an increase in the number of 'cribs'.[31] It seems likely that the number of 'cribs' increased in the third quarter of the century. In 1877 W. H. Packwood, the Central Secretary of the F.G.M.F.S., remarked at a joint meeting with the manufacturers' association that:

The growth of cribs is of serious importance, both to us, as a Society, and to you, as manufacturers. Our Society has little sympathy with cribs, and we consider it to be to our mutual interest to prevent, as far as possible, its spread. So far as employers are concerned, their part would be to refuse to supply the cribs with cullet, and then it would be impossible for them to obtain broken glass from hotels and elsewhere in sufficient quantities.[32]

In fact, the independent gaffer in his 'cribs' used the cheapest raw materials with a large proportion of cullet, or broken glass, which was added to the batch for remelting. Some used nothing but cullet to make cruets, ink-stands, medical, perfumery and other small articles.

The last operation in flint glass-making was annealing. It was simply a means of cooling the articles slowly, otherwise they would shatter at the slightest touch, or become so delicate as to be unfit for use. When finished, the objects were placed at once, and as hot as possible, on iron pans which travelled slowly on a miniature railway down from the heated end to the cooler end, a distance of about sixty feet. The time for annealing varied from six to sixty hours, the heavier articles requiring most heat and time. After that the products were sent to be cut, in the same premises in most cases, but sometimes to an independent glass cutting works. The work of glass cutting consisted of three stages—roughing, smoothing and polishing. The rougher, or grinder, received the glass, marked the pattern on it, and cut it, using a circular piece of iron. A visitor to the glass cutting works of John Smith of Leith wrote in 1866 that 'the cutters sat at frames to which spindles and wheels, varying in size from eighteen to one or two inches in diameter, were propelled by belts and drums driven by steam power'.[33] A stream of wet sand ran continually upon the glass when it was being cut or ground. The smoother received the articles from the rougher, and with stone, commonly called Warrington stone, smoothed the sharp edges. The article was then 'puttied' by the polisher. The putty was a white powder, formed by calcining an alloy composed of equal parts of tin and lead. The difference in effect of cutting and engraving lay principally in the depth of incision. Engraving wheels were copper discs ranging from two inches to an eighth of an inch. Instead of pumice, emery powder was used as the engraving medium. The wheels were adjusted in a small lathe, which was generally driven by a foot treadle. Obviously, engraving required higher skill than cutting.

Unlike flint glass makers, glass cutters had no relay system. Ten hours a day was usual in most regions in the 1850s and 1860s. The cutters were keen to shorten their working hours. In March 1872 the Stourbridge and Wordsley district of their union demanded fifty-four hours a week 'from 6 a.m. till 5 p.m. the first five days and from 6 a.m. till 1 p.m. on Saturdays, with the usual allowance for meals'.[34] The demand was accepted not only in Stourbridge but throughout the trade in 1872.[35] This was in the context of the engineers' nine-hour movement on Tyneside, begun in 1871. In 1878 the achievement was lost under the combined weight of the Midland employers, and the week came to fifty-eight hours.[36] All the other employers followed, and in some cases fifty-nine hours were demanded. It was not until 1891 that the working week was reduced to fifty-four hours again.[37]

In particular the relay system prevented the glass maker from getting a full night's sleep until the end of the week. It occasionally happened that if someone on the next turn was absent he had to carry on working. Henry Benham, a flint glass maker in Jackson's Flint Glass factory in London, stated that 'many a time, even while I was a boy (in the Pellatt's factory in London), I have been on 48 hours at a time, in these small places, till I could hardly hold my eyes open, and I have been that way so as I could not sleep because I was overtired'.[38] The relay system in flint glass making attracted the attention of Karl Marx. Quoting from the *Fourth Report* of the Children's Employment Commission of 1865, which recorded a boy working thirty-six consecutive hours and others getting only three hour's sleep before resuming work, he wrote in *Capital*:

Meanwhile, late by night perhaps, self-denying Mr. Glass-Capital, primed with port-wine, reels out of his club homeward, droning out idiotically, 'Britons never, never, never shall be slaves!'[39]

The Children's Employment Commission learned from some flint glass makers that 'they like the longer turn the best, as it gives them longer times unbroken for rest, and more of night sleep'.[40] It is notable, however, that they would not change the relay system. The F.G.M.F.S. made no attempt to change it before the first world war, and the six-hour shift was not generally abandoned until just before the second.[41] When any change was attempted, glass makers opposed it strongly. L. Percival, a manager of Osler's Flint Glass Works, of Birmingham, for instance, attempted to alter the six-hour shift to an eight-hour one, but failed. He stated:

Twelve hours at a time would be too severe for either boys or men to stand continuously, and would not answer so well as the relay system. I once proposed intervals of 8 hours, so as to alternate the day and night work, but the idea was disliked by the men.[42]

When the Factory and Workshops Acts of 1867 tried to enforce a change of the six-hour shift into a ten, twelve or fourteen-hour one, a deputation of glass manufacturers met Spencer Walpole, the Home Secretary, to put before him the difficulties they had to contend with.[43] The result was no change in working arrangements until the mid–1870s, when an inspector found that the glass trade was breaking the law. At once orders were given in Stourbridge, Birmingham and Manchester to change the shift to ten, twelve or fourteen hours. The Central Committee of the F.G.M.F.S. got in touch with the inspector and George Young, the secretary of the Royal Commission on the Acts, 'claiming to be heard, before any violation was done to our special industry'.[44] Before the commission W. H. Packwood insisted that 'we are satisfied with the present working of the Act; that is to say, with regard to our hours of work'.[45] T. J. Wilkinson, a Birmingham flint glass maker, also claimed that:

The Society as a union had nothing whatever to do with it [working hours]: it is merely a custom which has been in the trade for a great number of years, and I do not think it would be wise to alter it, but it is not a trade union question at all.[46]

The voice of the Birmingham district secretary, who 'urged the adoption of the Factory Act hours', was a lone one.[47] Probably flint glass makers felt that any change in the traditional pattern of working might have destroyed a barrier which had been helping to prevent less skilled men from entering the trade. The labour aristocrats did not necessarily want easier or even lighter work. They were proud of manly, intensive effort. Accordingly, they would not change the custom despite its inconvenience.

The attitude of flint glass makers to working hours in other trades was surprisingly different from their view of their own. It was T. J. Wilkinson, a delegate from the F.G.M.F.S., who proposed shorter hours at the first Trades Union Congress, in Manchester in 1868. He moved that 'this congress is of opinion that, in order to promote the well being of the working classes, and to neutralise the sad effects of the surplus labour of this country, it is highly essential that the hours of labour should be reduced'.[48] The proposition was carried. His motion also stated that:

this Congress recommends all trade councils and societies to bring before their members the serious consideration of a commutation of the hours of labour, and trade representatives present pledge themselves in the name of their respective societies to render such support as may be in their power, by the general circulation of printed information, and the interchange of delegates who shall address trade union meetings upon the question. (Applause.)[49]

But, returning to his own trade, he did nothing. Seven years later he declared that any change of working hours 'is not a trade union question at all'. The flint glass makers' union leaders saw the shortening of working hours as indispensable for reducing the supply of labour in other trades, but not in their own. They clung to their custom, and this distinguished them from other working men.

II *The environment of the factory*

'The glass house which I first entered,' J. E. White wrote in his impression of a flint glass works in South Shields, 'was dark and filled with a strong sulphurous vapour, said to be drawn into it by the strong draught of the furnace from some other furnace or kiln in the process of heating. One of the boys spoke of the smoke as a cause of his cough.'[50] The poisonous ingredients used in making the glass were also potentially harmful, particularly at mealtimes. A 'medical gentleman' stated that he had known 'one or two narrow escapes from arsenical poisoning from the food being dropped on the floor when arsenic is put into the pots'.[51] In particular lead, an indispensable ingredient of flint glass, made for 'a very unhealthy employment' if it was mixed with other materials by hand. Factories that used machines for mixing materials were very few, and hand mixing was almost universal.[52]

The heat was also a great concern. The temperature in the glass house at the mouth of the furnace was estimated at 172°F to 220°F; where the blowers stood, at 95°F to 118°F, and, at the place where boys 'took in', at 80°F to 196°F.[53] It might happen that a flint glass blower himself would faint, and other men had been known to 'turn faint and were obliged to knock off'.[54] Besides the extremely high temperature, 'the unequal temperature to which the workpeople are necessarily exposed'[55] was another condition peculiar to flint glass works and, of course, it was harmful to the workmen's health. Boys were exposed to much higher temperatures than others. The Children's Employment Commission reported in 1843 that 'the temperature of the place where the men stand to take the metal out of the furnace is 172°; and that where the boys stand when they "take in" the glass at the annealing oven is 196°'.[56] Because of the heat, takers-in working at night were 'very sleepy and have to sing to keep awake and the same in the day some times'.[57]

Taker-in work was totally auxiliary. As J. E. White reported in 1865, 'the greater part of their time is spent in passing to and fro to take glass to the annealing kilns, carrying and cleaning the men's irons, and in occasionally standing to help the men at their work in various ways, or holding irons with or without glass on at the mouth of a furnace'.[58] Takers-in were 'not commonly regarded as glass makers at all, but merely as attendants and helpers to those who are so'.[59] But menial work did not mean that little effort was involved. Takers-in 'journeyed' long distances within the works, normally thirty-two miles a day, sometimes thirty-six, occasionally without shoes or stockings.[60] The weight of each article was another nuisance. Items weighing some three pounds held at the end of an iron stick about seven feet long 'make him out of breath'.[61] As a workman put it, 'a man could not do a "taker-in's" work; it would kill him'.[62] In addition they were often ordered to run errands. 'Running out for men's drink is a very common errand.'[63] If the boys refused to do errands for the men they were ill treated; 'sometimes boxed on the head, if he did not haste for the men's errands'.[64]

Takers-in were occasionally treated badly in the workshops. Evidence of this is provided by the testimony of employers, glass makers and the boys themselves in the *Fourth Report* of the Children's Employment Commission. E. Moore, a pressed flint glass manufacturer in South Shields, stated: 'Boys in a glass-house, I am sorry to say, are very badly treated. The men are brutal and have horrid tempers. They often knock the boys about, i.e. kick them, cuff them too hard . . .'[65]

Men used to knock the boys about and the boys would run away. I have seen men knock boys down and hit them with the iron or tools, &c., e.g. if the boys did not come up right to their work. I have some nasty cuts on the top of my head now that I got when I was little, but I did not get knocked about much because I generally worked with my own relations, and they took care of me.[66]

It seems likely that takers-in working with their relatives were not only given more chance to learn the technique of glass making, but were treated more humanely. Testimony given by boys themselves shows ill usage more vividly. For instance, a boy who worked in a flint glass factory in Birmingham or Stour-bridge gave the following evidence:

Once I was taking in a glass and fell down and broke it, and when I came back and told the master [workman], he jumped up and ran at me and knocked me down and kicked me. There was a great bruise on my thigh from it. I saw a man hit a boy of about 12 on the back of his head with the blowing iron, which had some glass on the end of it, and cut his head open, and made it bleed. It did not bleed much. We all catched it sometimes. They leathered us sometimes.[67]

It is not surprising that the *Flint Glass Makers Magazine* did not report such 'dishonorable' behaviour by flint glass makers at all, and the local papers revealed the ill treatment only when the father of a taker-in sued glass makers for an assault on his son. The *Brierley Hill Advertiser* of 22 February 1862, for instance, reported that a glass maker named George Ridger, of the Hollo-way End Glass Works in Stourbridge, was sued by the father of a taker-in named George Green: Ridger had accused the taker-in of 'neglecting to clean his blow-pipe, and then struck him on the head with it. He was knocked down'.[68] The assault was judged in the Public Office and Ridger was fined 1s and costs.[69] Yet this was an exception. In most cases, glass makers who committed the assaults were not prosecuted and their misconduct was concealed. The society never tried to explore the matter ser-iously. The ill treatment of boys was the dark side of the respecta-bility the flint glass makers claimed.

It seems inevitable that such working conditions must have

led to much ill health, particularly in the case of boys. It was generally admitted that 'young people cannot bear this kind of work, and that it acts most injuriously on the youngest hands, who are generally pale, thin, ill-grown, and unhealthy, suffering severely from bad eyes, and stomachic, bronchial, and rheumatic afflications'.[70] Not only the young people were affected. Cold, influenza and fever accounted for 25·4% of 1,044 receiving sick allowance in Stourbridge between 1867 and 1880. Rheumatism and gout formed 18·8% and Bronchitis 9·1%. These were followed by injury (8·1%), dyspepsia (4·7%) and eye disease (3·3%).[71] The names of the diseases are not entirely reliable, because most of them were self-diagnosed by the men themselves as they claimed the sick allowance from the society. It seems likely, however, the 'injured eye' (2·3%) and 'injury' (8·1%), particularly 'burn' (0·8%), were assumed to be directly caused by the work. Even the glass manufacturers agreed that the effects of the working conditions on the health of the boys were bad. Lovibond Percivall, manager of Osler's Flint Glass Works, of Birmingham, remarked that 'the constant glare and heat of the glory-holes and furnace affect the eyesight at a comparatively early age, and the hand becomes tremulous prematurely'.[72] However, a Children's Employment Commissioner, Mr Horne, observed in Stourbridge that 'The endurance of the heat does not appear to injure the health of the boys, the ventilation being so well and amply provided'.[73] This view was shared by the leaders of the F.G.M.F.S. Richard Lester, secretary of the society, stated before the Commission on Factories and Workshops Acts in 1875 that 'the work is not very laborious. The heat does not at all affect them' (boys).[74] The leaders paid no attention to the health of the boys, simply because boys were not 'glass makers'.

Working conditions in glass cutting were worse than in glass-making. 'There is a general agreement among both employers and workpeople that flint glass cutting is less healthy than the glass house work, owing chiefly to the use of putty and the more confined and sedentary nature of the work'.[75] Flint glass cutting required 'a fixed leaning posture and close watching with the eyes, with a constant grasp of the glass to hold it properly against the cutting wheel'.[76] The hands of cutters were continually in water, which impaired the muscular power and paralysed the hands. The putty used in polishing was considered by the men to be injurious to the hand if it got under the nails. Horne pointed to the injury done by the putty:

I have seen a boy stand with his head close over the box or trough which contained the putty-powder, so that he was constantly inhaling it while he supplied the wheel of the man who sat or stood above him, and who of course also had his share of the injury, which, however, was of a less degree than that received by the boy. Want of cleanliness in the hands is also a great cause of injury. The putty is sure to get under the nails, and if suffered to remain there a few days it often causes the hand to contract. Meals eaten with unwashed hands in this condition are very injurious, and it is a common occurrence.[77]

As a result the disease called 'dropped hand' was very common among glass cutters. The *Morning Chronicle* reported in 1850 that a glass cutter 'who had twice been afflicted with "dropped hand" twice regained the use of it, after a twelve months' cessation of the work. It was stated that he had finally quitted the trade, being apprehensive that if he again lost the use of his hand he should never recover it.'[78]

It is notable that, unlike flint glass makers, glass cutters demanded a reduction in working hours on the ground that it would decrease diseases caused by their unhealthy working conditions. On 30 March 1872 glass cutters in the Stourbridge and Wordsley district of the cutters' union requested a nine-hour working day. The leaflet produced by the union ran:

You, Gentlemen, are fully cognizant of the fact of the unhealthiness of our Trade; we are constantly, or nearly so, in sitting posture, breathing vitiated air, causing in consequence, – Dropped Hands, Cholic, and almost innumerable diseases; . . . Gentlemen, we think a most conclusive argument in our favour for the shortening of the hours of labour. Terrible, Gentlemen, is it not? to suffer from diseases which for ever prevent us from supporting our Wives and Little-ones; many of us at all ages, are forced to leave the Trade through its unhealthiness. . . . We ask for the time for recreation and the improvement of our minds, which will tend to invigorate the frame so as to enable us the better to stand our daily toil, – it would inspire more confidence between the Employers and Employed, – raise us in the social scale, – and better fit us for the ordinary duties of life.[79]

But, as we have seen, flint glass makers intended neither to alter their peculiar working hours nor to improve conditions in the workshops.

Notes

1 D. Bremner, *The Industries of Scotland. Their Rise, Progress, and Present Condition*, Edinburgh, 1869, pp. 377–8.

2 'Many manufacturers make their own pots, the quality of which is of vital importance to them, and in these cases a few females and boys are employed in carrying or preparing clay' (*Children's Employment Commission*, 4th Report, 1865, p. 191, q. 85).

3 A visitor to a flint glass works in Edinburgh in the mid–1860s wrote that 'the clay is mixed and beaten into mortar, after which it is turned four or five times every week for six months, every time being cut into thin slices and tramped by men with bare feet' (*Scotsman*, 8 August 1866). The weight of clay required for one pot was nearly a thousand pounds.

4 'A day at a flint glass factory', *Penny Magazine*, X, February 1841, supplement, p. 83.

5 A. Ure, *Dictionary of Arts, Manufactures and Mines*, vol. I, London, 1853, p. 905. The finished pot was about three feet in height, being worth about £10. For the process of making the pot see Harrison, 'Stourbridge fire clay', p. 135.

6 William Gillinder, *A Treatise on the Art of Glass Making*, Birmingham, 1851, p. 128.

7 Ure, *Dictionary*, p. 911.

8 H. Martineau, 'Birmingham glass works', *Household Words*, V, No. 105, 27 March 1852, p. 35. The author of this article is confirmed by Anne Lohrli, *Household Words*, Toronto, 1973, pp. 357–61.

9 Ure, *Dictionary*, p. 905.

10 'Flint glass requires about 48 hours for its complete vitrification ... in consequence of the contents of the pot being partially screened by its cover from the action of the fire, as also from the lower intensity of the heat' (*ibid.*).

11 In Britain the four-man chair was typical in flint glass-making, but a five-man system was adopted in Manchester in the 1860s. On the other hand, in the 'cribs' the group consisted of fewer persons: two men and a boy or even one man and a boy. On the Continent 'each chair consists of as many as eight persons ... five boys are employed ... every provision is made to avoid needless waste of skilled labour' (H. J. Powell, *et al.*, *The Principles of Glass-making*, London, 1883, p. 76).

12 For instance, in Birmingham in 1867 there were 136 chairs with 300 men, sixty-six apprentices and 130 pots. Since the number of sets were divided by two, because of the two-shift system, there were about two pots to each chair (*Flint Glass Makers Magazine*, VI, p. 10).

13 *Ibid.*, V, p. 77.

14 *Ibid.*, V, p. 76.

15 *Royal Commission on Factory and Workshops Acts*, 1876, vol. II, Minutes of Evidence (P.P. XXX), p. 559, q. 11549.

16 For 'St Monday' in the Black Country see D. A. Reid, 'The decline of Saint Monday, 1766–1876', *Past and Present*, No. 71, 1976, pp. 76–101.
17 *Royal Commission on Factory and Workshops Acts*, 1876, vol. II, p. 348, q. 6911.
18 *Ibid.*, p. 421, q. 8658.
19 *Flint Glass Makers Magazine*, V, p. 75.
20 Working hours of takers-in were generally longer than those of higher-graded men, because 'boys sometimes come half an hour before the men, to get things ready' (*Children's Employment Commission*, 4th Report, 1865, p. 193, q. 101).
21 M. A. Bienefeld, *Working Hours in British Industry. An Economic History*, London, 1972, p. 25, and Guttery, *From Broad-glass to Cut Crystal*, p. 9.
22 *Children's Employment Commission*, 4th Report, 1865, p. 193, q. 99. The reason for the existence of six-hour shifts in flint glass-making is explained by Bienefeld by the fact that 'the six-hour spells were not broken for meals' (Bienefeld, *Working Hours*, p. 65). The two explanations are not mutually exclusive.
23 *Royal Commission on Factory and Workshops Acts*, 1876, vol. II, p. 559, q. 11548, statement of W. H. Packwood, of Stourbridge.
24 Bienefeld, *Working Hours*, p. 77, table I.
25 *Children's Employment Commission*, 4th Report, 1865, p. 197, q. 128.
26 A taker-in (boy), two stickers-up (boys), a gatherer (generally as old as sixteen or more), a presser (man), and a melter (man).
27 *Pressed Glass Makers of Great Britain — Factory Working Rules*, Newcastle, 1872, (Webb Trade Union Collection, Section C, vol. 42, XV), rule I. Rule I includes that they 'work 8 hour turns alternately'.
28 *Ibid.*, rule I.
29 *Children's Employment Commission*, 4th Report, 1865, p. 193, q. 98.
30 *Flint Glass Makers Magazine*, III, p. 16, Joseph Leicester's report.
31 *V.C.H.*, Stafford, vol. II, 1967, p. 228.
32 *Flint Glass Makers Magazine*, IX, p. 241. The joint meeting held on 12 October 1877.
33 *Scotsman*, 8 August 1866. An observer viewed Bower & Sons, of Hunslet, in 1828 and wrote of the cutting shop, 'urged by a small steam engine, the most elegant ornamented articles are finished for sale' (Richard Phillips, *A Dictionary of the Arts of Life and Civilization*, London, 1833, p. 770). By the 1860s the application of steam to the processes of cutting and grinding was universally adopted in the larger manufactories (Timmins (ed.), *Birmingham and the Midland Hardware District*, p. 530).
34 *To the Glass Masters of the Stourbridge and Wordsley Districts* (leaflet), dated 30 March 1872, issued by 'The Committee. Isaac Coakley, Chairman' (Brierley Hill Library).

35 S. Webb, *Questionnaire for the Flint Glass Cutters' Society* (Webb Trade Union Collection, Section A, vol. XLIII, 5), p. 393.
36 In June 1879 'the 9 hours gained in 1871–72 is now practically extinct the Midland associated employers having met and determined to raise the week's work to 58 hours' (S. Webb, *Flint Glass Cutters*, Ms, Webb Trade Union Collection, Section A, vol. XLIII, 5, p. 360).
37 Webb, *Questionnaire for the Flint Glass Cutters' Society*, p. 393.
38 *Children's Employment Commission*, 4th Report, 1865, p. 235, q. 130.
39 Marx, *Capital*, vol. I, English edn, pp. 248–9, n. 1.
40 *Children's Employment Commission*, 4th Report, 1865, p. 193, q. 99.
41 Guttery, *From Broad-glass to Cut Crystal*, pp. 9, 38. The first firm to abandon the six-hour shift in Stourbridge was the Stevens & Williams factory, in 1936.
42 *Children's Employment Commission*, 4th Report, 1865, p. 221, q. 57.
43 *Flint Glass Makers Magazine*, VIII, p. 387.
44 *Ibid.*
45 *Royal Commission on Factory and Workshops Acts*, 1876, vol. II, p. 558, q. 11544.
46 *Ibid.*, p. 457, q. 9217.
47 *Flint Glass Makers Magazine*, VIII, p. 387.
48 *Manchester Guardian*, 4 June 1868.
49 *Ibid.*
50 *Children's Employment Commission*, 4th Report, 1865, p. 238, q. 143.
51 *Ibid.*, p. 186, q. 42.
52 In the mid–1860s only two factories used machinery for mixing materials—the Sowerby & Neville Glass Works in Newcastle and Stone's Flint Glass Works in Birmingham (*ibid.*, p. 229, q. 96, and p. 239, q. 153).
53 *Children's Employment Commission*, 2nd Report, 1843, appendix I (P.P. XIV), p. F 24, q. 230.
54 *Children's Employment Commission*, 4th Report, 1865, p. 200, q. 149.
55 *Children's Employment Commission*, 2nd Report, 1843 (P.P. XIII), p. 36, q. 234.
56 *Children's Employment Commission*, 2nd Report, 1843, appendix I, p. F 24, q. 230. The report of the Commission of 1865 also stated that 'in the flint glass house my thermometer at the mouth of the kiln, where the boys put in articles to anneal, standing there, each time only while they set down the articles, rose quickly to the top, viz., 150°' (*Children's Employment Commission*, 4th Report, 1865, p. 187, q. 46).
57 *Children's Employment Commission*, 4th Report, 1865, p. 200, q. 151.
58 *Ibid.*, p. 189, q. 67.

59 *Ibid.*, p. 188, q. 60.
60 *Ibid.*, p. 240, q. 157.
61 *Ibid.*, p. 191, q. 79.
62 *Quarterly Review*, vol. 119, 1866, p. 390.
63 *Children's Employment Commission*, 4th Report, 1865, p. 191, q. 78. 'These errands, however, when they take boys out long distances in cold weather, when "sweaty" and with "only shirt and trousers on" or if "the men won't let you stop for that (i.e. to slip a waistcoat on)", – it may be in a winter midnight – amount to unpleasant work, and are apt to cause colds' (*ibid.*).
64 *Ibid.*, p. 86, q. 478.
65 *Ibid.*, p. 238, q. 148.
66 *Ibid.*, p. 236, q. 134.
67 *Ibid.*, p. 258, q. 220. Neither his name nor the name of the factory was given in the report, to prevent his master from taking revenge.
68 *Brierley Hill Advertiser*, 22 February 1862.
69 *Ibid.*
70 *Children's Employment Commission*, 2nd Report, 1843, p. 109, q. 596.
71 Compiled from lists of the recipients of sick allowance in the Quarterly Report of the F.G.M.F.S. between 1867 and 1880. The sick allowance began in September 1867 and stopped in September 1880. A flint glass maker who received the allowance for more than one week in three months is regarded as one case of sickness, irrespective of the duration.
72 *Children's Employment Commission*, 4th Report, 1865, p. 220, q. 57.
73 *Children's Employment Commission*, 2nd Report, 1843, p. 46, q. 286.
74 *Royal Commission on Factory and Workshops Acts*, 1876, vol. II, p. 455, q. 9201.
75 *Children's Employment Commission*, 4th Report, 1865, p. 201, q. 162.
76 *Ibid.*, p. 191, q. 83.
77 *Children's Employment Commission*, 2nd Report, 1843, p. 46, q. 286.
78 *Morning Chronicle*, 23 December 1850.
79 *To the Glass Masters of the Stourbridge and Wordsley District* (leaflet), 30 March 1872.

Chapter three

Stratification

I *Methods of payment and wage differentials*

The wages of flint glass makers were put together in an extremely complicated fashion. They were really piece rates,[1] depending on the kind of articles produced and the number made, but took the 'fictitious' form of time wages. David Schloss wrote in 1892 that 'an interesting example of a piece-wage rate expressly fixed on a time-basis, which is admitted to be fictitious, is to be found in the flint glass trade'.[2] This meant that in a dispute, as Schloss pointed out, the argument was not about how much per hour should be paid, but about the 'number' of articles that should be made per hour in order to earn the current standard minimum wage.[3] In so far as the F.G.M.F.S. forbade the glass makers to produce more than a specified quantity of work in each turn and strictly regulated the number of articles produced in a given time, the amount of work could be shown on a time basis. The concept of 'move' was used in the flint glass trade as a means of transforming a piece wage to a time wage. The number of articles produced by a glass maker in a week was first translated into 'moves', according to the proportions agreed between the employers and the society. The figures thus obtained were then transformed into hours, according to the principle of 'two moves per turn'. Since one turn was six hours, one move usually meant three hours.[4] It was a custom in the flint glass trade that the *nominal* week's work of thirty-three hours consisting of eleven moves was paid for as a weekly wage and anything worked over the eleven moves was paid as 'over work'.[5] Since actual work was sixteen moves or more a week, the overtime was often in excess of the nominal work by about 50%. Hence the 'over work' in flint glass-making never meant the actual overtime payment as in other industries such as building, but meant a purely fictitious difference between the actual week and the eleven moves.[6] In other words, it meant the difference between the amount of glass actually produced per hour and the fictitious amount of glass per hour agreed between the employers and the society. As Schloss put it, in flint glass-making 'the time allowed for doing a specified amount of work is far greater than that which is actually spent in the performance of this work by an operative of average capacity'.[7] The origin of this peculiar custom in the trade is obscure, but it is likely that in flint glass-making, as a result of earlier technical innovations, a week's work came to be done in about three days and the eleven moves remained a week's nominal work over centuries. The fact that flint glass makers depended on simple tools which had been unchanged for centuries and introduced only small items of new machinery helped to preserve this system.

It is of great importance, however, that the fictitious time wage had a certain reality. Flint glass makers considered that, although they actually worked until Friday, their week's work ended on Wednesday, so that on Thursday and Friday they were not bound by the contract with their employers. This delusion became a point of dispute in a judgement on breach of contract in court. In July 1874 Thomas Dykes, a Birmingham glass maker, was discharged 'at a minute's notice', without receiving a fortnight's wages, on the ground that he produced many spoilt glasses which were not fit for sale. He sued his employers, Lloyd & Summerfield of Birmingham, and the following cross-examination took place between the judge and a witness, another flint glass maker, in court on 28 July 1874:

Judge. I want to know whether, after he has been paid his proper week's wages, he should be paid for overtime work when he had not worked at all?

Witness. He has to be paid for the extra time, because, if not, his week's work would be done on Wednesday evening.

Judge. But is it invariably the custom to finish the rest of the week?

Witness. A man always goes on after Wednesday.

Judge. Is it compulsory?

Witness. No, he need not unless he likes. It is optional, it is called over work.

Judge. My difficulty is to see what right there can be for the man to do the over work.

Witness. He can stay to work if he likes, or he can go away.

Judge. Then he need not be paid for the over work?

Witness. But he always remains. I have never known a case where a man has not been paid for over work.[8]

A similar kind of dispute occurred in 1858. In November that year, at the Wordsley police court, five flint glass makers were charged with illegally absenting themselves from the Graze-brook Glass Works at Stourbridge. Their discharge was the flashpoint of the long-term strike and lock-out of flint glass makers in 1858–59. When the length of their working week became a point of dispute between the employers and the workers in reference to the validity of a fortnight's notice, Mr Walker, retained for the defence, stated that:

It was customary to give the fourteen days' notice on the ordinary pay day, or before going to work in the ensuing week, and that in this instance the notice was given before the men went to work; that eleven 'moves' constituted a week's work, and that the employer had no control over the men after that number was made.[9]

This was accepted by the court. The court ruled that after finishing eleven moves the glass makers were beyond the control of the employers and consequently 'were at liberty to obtain employment elsewhere'.[10]

An additional complication was that wage rates during the 'over time' period were less than those during the nominal working hours, particular in the case of servitors and foot-makers. One may conjecture that this curious tendency to pay less for over work originated in the employers' inability to control closely the quantity and quality of the metal beyond the first thirty-three hours. The quality of production probably tended to deteriorate. This would afford a reason, in his view, for rewarding the work less well than he did in the earlier part of the week. The Central Secretary of the F.G.M.F.S. stated in the campaign for assimilation of the 'over work' wages in 1873 that 'it seems a ridiculous system for men to be paid less for the work they make at the latter part of the week than the former, and the more so as the work becomes more laborious and difficult with the metal getting done'.[11] The campaign started in Stourbridge and Birmingham, and both Districts accomplished the assimilation after negotiation with the employers.[12] By March 1873 Lancashire had followed, and by July of that year 'nearly the whole trade is paid by that system'.[13]

Apart from this partial improvement, flint glass makers had no intention of changing the 'fictitious' wage system. Firstly because the 'move' system was closely connected with the six-hour shifts. 'Two moves per turn' was their principle. Why flint glass makers opposed any attempt in changing the six-hour shifts has been explained in terms of their labour-aristocratic consciousness. Secondly, they feared that the abandonment of the system might lead to a loss of control over the amount of their labour.

The next step is to trace wage differentials in the flint glass factory. The differentials between flint glass makers and cutters were wide. The wages of the highest rank both of glass makers and of cutters are shown in table 3:1. According to the table flint glass cutters received wages one-third or one-fourth less than glass makers. But the actual wages glass cutters received were less than the amount shown in the table, because there was a strange custom in the cutting shops that employers deducted more than 12*s* a week for the steam power from each cutter. This custom derived from the fact that, before the application of steam power to glass cutting, each cutter had to pay from his wages men or boys to turn the wheel for them. Even after the introduction of steam power the employers insisted that the men should pay for the turning of the wheel. The *Morning Chronicle* reported in 1850 that 'in some establishments the "turning" or steam power is reckoned at one-third of a man's earnings; so that, if a man nominally earns 36*s* a week, he only receives 24*s*'.[14] Hence, it seems likely that the actual wage differentials between glass makers and cutters were much wider than the table indicates.

TABLE 3:1 Wage differentials between glass makers and cutters
(weekly wages)

Region	Year	Glass maker	Glass cutter
Birmingham	1850	40s–48s	20s–34s
"	1866	49s	32s
"	1877	54s	28s
Manchester	1849	45s	32s
"	1859	45s	32s
Newcastle	1867–8	36s–39s	24s–40s
Sunderland	1883	40s	30s
Glasgow	1883	40s	30s

Source. Labour Statistics — Return of Rates of Wages, Part II, 1887 (P.P. LXXXIX), pp. 243–7, except data for Birmingham 1850. (Some scholars have cast doubt on the reliability of those figures. See, for example, Hobsbawm, *Labouring Men*, p. 281.) *Morning Chronicle*, 23 December 1850.

Moreover, flint glass makers distinguished themselves not only from glass cutters but from bottle makers, teasers, learmen, founders, moulders, smiths, stopperers, claymen, yardmen and warehousemen in the factory. The average weekly wages of flint glass makers in Beatson & Clark's works at Rotherham tended to decline from 39s 10d in the 1860s to 37s 10d in the 1870s and to 28s 7d in the early 1880s. On the other hand, those of flint bottle makers ranged between 23s and 27s in the same period. Thus bottle makers received 57·7% of flint glass makers' wages in the 1860s, 71·7% in the 1870s, and 87·2% (88·4% in the Wood Bros factory) in the 1880s.[15] Though wage differentials between the two were narrowing between the 1860s and 1880s, the differentials were still wide. In the same period teasers and learmen were paid approximately 14s to 20s but occasionally over 20s. Founders were paid between 16s and 24s. Mouldmakers, smiths, stopperers and claymen were paid between 14s and 27s. Yardmen and warehousemen were almost always paid less than 20s.[16] On the whole, flint glass makers in the chairs enjoyed markedly higher wages than these workers.

Yet more significant in terms of the formation of the labour aristocracy were wage differentials within each chair. The differentials were fairly wide, to the extent that the lower wages of the superior status overlapped the higher wages of the inferior status. This structure derived partly from the difference in the duration of service in the same status and partly from the fact that different chairs produced different articles, such as tumblers, goblets and wineglasses of various kinds. Nonetheless the wage stratification according to each status can be isolated. Of the wages of workmen, servitors had about two-thirds, journeymen footmakers about one-third, apprentice footmakers about a quarter and takers-in about a tenth.

The next step is to trace changes both in wage levels and in wage differentials in Stourbridge and in Rotherham. As table 3:2 shows, between 1840 and 1862 the wages of workmen and servitors in Stourbridge tended to increase substantially.[17] Weekly wages of workmen were 65·9% higher in the early 1860s than in the first half of the 1840s, and those of servitors 64·0% higher. Wages within two groups (workmen and servitors) tended to disperse over the period. Nonetheless, wage differentials between workmen and servitors (median) widened until

TABLE 3:2 Wages of flint glass makers in Stourbridge between 1838 and 1862.

(a) Weekly wages: interquartile range

Year	No. of Chairs	Workman			Servitor			Footmaker			Taker-in		
		s d	s d (Median)	s d	s d	s d (Median)	s d	s d	s d (Median)	s d	s d	s d (Median)	s d
1838–39	8	38 3	31 8	26 2	24 8	22 3	14 11	11 6	8 2	5 0	4 10	4 7	4 3
1840–44	8–10	28 1	26 5	24 1	20 4	19 0	16 0	10 6	9 0	7 10	4 8	4 3	3 0
1845–49	7–8	31 8	28 0	25 0	20 10	18 11	17 2	11 9	10 11	9 2	3 7	3 3	3 1
1850–54	7–9	39 10	34 1	29 – 3	21 11	20 0	12 0	12 0	11 0	10 6	4 8	4 3	3 10
1855–59	8–10	45 8	38 0	33 1	26 10	23 2	13 11	13 11	11 11	8 9	4 4	4 2	3 11
1860–62	9–10	46 7	40 3	34 7	31 2	24 2	11 1	11 1	8 9	6 0	4 7	4 3	4 3

Notes

(a) The wages in the first week of January and July each year are chosen, but when one (or both sets) is estimated to have been obtained by working less than eleven moves a week, then these figures are excluded in the average calculation. These are not nominal wages (eleven moves) but weekly wages actually paid.

(b) The number of chairs are those in the first week of January each year.

(c) The wages in 1859 are those for July so as to exclude the effects of the strike and lock-out of flint glass makers.

Source. Wages book of Stevens & Williams.

TABLE 3:2(b) Index: interquartile range (1840–44 = 100)

Year	Workman			Servitor			Footmaker			Taker-in		
		Median			Median			Median			Median	
1838–39	136·2	117·4	109·7	130·8	129·8	139·1	142·1	127·8	104·3	139·5	120·0	125·0
1840–44	100·0	100·0	100·0	100·0	100·0	100·0	100·0	100·0	100·0	100·0	100·0	100·0
1845–49	112·8	106·1	103·8	101·7	107·3	111·9	121·3	119·6	102·5			102·8
1850–54	141·8	129·0	121·5	124·2	115·4	125·0	114·3	87·0	90·2	130·2	127·5	127·8
1855–59	162·6	143·8	137·4	148·3	141·2	144·8	132·5	131·5	107·6	120·9	125·0	130·6
1860–62	165·9	152·4	143·6	163·8	164·0	151·0	105·6	97·2	78·3	130·2	137·5	141·7

TABLE 3:2(c) Wage differentials of flint glass makers in Stourbridge (index: median)

Year	Workman	Servitor	Footmaker	Taker-in
	Median	Median	Median	Median
1838–39	100·0	79·6	37·1	12·9
1840–44	100·0	71·9	34·1	12·6
1845–49	100·0	67·6	39·0	12·2
1850–54	100·0	64·3	23·0	12·5
1855–59	100·0	70·6	31·1	11·0
1860–62	100·0	77·4	21·7	11·4

TABLE 3:3 Wages of flint glass makers in Rotherham between 1856 and 1882

		Status		
Year	Workman	Servitor journeyman	Servitor apprentice	Workman in the best paid chair
		Average weekly wages		
1856–59	50s 0d	30s 5d	15s 4d	56s 8d
1860–69	43s 7d	27s 11d	14s 0d	52s 6d
1870–79	50s 10d	38s 7d	14s 7d	59s 10d
1880–82	41s 6d	30s 10d	12s 7d	51s 4d
		Index		
1856–59	100·0	60·8	30·7	113·3
1860–69	100·0	64·1	32·1	120·5
1870–79	100·0	75·9	28·7	117·7
1880–82	100·0	74·3	30·3	123·7

Notes
(a) The wages books of Beatson & Clark for the years 1875–78 are missing.
(b) The method of calculation is the same as was used for the wages book of Stevens & Williams. See table 3:2.
(c) The wages of the takers-in are included in the workmen's wages and not separately listed.
Source. Wages book of Beatson & Clark.

the first half of the 1850s (64·3%) and thereafter narrowed. In the early 1860s servitors received 77·4% of workmen's wages.

The movement of wages in the Rotherham factory between 1856 and 1882 is shown in table 3:3. Only in the 1850s and early 1860s are the wages comparable with the Stourbridge data. In the 1850s the differences in wage levels were wide between the two areas. Workmen in Rotherham had wages about a third higher than those in Stourbridge (Rotherham 50s 0d and Stourbridge 36s 1d).[18] Servitors had one quarter higher wages than those in Stourbridge (Rotherham 30s 5d and Stourbridge 24s 5d). Probably these regional variations derived from different situations in the labour market and trade structure as between the two areas: with its long tradition of flint glass making, skilled men had become more numerous in Stourbridge; in Rotherham a high level of wages was necessary to attract them, as Yorkshire was somewhat late in developing a glass industry and it concen

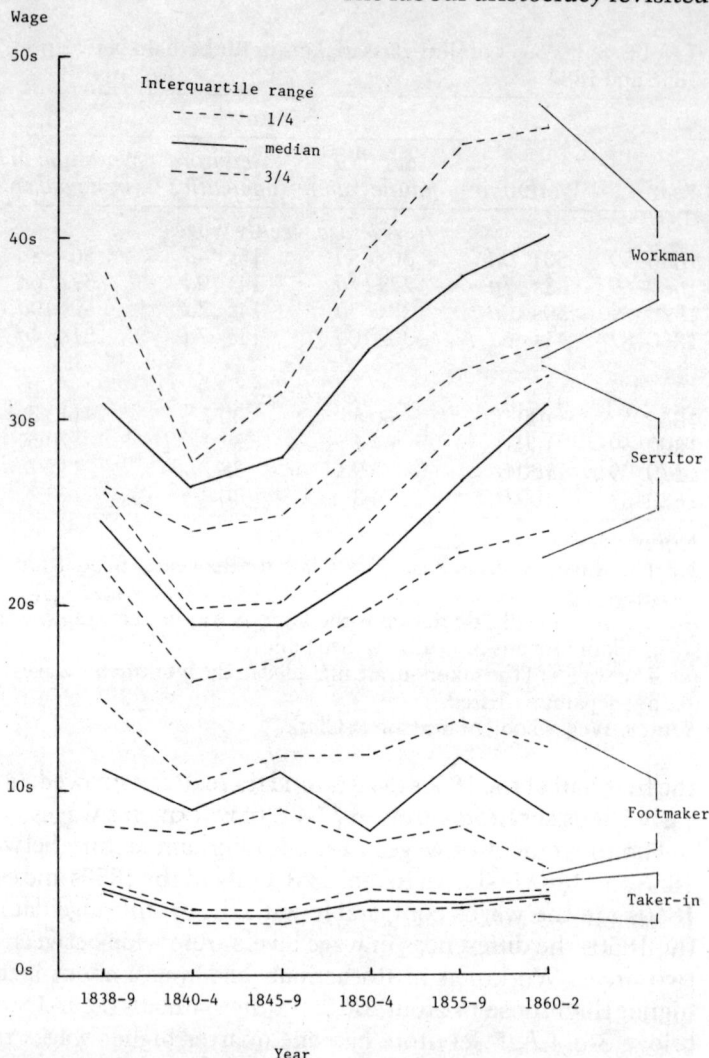

Fig. 1 Wages of flint glass makers at Stevens & Williams, Stourbridge, 1838–62

trated mainly on bottle glass. Soon after, however, these regional differences disappeared. By the 1860s wages in both areas were very similar. Certainly the role the society played in this equalisation cannot be ignored. In addition, the law of competition in the market seems to have begun to penetrate and helped equalise wage levels. Higher pay in Rotherham pushed up costs so that Rotherham flint glass became less competitive. In the 1870s the wages of workmen and servitors in Rotherham rose again, probably at the same pace as in Stourbridge. The movement of wages for footmakers and takers-in was most significant. Particularly in the first half of the 1850s in Stourbridge they fell below 8s, being 23·0% of workmen's wages. The wages of apprentice servitors in Rotherham, corresponding to footmakers in Stourbridge, moved irregularly too. Those of apprentice servitors in Rotherham gradually declined between 1867 and 1882, although there was a slight increase in the 1870s. It is of great importance to recognise not only that the movement of the wages of footmakers was different from those of both workmen and servitors, but that footmakers' were, in absolute terms, distinguished from those of workmen and servitors. Clearly the low wages of footmakers made it difficult to keep a family. According to George Barnsby, wages 'just to subsist in the household budget in the Black Country' were 14s 7½d in 1840, 12s 6d in 1850, 14s 0d in 1860, and 13s 4½d both in 1870 and 1880.[19] It is clear that the Stourbridge footmakers' wages were below subsistence level in the 1840s and 1850s. The low wages of footmakers became a serious problem for the F.G.M.F.S., and it was the demand of 14s as a minimum wage for them which precipitated the long strike and lock-out of 1858–59. The strike ended in April 1859 with an agreement recognising 14s as footmakers' minimum wage. In the early 1860s it reached, at most, subsistence level. But afterwards footmakers continued to move out of the industry because of their low pay. Benjamin Smart, the Central Secretary of the society, said in a letter to George Lloyd, chairman of the Midland Glass Manufacturers' Association, in 1863 that 'the small wages received by footmakers have caused many of them to leave the blowing'.[20] When wages of apprentice footmakers were included, in the early 1860s footmakers' wages were still less than 9s and they could not regain their level of the 1840s.

The census enumerators' books for Stourbridge in 1861, with other sources, suggest that the average age of footmakers was 28·14 years, and 73·3% were married, with, on average, 1·41 children per family.[21] And 73·4 per cent of all footmakers were responsible for the maintenance of the family as head of the household. As Joseph Leicester, a London flint glass maker, put it, footmakers 'really are men, and not boys, and they are men with families'.[22] Their children were still too young to work, so that footmakers' earnings were not supplemented by that source.[23] Although some wives had to work, it was inconvenient for them to have jobs outside the home because of the peculiar working hours in flint glass making. The harshness of the footmakers' life was repeatedly stressed in the society. At the Edinburgh conference, held in 1867, for instance, it was regretted that 'any branch of the glass manufacture should be so low paid as the footmakers – whose wages are not sufficient to enable them to support a family and educate their children'.[24] In the 1870s the situation remained unchanged. In 1873 Richard Leicester, a Manchester flint glass maker, remarked that the footmaker 'has been greatly underpaid',[25] and justified the appeal of footmakers in the District which demanded an increase in wages without the sanction of the executive committee of the society. The appeal well illustrates the footmakers' standard of living.

Look at our homes – many amongst us are married and have children. We have to send our wives to the factory, when we would willingly keep them at home, in order to make all ends meet. The consequences are, children are neglected, and home becomes more like a place to run away from, than a home in reality as well as in name, where, when our toil is over, we could repair with feelings of pleasure and recruit [sic] our exhausted strength . . . Are we of less importance to the glass maker than what the hod carrier is to the bricklayer, or the teaser as an accessory to glass making?[26]

Footmakers' wages were considered low even for a labourer. In 1876 a letter from a member of the society pointed out that 'it is a well known fact that plenty of good footmakers leave our trade as soon as they are out of their time. Because they can get more as labourers than they can as Footmakers . . . Eighteen shillings is considered low wages for a labourer.'[27] Clearly then, a sharp distinction existed within chairs between workmen and servitors on the one hand, and footmakers and takers-in on the other. This was well realised by a contemporary flint glass maker, who stated that footmakers, 'as a class, cannot mix with more favoured shopmates, not being able to appear respectable'.[28]

II *Promotion and lifetime wage curve*

Changes in the wages of the different groups of workers in chairs, and changes in wages during the lifetime of individual working men, are related but different issues. In any study of the labour aristocracy the analysis of the lifetime change is crucial, because with promotion wages might increase more rapidly.

David Bremner wrote in 1869 that 'the flint-glass makers have a union, which is understood to be one of the strictest associations of the kind in the United Kingdom'.[29] In particular, apprentice restriction was strictly enforced and 'much more successful than in other trades'.[30] The rule of the newly organised society provided that the ratio between journeymen and apprentices should be six to one. If 'unauthorised' apprentices came in, the society men often went on strike until the newcomers were expelled. In 1858, for instance, Francis Bate, who apprenticed his son to the Webbs' glass factory at Wordsley, summoned Joseph Webb, the proprietor, for the sum of £3 15s, because soon after his son had entered employment 'the men at the work struck against the boy, stating that there were too many apprentices employed, and consequently would not allow him to proceed with his work . . . Complainant had offered the sum of £5 if the men would cease their opposition; but they still refused to allow the boy to work'.[31] It is clear that the apprentice restriction was stringent.

In order to make the demand for labour exceed the supply, the society's conference in June 1858 decided to restrict the apprentice ratio more stringently than ever before, believing that 'our success depends in a very great measure on regulating the supply for the demand'.[32] The new rule of one apprentice to three chairs precipitated the strike and lock out of 1858–59, and at the end of the lock-out the rule was revised to one apprentice to two chairs.

In the 1860s the apprentice restriction of the society began to be violently criticised by the employers. At the conference of the Social Science Association in Newcastle in 1863 R. W. Swinburne, a plate glass manufacturer of South Shields, read a paper in which he made 'a most unfounded attack on the principles, object, and practice of the Flint Glass Makers' Friendly Society'.[33] He remarked that:

A great impediment to the progress of glass manufacture in this district is the trades' union among the workmen. In the blown flint trade the union exercises a power which amounts to a domination over the employer. In one case at least a manufacturer permanently gave up his business from this cause, and in other cases large works have been for a time wholly suspended.

A respectable flint glass manufacturer makes the following statement: – 'The glass makers' society decides upon the number of apprentices the master shall employ, and the rate of wages he must pay his men'.[34]

The paper created a sensation. William Caine, a Manchester glass manufacturer, wrote in the *Alliance News* that 'to my great gratification the author, Mr. Swinburne, did not shrink from mentioning one great impediment to the progress of the glass manufacture'.[35] On the other hand, the *Bee-Hive* wrote that 'this paper contained all the used-up, worn-out statements against Trades' Unions which have appeared in the columns of the *Times* and *Telegraph* and other papers of the like kidney', and saw Swinburne's paper as 'a condemnation of Trades' Unions generally'.[36] Benjamin Smart, the Central Secretary, also counter-attacked, stressing that the consensus on apprentice restriction had come at the end of the great strike in April 1859 between the society and the manufacturers' association and that agreement was still in effect.[37] It seems likely that Swinburne's paper was based on information given by Nevill, who had been hostile to the society since the early 1850s.[38] The problem was resolved officially at the next conference of the Social Science Association,[39] but the obloquy of the apprentice restriction had been widely spread by the paper and was not soon forgotten.

Thus, if boys entered the flint glass trade between the age of eleven and thirteen as takers-in, the vast majority of them left at about fourteen or fifteen without becoming apprentices. At a flint glass factory in Birmingham, for instance, out of a total of eighty or ninety boys who had been employed as takers-in for eight or nine years, only four were taken on as apprentice foot-makers.[40] In the Stevens & Williams factory at Stourbridge sixty-six boys were employed as takers-in over fifteen years between 1847 and 1862, but only nineteen were taken on as apprentice footmakers. The other forty-seven left the factory without being apprenticed.[41]

Together with apprentice restriction, the workmen's control of promotion proved very effective in the flint glass industry. The manufacturers had little or no power over promotion. A rule of the society provided that 'any servitor or footmaker applying to be put on without the consent of the men in the factory where he works, and of the District, shall be fined one pound and not allowed to work if he gets the situation. Districts to have power to increase these fines, but not to exceed five pounds'.[42] The following cross-examination occurred before the Royal Commission on Trade Unions in 1868 between a commissioner and George Lloyd, chairman of the manufacturers' association:

Question. So that the master has no voice in the promotion of his men without consulting the union?
Lloyd. He may do it sometimes, and he does do it, but there is a risk.
Question. Of getting his shop struck?
Lloyd. Yes, or blocked; that means an impediment put in the way of employers or workmen filling up the vacant situation.
Question. So that the union assumes the power of control over the advancement of the men, irrespective of the wishes of the master?
Lloyd. Entirely.[43]

If there was a vacancy for a workman, it could not be filled with a servitor unless there were no workmen on the unemployment roll. The *Flint Glass Makers Magazine* openly insisted that 'servitors ought not to be allowed to take workmen's situations when there are men on the roll who can fill the vacant situation'.[44] A factory inspector reported in 1879 that:

No promotions are permitted or take place until the funds of the society are relieved of the unemployed; therefore however deserving a young servitor or footmaker may be for promotion on any opportunity occurring, notwithstanding his having been trained to making a special class of goods, it is never accomplished without a struggle, and is scarcely possible by reason of the unemployed subsisting on the funds.[45]

In this way the position of highly graded flint glass makers was carefully protected. The *Pottery Gazette*, the glass manufacturers' journal, condemned the society in 1880, claiming that 'although there are 500 glass makers out of employment, there is a difficulty even now in filling applications for first-class men'.[46]

One of the most important criteria of whether a worker is a

labour aristocrat or not is his chances of promotion. The national data relating to the promotion of flint glass makers are obtained from the *Flint Glass Makers Magazine* in the mid–1860s. As table 3:4 shows, the annual rate of promotion for apprentices put on as journeymen (normally footmakers but sometimes they moved up direct to servitor) was 45·6% of all apprentices. Since apprentices who had served five or six years were allowed to be members of the society, the rates imply that almost all apprentices were promoted to journeymen after a seven-year apprenticeship. The rate of promotion from footmaker to servitor was 9·3% of all footmakers. It is notable that promotion to workman was extremely difficult; in any one year a servitor had only a 2·2% chance of becoming a workman. Thus it is clear that once a taker-in was apprenticed he could normally expect to be promoted to journeyman footmaker and, after a number of years, to servitor. But there was a surprisingly strong barrier between servitors and workmen; some were promoted to workman but some remained a servitor until death or retirement.

TABLE 3:4 Differences in the rate of promotion of flint glass makers in chairs in the 1860s

Status	No. of members of F.G.M.F.S.		No. promoted during 3½ years		Rates of promotion per annum (%)	
	Great Britain	Stour-bridge	Great Britain	Stour-bridge	Great Britain	Stour-bridge
Apprentice	52	13	83	10	45·6	22·0
Footmaker	236	39	77	14	9·3	10·3
Servitor	623	104	49	2	2·2	0·5

Notes
(a) The number of membership is that of 1865 and this excludes the number of workmen.
(b) The number of the promoted is that between the second quarter of 1864 and the third quarter of 1867. The status prior to promotion is here described.
(c) The rate of promotion per annum is: the number of the promoted divided by the number of membership of the F.G.M.F.S. in the status divided by 3½ × 100.
Source. Calculated for Quarterly Report of the F.G.M.F.S., *Flint Glass Makers Magazine*, V, p. 248–VI, p. 40.

It is also useful to examine regional differences in the frequency of promotion. As table 3:5 suggests, in Stourbridge the

TABLE 3:5 Regional differences in promotion of flint glass makers in the 1860s

District	No. of members of F.G.M.F.S.	No. promoted during 3½ years	Rates of promotion per annum (%)
Stourbridge	279	26	2·7
Birmingham	297	32	3·1
Manchester	268	44	4·7
Newcastle	70	13	5.3
All districts	1611	209	3·7

Notes
(a) The number of the F.G.M.F.S. is all membership including workmen in 1865.
(b) The number of the promoted is the total of all promotions, that of apprentices put on, footmakers advanced and servitors advanced.
(c) The rate of promotion per annum is: the number of the promoted divided by the number of membership of District by 3½ × 100.
Source. Ibid.

society restricted promotion most successfully, with Birmingham second. The average rates of promotion per annum in these Districts were respectively 2·7% and 3·1% of the members in each District. On the other hand, in both Manchester and Newcastle the rate of promotion was far beyond the average for the society as a whole, particularly in Newcastle, where it was 5·3%, almost twice as high as in Stourbridge. Certainly these regional differences were related to the degree of the society's discipline, which varied in each region. Newcastle was a declining force in blown flint glass making over the period, and Manchester was growing rapidly, so that the society was able to exert less control over promotion. In contrast in the West Midlands the society could exercise a fair degree of control. In Stourbridge it was most stringent. The rate of promotion of apprentices, footmakers and servitors there was, respectively, 22·0%, 10·3% and 0·5% per annum.

A limitation of these data obtained from the *Flint Glass Makers Magazine* is that takers-in are not included, simply because they were not members of the society. However, the wages book of Stevens & Williams factory in Stourbridge provides some additional information. In the period between 1847 and 1862 sixty-six boys were employed as takers-in. The other eighty employees were footmakers, servitors or workmen. The

average rate of promotion for all these workers in the factory
was 2·3% per annum,[47] approximately the same as the Stourbridge rates in the mid–1860s calculated from the *Magazine*
(2·7%). In the period twenty-eight promotions out of 146
workers took place:[48] takers-in who were apprenticed numbered sixteen, and journeymen footmakers advanced to servitor
numbered nine. But the number of servitors advanced to workman was only three. The rate of promotion per annum in each
status was 11·6% to takers-in, 6·5% for footmakers and 2·2% for
servitors (table 3:6). It is clear that to be promoted from servitor
to workman and enter the top league of the labour aristocracy
was extremely difficult. This fact must have strengthened
labour-aristocratic consciousness when any glass makers
passed down the narrow road to the highest status in the factory.
Since promotion was most difficult in Stourbridge, it seems not
unreasonable to suggest that it was there that feelings of
superiority were most marked.

TABLE 3:6 Promotion of flint glass makers at Stevens & Williams,
Stourbridge, between 1847 and 1862

	Average No. of men in the factory	No. of promotions during 16 years	Rates of promotion per annum (%)
Taker-in	8·6	16	11·6
Footmaker	8·6	9	6·5
Servitor	8·6	3	2·2

Notes
(a) The number of men in the factory was the average per annum,
    estimated from the average number of chairs in the factory between
    1847 and 1862.
(b) The number of promotions is obtained from the checking of each
    name in the wages book every six months in the period between
    1847 and 1862.
Source. Wages book of Stevens & Williams.

The next investigation is an attempt to examine the lifetime
experience of an average glass maker, who passed through the
restricted promotion in the chairs in Stourbridge. By combining
the census enumerators' books of 1861 with a list of the
membership of the F.G.M.F.S. which indicates the status of
glass makers in chairs, it is possible to calculate the average age
of glass makers according to status. The age distribution of flint
glass makers thus obtained is set out in table 3:8. It is not

surprising that under the restricted control of promotion by the Society, socio-economic status in chairs correlated with years of service. As figure 2 suggests, workmen under thirty were only 7·8% of all workmen, those between thirty and thirty-nine were 45·5%, and those over forty were 46·8%. So far as servitors were concerned, 69·3% were concentrated in the age group between twenty-five and thirty-nine. Only 24·3% were over forty, about half the percentage of workmen past that age. On the other hand, 80% of all footmakers were under the age of thirty. As a result, the average ages of workmen, servitors, and footmakers were respectively 41·7, 34·7 and 28·1. Meanwhile the wages book of Stevens & Williams of Stourbridge provides the wages over the period between 1840 and 1862, which has already been presented in table 3:2. If we regard the data from the factory as the average wage of flint glass makers in Stourbridge, it is thus

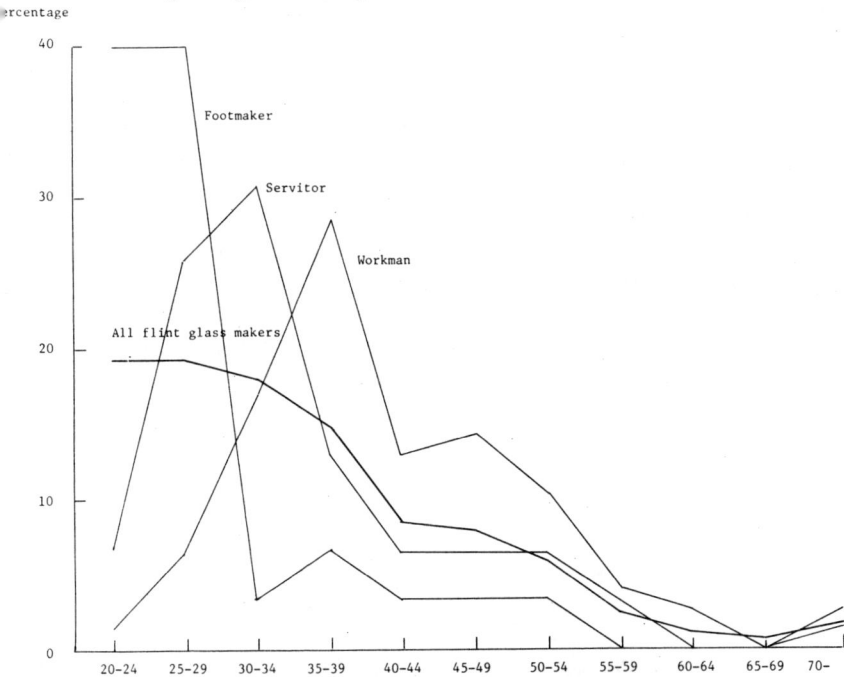

Fig. 2 Age distribution of flint glass makers in Stourbridge, 1861. Source: census enumerators' books for Stourbridge, 1861; list of membership of the F.G.M.F.S. in 1857, *Flint Glass Makers Magazine*, III, pp. 238–43

possible to estimate the changing wages of individual glass makers during their lifetime, by combining the data of ages with those of wages in each status. In the estimation it is assumed that glass makers began to work at the age of twelve and that there was little or no change in the average of each status in the period concerned.

If a glass maker started in 1830 with 3s–4s as taker-in,[49] his wage increased to 10s 11d when he was a footmaker and to 21s 11d when he was a servitor. When he was a workman in the late 1850s his wages became 38s 0d. Similarly, if he started with 3s–4s in 1845, his wages passed 7s 10d and 26s 10d and became 40s 3d in the 1860s. If he started in 1840 with 3s–4s his wages went through 11s 10d and 31s 2d and reached probably more than 42s in the late 1860s. This result indicates what amount of wages the *average* glass maker received *after* passing through the restricted promotion in the chairs. Since the above wage data are nominal wages, they must be converted into real wages. But the cost of living in Stourbridge was, according to Hopkins's calculation,[50] almost stable both in the 1840s and the 1850s and increased less than 10 per cent in the 1860s over the previous two decades. So it is clear that the rise of wages of individual glass makers in a lifetime was still extremely sharp, if they obtained average promotion, probably incomparably sharper than that of the labourers.[51]

As was noticed above, many takers-in left the factory without being apprenticed. Once apprenticed, they were promoted towards workmen. But some glass makers remained of the same status for a much longer period, while others were promoted much more quickly than the average. Even glass makers of the same status had different wages according to different chairs. Accordingly, the wages of individual glass makers moved in a complicated manner. The weekly wages and status of individual glass makers over the period between 1847 and 1862 are shown in table 3:7. Nine glass makers among them were employed there for at least the full sixteen years. H. Scriven was the only one to rise from taker-in to workman during the period. In 1847, as a taker-in, he earned 3s a week. The following year he was apprenticed and thereafter served as apprentice footmaker, receiving 5s for seven years. Then he became a journeyman footmaker. As a result his wages rose sharply to 20s. After six years as servitor he was promoted to workman in 1861 and received 25s. A similar advance after serving an apprenticeship can be found in the case of B. Scriven. But normally an apprentice footmaker became a journeyman footmaker without such a sharp rise in wages. When G. Rider was apprenticed, his wages

TABLE 3:7 Weekly wages of individual glass makers in Stourbridge

Year	J. Scriven		G. Scriven		J. Rockes		W. Scriven		I. Scriven	
	s	d	s	d	s	d	s	d	s	d
1847	20	0 W	28	0 W	20	0 W			17	0 S
1848	22	0 W	28	0 W	21	0 W			20	0 W
1849	24	0 W	28	0 W	22	0 W			21	0 W
1850	26	0 W	28	0 W	25	0 W	22	0 W	22	0 W
1851	33	0 W	28	0 W	27	0 W	22	0 W	27	0 W
1852	35	0 W	28	0 W	27	0 W	24	0 W	28	0 W
1853	35	0 W	28	0 W	27	0 W	26	0 W	28	0 W
1854	40	0 W	33	0 W	28	0 W	36	0 W	28	0 W
1855	40	0 W	33	0 W	28	0 W	36	0 W	28	0 W
1856	40	0 W	33	0 W	28	0 W	40	0 W	28	0 W
1857	40	0 W	33	0 W	28	0 W	40	0 W	28	0 W
1858	40	0 W	33	0 W	28	0 W	40	0 W	28	0 W
1859	40	0 W*	33	0 W	28	0 W	40	0 W*	28	0 W*
1860	40	0 W	33	0 W	28	0 W	40	0 W	28	0 W
1861	40	0 W	33	0 W	28	0 W	40	0 W	28	0 W
1862	40	0 W	33	0 W	28	0 W	40	0 W	28	0 W

Year	W Scriven (J)		T. Sheldon		T. Scriven		J Cartwright		G. Compson	
	s	d	s	d	s	d	s	d	s	d
1847	17	0 S			20	0 S	16	0 S	7	6 F
1848	18	0 S			20	0 S	17	0 S	8	6 F
1849	18	0 S			20	0 S	18	0 S	9	6 F
1850	18	0 S			20	0 S	18	0 S	10	6 S
1851	18	0 S	17	0 S	20	0 S	18	0 S	16	0 S
1852	20	0 W	17	0 S	20	0 S	18	0 S	16	0 S
1853	21	0 W	17	0 S	20	0 S	18	0 S	17	0 S
1854	22	0 W	20	0 W	22	0 S	20	0 S	18	0 S
1855	28	0 W	22	0 W	22	0 S	20	0 S	22	0 S
1856	28	0 W	23	0 W	22	0 S	20	0 S	22	0 S
1857	28	0 W	23	0 W	22	0 S	20	0 S	22	0 S
1858	28	0 W	23	0 W	22	0 S	20	0 S	22	0 S
1859	28	0 W	23	0 W	23	0 S	21	0 S	22	0 S
1860	28	0 W	25	0 W	23	0 S	21	0 S	22	0 S
1861	28	0 W	26	0 W	23	0 S	21	0 S	22	0 S
1862	28	0 W	26	0 W			21	0 S	22	0 S

TABLE 3:7 *concluded*

Year	W. Wild			G. Rider			J. Thompson			H. Scriven			B. Scriven		
	s	d		s	d		s	d		s	d		s	d	
1847				3	0	T				3	0	T			
1848				3	0	T				5	0	F			
1849				3	0	T	3	0	T	5	0	F	3	0	T
1850	3	0	T	3	0	T	3	0	T	5	0	F	3	0	T
1851	3	0	T	5	0	F.	3	0	T	5	0	F	5	0	F
1852	5	0	F	5	0	F	3	0	T	5	0	F	5	0	F
1853	5	0	F	5	0	F	3	0	T	5	0	F	5	0	F
1854	6	6	F	5	0	F	3	0	T	5	0	F	5	0	F
1855	7	6	F	5	0	F	3	0	T	20	0	S	5	0	F
1856	8	0	F	5	0	F	3	0	T	20	0	S	5	0	F
1857	9	6	F	9	6	F	6	0	F	20	0	S	5	0	F
1858	10	0	F	12	0	F	7	6	F	22	0	S	20	0	S
1859	13	0	F	13	0	F	9	6	F	24	0	S	20	0	S
1860	13	0	F	13	0	F	10	6	F	24	0	S	20	0	S
1861	16	0	S	14	0	F	14	0	F	25	0	W	23	0	S
1862	17	0	S	14	0	F	14	0	F	26	0	W	27	0	S

Notes

(a) W Workman, S Servitor, F Footmaker, T Taker-in. *Strike-breaker.

(b) The wages in 1858 and 1859 do not include the effects of the strike and lock-out.

Source. Wages book of Stevens & Williams.

rose from 3s to 5s. In the last year of a seven-year apprenticeship they rose to 9s 6d. The following year he became a journeyman footmaker and received 12s. Thereafter his wages went on rising gradually and in 1861 reached 14s, probably as a result of the agreement regarding the minimum wages of footmakers between the Glass Manufacturers' Association and the society.

Some servitors remained without promotion to workman for years. For instance, J. Cartwright was a servitor for sixteen years, during which his wages rose from 16s to 21s. G. Compson was a servitor for thirteen years and T. Scriven for fifteen years. Servitors, including these three men, met a wage 'ceiling' around 21s–24s. Only those who were promoted to workman were able to break through it. There seem to have been two types of workmen. On one hand, G. Scriven and J. Rockes were workmen for sixteen years but their wages did not rise so sharply and rather tended to stay on a plateau; Scriven's increased by only 5s and Rockes's by 8s in sixteen years. Both wages failed to increase for nine years after 1854. Though W. Scriven (junior),

T. Sheldon and I. Scriven received respectively 28s, 26s and 28s in 1862, the rise in their wages after becoming workman was not so great. On the other hand, the wages of other workmen rose appreciably. J. Scriven's increased from 20s in 1847 to 40s in 1854 and W. Scriven's from 22s in 1850 to 40s in 1856. It is interesting that the two best-paid workmen became strike-breakers at the time of the long strike in 1858–59. These concrete examples of wage curve suggest that with promotion wages rose and continued to increase, but only gradually, and then ceased to rise if there was no promotion to a high status. Some of the upward movement in the 1850s and '60s would have been due to a general increase in wages.

The wage curve of flint glass makers in a lifetime must be considered in relation to family size, because the increase of earnings with promotion might be offset by the increasing number of dependent children, but it might, on the other hand, be supplemented by those children's earnings or those of the wife. The results obtained from the census enumerators' books of 1861 for Stourbridge are summarised in table 3:8. Out of a total of 389 flint glass makers 165 were single (42·3%) and 224 were married (57·6%). The relatively high proportion of those who were single stems from the fact that the figures obtained from the census enumerators' books included many takers-in and apprentices. According to the marriage registers in Stourbridge's four churches[52] the average age of marriage for flint glass makers between 1850 and 1885 was 23·78. About three-quarters of them married at between twenty and twenty-five in the same period. The fact that 73·3% of footmakers were married has been established. As table 3:8 shows, for servitors the proportion became higher (88·7%), and as for workmen, all were married. The same tendency can be found in the household structure. Out of a total of 389 flint glass makers there were 217 heads of households (55·8%) and 125 sons (32·1%), forty-four lodgers (11·3%) and three others (0·8%). According to work group, the percentage of heads varied from 73·4 for footmakers to 83·8 for servitors and 98·7 for workmen.

The average number of children per family was 2·38. Mainly because of the difference of ages in each work group, the number of children varied from group to group, as table 3:7 shows: 2·84 for a workman, 2·13 for a servitor and 1·41 for a footmaker. It is

TABLE 3:8 Average of ages, marital status, household position and number of children of flint glass makers in Stourbridge in 1861

Status	Age	Married (%)	Head of household (%)	No. of children (per family)	No. of children working (per family)
Workman	41·7	100·0	98·7	2·8	0·58
Servitor	34·7	88·7	83·8	2·1	0·24
Footmaker	28·1	73·3	73·4	1·4	0·09

Source. Census Enumerators' Book of 1861, Stourbridge.

difficult to give an exact answer to the question of the extent to which the increased earnings were offset by the growing number of dependent children, because no data for the household budget of glass makers are obtainable. Clearly the number of children working is an important element in the calculation. Families in which more than one child was working formed only 23·7% of all glass makers' families. But 33·8% of workmen's families had more than one child working, and 16·7% of families had more than two children at work. Out of forty-five children working in workmen's families, thirty were sons and fifteen were daughters. Of the thirty sons, twenty-five followed their father's job and were employed in the glass factories as takers-in. Although the wages of takers-in were as low as 4s to 5s a week, such a supplement of the family budget was better than nothing. If more than two children were working (16·9% of workmen's families), the family income was probably increased by as much as 8s–10s a week. Of the servitors' families 18·5% had more than one child working, but only 5·5% had two children working. It is absurd to imagine that the increase of 16s–18s a week on promotion from journeyman footmaker to servitor was completely offset by an increase in consumption for on average 0·72 children. It is more likely that after promotion the standard of living improved to a considerable extent and began to enter the realm of the labour aristocracy.

The peculiar working system in flint glass making was inconvenient for the housewife. The inconvenience was increased when children in the family had jobs on different shifts in the glass or other trades. In Stourbridge in 1861, for instance, eighty-five children of flint glass makers were working. Out of these thirty-eight were working in glass making itself, three in glass cutting, fourteen in other jobs in the glass trade, and thirty-two in other trades. Assuming that in thirty-eight cases fathers and children were working on the same shift in flint glass making, it is estimated that wives of glass makers in forty-seven families had children and husbands working on different shifts. On the other hand, out of 125 young glass makers living with their parents, seventy-two parents were employed in other trades. Those who were engaged in glass making, cutting and other jobs in the trade are respectively thirty-eight, six and ten.[53] Therefore, at least in eighty-seven families, mothers of glass makers suffered from the irregular working hours of their sons. In all, glass makers living with other workers in the same family amounted to 137, equivalent to 35·2% of the total 389 flint glass makers in the district. We can assume that, apart from the 'pure' flint glass makers' families, about a third of the wives or mothers of flint glass makers experienced with peculiar intensity the inconvenience due to the shift system. It was difficult for the wife in this kind of family to work outside the home, and her role was necessarily limited to housekeeping. In fact, out of the whole 224 families of flint glass makers in Stourbridge only seven wives had occupations (3·1%).[54]

The age at marriage of the children of flint glass makers is also an important indicator of the time of their independence from parents' household budgets. According to the marriage registers in Stourbridge, the average age of marriage between 1858 and 1885 was 23·64 years for sons and 22·77 for daughters.[55] About four in five sons and daughters married before the age of twenty-five and about one in three daughters married before twenty. We can therefore assume that children began to be independent when glass makers reached about fifty. According to the quarterly report of the Death Fund of the F.G.M.F.S., the average age at death of all flint glass makers in Stourbridge between 1858 and 1882 was 48·9, 2·4 years higher than the national average for flint glass makers.[56] Since the data obtained from the report do not include the deaths of takers-in or most of the apprentice footmakers, the real figures may be slightly higher than those for all glass makers. But table 3:9 shows that about 30% of glass makers in Stourbridge died before the age of forty, and about half before fifty, when their children began to be independent. About 39% of all glass makers lived to be over fifty-five and 28% lived to be over sixty. As T. J. Wilkinson observed, 'the whole of those men [who died] have worked up to a very recent period of the time of their death'.[57] So it is likely that from fifty until their death workmen really enjoyed increasing wages without having to maintain their children. It is generally accepted that not only in childhood and early middle life, when they had a family of dependent children, but in old age Victorian labourers were underfed. In contrast to the labourers, flint glass makers, skilled workers, were able to enjoy the highest standard of life in the later stages of life.

TABLE 3:9 Distribution of age at death of flint glass makers between 1858 and 1882 (%)

Age	Stourbridge		All Districts	
20–24	5·1		6·1	
25–29	3·9	(9·0)	8·8	(14·9)
30–34	9·0	(18·0)	10·1	(25·0)
35–39	12·8	(30·8)	12·4	(37·4)
40–44	14·1	(44·9)	11·5	(48·9)
45–49	6·4	(51·3)	9·7	(58·6)
50–54	11·5	(62·8)	8·5	(67·1)
55–59	9·0	(71·8)	9·9	(77·0)
60–64	11·5	(83·3)	9·5	(86·5)
65–69	11·5	(94·8)	5·9	(92·4)
70–	5·1	(100·0)	7·6	(100·0)
Totals (N)	78		444	

Notes
(a) Age at death unknown (seventeen in Stourbridge and 150 in all Districts) is not included.
(b) The death fund of the F.G.M.F.S. started in September 1858.
Source. Quarterly Report of the Death Fund, published in *Flint Glass Makers Magazine*, September 1858 to May 1882.

They could also contemplate relatively bright prospects for their children. Glass-making was said to be an hereditary job. George Lloyd, a Birmingham flint glass manufacturer, stated in the mid–1860s that 'we have had in our glass-house at the same time members of three successive generations, one, a man of 74, who began at the age of 10, whose father, also a glass-blower, lived to upwards of 100'.[58] It is not surprising that glass makers of superior status wished their sons to follow them. A boy aged eleven working at the Birmingham glassworks said that 'Mother wished me to come to glass making as soon as I was big enough'.[59] As J. E. White noted, 'the wish of the mother arose from her husband having held a good position as a glass worker'.[60] Indeed, the son's work was probably considered by his parents in terms of its potential rather than its addition to the parental income.

That consideration might be further reinforced if there was a hereditary component in promotion. Sons of glass makers appear to have received preferential treatment. The Children's Employment Commission reported that:

boys seldom get to any regular blowing work before the age of from 14 to 16, even in the lighter kinds of glass. Young boys, however, who work with fathers or men well disposed to help them in the trade, are constantly getting their hand in by handling the men's tools and trying to make things in spare times, such as the stoppages for meals. This is the way in which they are able first to show their capabilities, and learn the work enough to be put on.[61]

It is difficult to measure precisely the extent to which the promotion of flint glass makers was affected by their father's occupation. However, the combination of data relating to the occupational continuity between fathers' and children obtainable from the census enumerators' books with that obtainable from the marriage registers provides a way of measuring the extent.

The census enumerators' books list the fathers' occupation of teenage glass makers who can be assumed to have been takers-in or apprentices, and the marriage register shows the father's occupation of bridegrooms, who can be assumed to have been journeymen footmakers or journeymen servitors.[62] The gap in occupational continuity between these two sources, if any, can be regarded as a result of preferential treatment in promotion for the sons of glass makers. The result is set out in table 3:10. According to the table, 29·6% of the takers-in or apprentices came from glass makers' families, but 57·6% came from families outside the glass trade. However, journeymen glass makers coming from glass makers' families in the marriage register formed 61·0%. Only 28·5% of those who had come from the families of other trades survived in the glass trade as journeymen. This large gap implies that glass makers' sons had a better chance of promotion from taker-in or apprentice to journeyman footmaker or servitor. Since, once they were apprenticed, flint glass makers were normally promoted to journeyman, it can be assumed that preferential treatment for the sons of glass makers was a crucial factor when promotion from taker-in to apprentice took place. It is therefore assumed that a large proportion of the takers-in who had left the trade without being apprenticed had come from families who worked in other trades. Takers-in who had come from families in which the father had a different job in the glass trade suffered the same fate. But boys coming from glass cutters' families received the same treatment as sons of glass makers, although the number was extremely small.

TABLE 3:10 Occupational continuity between flint glass makers and their parents in Stourbridge (%)

		Occupation of parents				
Source	Case (N)	Glass maker	Glass cutter	Other jobs in glass trade	Other trades	Total
Census of 1861	125	29·6	4·8	8·0	57·6	100·0
Marriage register 1850–85	123	61·0	8·1	2·4	28·5	100.0

Source. See tables 6:2 and 6:3.

Real wages in absolute terms and wage differentials in the chair must have been the main concern of individual working men. In addition they must have paid much attention to the course of wages in the past and the wages expected in the future. The rise in wages for glass makers over a lifetime was considerable, but it was closely related to promotion. It is also clear that a factor determining membership of a 'labour aristocracy' was not only the workers' chances of promotion but the job opportunities open to the children. These two features of flint glass makers — the rise in wages over a lifetime and the occupational continuity between generations — characterise them as a labour aristocracy, at least so far as the economic dimension is concerned. Their privileges were secured by their union, so that it is necessary to examine its structure and policies more closely.

Notes

1 S. and B Webb, *Industrial Democracy*, 1920 edn, London, p. 286, table I, and G. D. H. Cole, *The Payment of Wages*, London 1918, p. 13.
2 D. F. Schloss, *Methods of Industrial Remuneration*, London, 1892, p. 25. Charles Booth also wrote of flint glass makers' wages that 'the wages are paid upon a complicated system, nominally by time, but actually by piece' (C. Booth, *Life and Labour of the People in London*, 2nd ser.: Industry, vol. II, London, 1902–04, p. 82).
3 E. A. Pratt wrote: 'One of the peculiarities of the [flint glass] trade, and one of the greatest grievances of the employers, is that the men themselves fix the precise amount of work that shall be done in the six-hour turn. In the case of an established design the "number" is given by the union officials in the district, and becomes a "district number". In the case of a new design the master is allowed to ask his own men how many they will consent to produce in a turn, and a half-hour's discussion may follow, in which the men will show a tendency to get as low a number arranged as possible, while the employer will try to get as high a number as he can' (E. A. Pratt, *Trade Unionism and British Industry*, London, 1904, p. 97).
4 Originally the term 'move' meant a certain quantity of glass produced. H. J. Powell writes of a 'turn' as 'the period, usually six hours', and a 'move' as 'a piece work term for an agreed number of glass to be made for an agreed price' (Powell, *Glass-making*, p. 41). But since 'two moves per turn' was fixed and the fictitious time wages had a reality as actual time, a 'move' became a synonym for three hours.
5 The following table provides a good illustration of the process of the complex calculation:

Name of glass maker	Number produced	Moves	Nominal weekly wages, 11 moves	'Over work' Wages per move	actually paid
A	1,560	15½	40s	3s 6d	55s 9d
B	1,595	16	28s	2s 8d	41s 4d
C	1,415	14¼	26s	2s 4d	33s 7d

The table is made up from the wages of three workmen chosen at random from the wages book of Stevens & Williams for the week ending 5 January 1861. The wages book shows only names and figures, and I have suggested the column headings.
6 A similar 'fictitious' form of time wages could be found in the handicraft (bespoke) section of the tailoring trade, in which the concept of the 'log' was used, instead of the 'move' (Schloss, *Methods of Industrial Remuneration*, p. 26). The method of payment known as the 'log' was 'really a schedule of piece-rates masquerading under the guise of time-rates' so that 'there is no pretence that the "log" hour is equivalent to a real hour' (S. P. Dobbs, *The Clothing Workers of Great Britain*, London, 1928, pp. 116–18).

7 For instance, if the glass makers agreed to work at six glasses per hour, then in each turn of six hours thirty-six glasses were to be produced. But the chair was actually making, say, fifty glasses in each turn, fourteen glasses more than the fictitious amount. In this example thirty-six glasses were paid for as nominal work and fourteen glasses as 'over work'. If this was done through the week, besides the nominal weekly wages (eleven moves), 4·3 moves would be paid for as 'over work'.

8 *Flint Glass Makers Magazine*, VIII, p. 642. The verdict given was that the full amount of £3 should be paid to the plaintiff, because of the default of a fortnight's notice.

9 *Brierley Hill Advertiser*, 20 November 1858.

10 *Ibid.* In Birmingham in 1850 during the 'overtime' period, workmen got 7% less than during the nominal working hours. Servitors got 22% less and footmakers got 10% less (calculated from the wages in *Morning Chronicle*, 23 December 1850). In 1861 at the Stevens & Williams factory in Stourbridge workmen got 1% more, servitors 4% less and footmakers 23% less (calculated from the wages book of the factory). The numbers in the sample are nine for workmen, seven for servitors and eleven for footmakers.

11 *Flint Glass Makers Magazine*, VII, p. 392.

12 *Ibid.*, VII, p. 170. In July 1872 J. Griffin, District secretary of Stourbridge, said that 'the system of paying the overwork in the same proportion as is received per move on the first part of the week is a new feature.'

13 *Ibid.*, VII, p. 443.

14 *Morning Chronicle*, 23 December 1850.

15 Calculated from wages book of Beatson & Clark of Rotherham and that of Wood Bros of Barnsley. Flint glass makers included workmen, servitors (both journeymen and apprentice), but do not include takers-in. Bottle makers included all men from first class to fifth class. The figures are the average weekly wages. For the method of calculation, see note (a) in table 3:2 (a).

16 Wages book of Beatson & Clark of Rotherham.

17 Unfortunately we have no wages book after 1863 in Stourbridge which cover the period under consideration. Eric Hopkins's figures ('Small town aristocrats of labour and their standard of living, 1840–1914') appear to overestimate the increase of workmen's wages (*Economic History Review*, 2nd ser., XXVIII, 1975, pp. 226–7). His overestimation stems from his use of the workman's wages in the best-paid chair. According to Hopkins, the wages of a workman in the Stevens & Williams factory were 49·6% higher in the 1850s and 72·8% higher in the 1860s than in the 1840s. But according to my calculation the wages of a (median) workman were 32·4% higher in the 1850s and 47·7% higher in the 1860s than in the 1840s (not in the first half of the 1840s). In addition, according to Hopkins, the year 1859 recorded especially high wages, the workman named John Scriven earning annually £171 2s 0d (*ibid.*, p. 242). But Hopkins

disregarded the fact that John Scriven was a *strike-breaker.* The F.G.M.F.S. labelled him a 'Traitor' together with another twenty-six members (*Flint Glass Makers Magazine*, III, p. 424). Hopkins also neglected the wages of servitors, footmakers and takers-in, assuming that 'the other members of the chair, were paid proportionately' to workmen (Hopkins, *op. cit.,* p. 226). But an examination of the wages of other members in the chairs is of importance for any study of the labour aristocracy, and in fact they were not necessarily paid proportionately.

18 The wages of workmen and servitors both in Stourbridge and in Rotherham are average weekly figures.

19 G. Barnsby, 'The standard of living in the Black Country during the nineteenth century', *Economic History Review*, 2nd ser., XXIV, 1971, p. 229. A family is assumed to consist of man, wife and two small children. Subsistence wages were calculated by halving the standard-of-comfort wage, excluding food, rent and fuel, which were necessities.

20 *Flint Glass Makers Magazine*, V, p. 129.

21 The area which the census enumerators' books for Stourbridge encompassed will be noted on p. 149. Although the books distinguish 'glass makers' from other glass workers, they do not indicate the glass makers' position in the chairs. The membership list of the Stourbridge District of the F.G.M.F.S. for 1857 is here used to identify their position, on the assumption that promotions which took place between 1857 and 1861 were negligible. By tracing each name in the list of 249 members of the F.G.M.F.S. in the area, 169 glass makers (seventy-seven workmen, sixty-two servitors and thirty footmakers) can be identified and linked up with those in the enumerators' book, which list 297 glass makers over the age of tv enty. The position of non-society glass makers cannot be identified, but those who are not identified are not necessarily the non-society men.

22 *Royal Commission on Trade Unions*, 10th Report, 1867–68, p. 454, q. 492.

23 The number of children working was 0·09 per family in the case of footmakers. See table 3:8.

24 *Glasgow Sentinel*, 15 June 1867.

25 *Flint Glass Makers Magazine*, VII, p. 357.

26 *Ibid.,* VII p. 356. The Manchester District gave the footmakers 15s per man, or a sum total of £24 from the local funds, with the following statement from the District secretary: 'when they asked us for very bread, we should have been something inhuman if we had offered them a stone' (*ibid.,* VII, p. 357), but the Central Committee of the society did not sanction the decision.

27 *Ibid.,* VIII, p. 657.

28 *Ibid.*

29 Bremner, *The Industries of Scotland.,* p. 383.

30 George Howell, *The Conflicts of Capital and Labour,* 2nd edn, London, 1890, p. 240.

31 *Brierley Hill and Stourbridge Gazette*, 20 February 1858. The Bench judged that 'stopping the boy from work was a misdemeanour on the part of the men; and the boy in consequence was not only losing his wages, but the opportunity that ought to be afforded him by his master for learning his business', because 'the men had no right to dictate terms to their employers' (*ibid.*).

32 Address of the Delegates, in *Rules and Regulations of the F.G.M.F.S.*, 1858, p. 20.

33 *Flint Glass Makers Magazine*, V, p. 15.

34 *Report of the Social Science Association, 1863*, 1863, p. 181. Swinburne's paper was reprinted in Armstrong *et al.* (ed), *The Industrial Resources*, pp. 197–204.

35 *Alliance News*, 12 September 1863.

36 *Bee-Hive*, 19 September 1863.

37 *Glasgow Sentinel*, 16 September 1863, and *Newcastle Daily Journal*, 11 September 1863.

38 Swinburne wrote that in preparing the paper he had been assisted by Sowerby & Neville of Gateshead and other glass manufacturers in the area (*Report of the Social Science Association, 1863, op. cit.*, p. 176).

39 At the seventh annual meeting of the Social Science Association in Edinburgh in October 1863 Alexander Campbell, a representative of the F.G.M.F.S., 'rebutted the unprovoked and unjustifiable attack lately made by a Mr. Swinburne on the Flint Glassmakers' Society, in a paper read before the British Association at Newcastle-on-Tyne' (*Flint Glass Makers Magazine*, V, p. 66).

40 *Children's Employment Commission*, 4th Report, 1865, p. 219, q. 57.

41 Calculated from wages book of Stevens & Williams. Every January and July each year takers-in employed in the factory are checked to see whether they were apprenticed or left the factory.

42 *Rules and Regulations of the F.G.M.G.S., 1858*, rule XXXII.

43 *Royal Commission on Trade Unions*, 10th Report, 1867–68, p. 23, q. 18402–404.

44 *Flint Glass Makers Magazine*, II, p. 194.

45 *Factory Inspectors' Report, ending October 31 1879*, 1880 (P.P. XIV), p. 32.

46 *Pottery Gazette*, 1 December 1880, p. 788.

47 The rate of promotion per annum in the factory comparable to the rate obtained from the *Magazine* is given as follows: twenty-eight promotions out of eighty workers excluding takers-in in fifteen years. The number of takers-in employed is not included, because the figures obtained from the *Magazine* excluded the non-society men. But takers-in apprenticed are included in the calculation, because most of them were promoted journeyman footmaker after a seven-year apprenticeship.

48 Among twenty-eight promotions there were three who were promoted twice from taker-in to footmaker and up to servitor in the

same period, and only one was promoted three times, from taker-in
to workman.

49 Though we have no wage data for 1830 and 1835, it is most unlikely
that takers-in's wages were over 4s.

50 Hopkins, 'Small town aristocrats of labour', p. 225.

51 Neale shows that the wages of the long-serving labourers in Bath
increased from 10s to 12s in the period between 1836 and 1851 (R. S.
Neale, 'The standard of living, 1780–1844: a regional and class
study', *Economic History Review*, 2nd ser., XIX, 1966, pp. 590–606).

52 Marriage registers used are as follows: (1) Old Swinford, Stourbridge,
1850–75. (2) St Mary's Church, Kingswinford, 1851–85. (3) St James's
Church, Wollaston, 1860–85. (4) Trinity Church, Amblecote,
1850–85. In the calculation of the average age at marriage of glass
makers, remarriage or widowers were excluded. 'Glass blowers' are
included but glass cutters and other glass workers are excluded. The
number of marriages in each register relating to glass makers is
respectively fifty-seven, twenty-nine, eleven and twelve. In the
calculation of the marriage age of children of glass makers the same
procedure is used. The number of marriages in each register is: in the
case of a son fifty-four, twenty-seven, ten and eleven respectively and
in the case of a daughter sixty-five, thirty, sixteen and twenty-three.

53 Census Enumerators' Books of 1861, Stourbridge.

54 *Ibid.* The occupations of the wives of glass makers were: tailoress
(two), pressmaker (one), nailmaker (one), laundress (one), shop-
keeper (one) and dressmaker (one). Eric Hopkins pointed out that
glass makers' wives with no occupation in Stourbridge contrast
with the wives of nailmakers, who worked with their husbands in
their domestic workshop in Lye and Wollescote (in the Stourbridge
area) (Eric Hopkins, 'The Working Classes of Stourbridge and
District, 1815–1914', Ph.D. thesis, University of London, 1972, p.
351). The wives of glass cutters also tended not to have occupations
but the proportion of the wives with occupations was slightly
higher than those of glass makers. Out of 255 glass cutters' families
twenty-one wives had occupations (8·2%), of which seven were
dressmakers and five were shopkeepers.

55 See n. 52.

56 Before the Royal Commission on Factory and Workshops Acts of
1876, Richard Leicester, one of the secretaries of the society, stated
that 'the average life is 46 years which I think is a very good average
compared with other trades in the country' (*Royal Commission on
Factory and Workshops Acts*, 1876, vol. II, p. 457, q. 9221). My
calculation of the national average age at death age as 46·5 is therefore approximately the same as Leicester claimed. The total number
of deaths of glass makers between 1858 and 1882 was 594 and the
average membership of the society in the same period was 1,725, so
that the death rate was 14·3 per 1,000 per annum. T. J. Wilkinson's
statement before the same commission that 'the death rate does not

amount to 12 per 1,000 per annum' (*ibid.*, p. 455, q. 9201) seems a slight underestimate.

57 *Ibid.*, p. 455, q. 9201.
58 *Children's Employment Commission*, 4th Report, 1865, p. 227, q. 89
59 *Ibid.*, p. 221, q. 58.
60 *Ibid.*
61 *Ibid.*, p. 191, q. 81.
62 See Fig. 2, p. 65.

Chapter four

The structure and policies of the Flint Glass Makers' Friendly Society

I *A 'New Model' union supporting George Potter's group*

The Webbs characterised the trade union movement in the third quarter of the nineteenth century as possessed by 'the New Spirit and the New Model', under which 'Trade Unionism obtained a financial strength, a trained staff of salaried officers, and a permanence of membership hitherto unknown'.[1] They thought that this period clearly differed from the 'Revolutionary Period' between 1829 and 1842. The Amalgamated Society of Engineers, organised in 1851, provided them with the leading example of the 'New Model' union. They interpreted the conflicts between Potter and the Junta[2] in the 1860s in terms of a struggle between the old and the new trade unionism. The Webb's view that the years around mid-century saw a turning point in the structure of the unions strongly influenced later historians of opposite political persuasions like Rothstein and Perlman.[3]

G. D. H. Cole was the first to revise the Webbs' view. He denied that the Amalgamated Societies could be regarded as representative of the entire trade union movement, or even most of it, during this period, and that even the Amalgamated Societies were nearly so 'capitalist-minded' as historians of the trade union movement commonly suggest'.[4] They 'covered only a fraction of the total Trade Union membership', and 'the leadership of the "Junta", so far from being complete, was in fact challenged by a larger number of important Unions, and did not amount to an ascendancy at any rate until after 1871 – if even then'.[5]

Cole reinstated Potter, the editor of the *Bee-Hive*, 'the most important Labour and Trade Union journal of the day', and gave him credit for his role in the origin of the Trades Union Congress. Thus besides building, engineering and shipbuilding, there were other industries in which trade unions existed, including mining, cotton and other textiles, printing and book-binding, cabinetmaking, coach-building, iron and steel manufacture, glass and glass bottle making, pottery, tailoring, and boot and shoe manufacture.[6] Cole showed that among these other unions little or no attempt was made to follow the 'New Model'. Even the builders were not conquered 'nearly so completely' as the engineers. An examination of the mining, iron and steel, and textile trades led him to conclude that 'in none of them did the "New Model" influence show itself of much account'.[7]

Cole understood the difference between the 'New Model' unions and the others in terms of the existence of 'a clear division among the workers themselves. In engineering, building and shipbuilding, the skilled craftsmen who finished apprenticeships were always trying to keep the division rigid as the only means of ensuring the maintenance of their higher standards'. Meanwhile, in mining, metal manufacture and the textile trades, 'no similar class cleavage generally exists, or has existed'.[8] In other words, Cole explained the preconditions for the existence of the 'New Model' unions in terms of the stratification between the workers in the industry concerned and saw the 'New Model' unions as the skilled workers or upper order of workers' institutions. However, he neglected many unions, unions in which skilled workers with apprenticeship controls were not influenced by the Junta.

The Webbs' treatment was not entirely satisfactory, particularly where the flint glass makers' union was concerned. They first pointed to the F.G.M.F.S. as a 'New Model' union and often used articles from the *Flint Glass Makers Magazine* to demonstrate how deeply the 'New Spirit' pervaded the trade union world after mid—century, then pushed it out of sight when they came to discuss the Junta v. Potter.[9] From the Webbs' point of view the F.G.M.F.S. ought to have supported the Junta. In fact, the reverse was the case.

The relation of the F.G.M.F.S. with George Potter began with the *Bee-Hive*, which first appeared on 19 October 1861. In spite of financial difficulties it was helped by expert journalists such as George Troup and Robert Hartwell, and with Potter's vigorous salesmanship it made a promising start. The paper was adopted as the organ of the London Trades Council in November that year, when the circulation had already reached 5,000.[10] At the conference of the F.G.M.F.S. in March 1864 it was resolved that the society should take 100 shares in the *Bee-Hive* and would 'recommend it to the members of our Society',[11] The London District paid £25 for 100 shares.[12] The F.G.M.F.S. strove to sell the *Bee-Hive* among its own members. On 9 April 1864 Benjamin Smart, the Central Secretary, remarked, 'I can further recommend it as a first-class newspaper, which besides containing all information on trades affairs, is also a first-class paper for all other general news . . . We might easily increase its circulation at least 500 copies.'[13]

The F.G.M.F.S. also decided at the 1864 conference that 'Joseph Leicester, of London, represent our interest in the management for the present',[14] and at the half-yearly meeting of the *Bee-Hive* on 31 May Leicester was elected to the board of directors. Although the actual circulation of the *Bee-Hive* among glass makers is not known, it is clear that after Leicester joined the board the relationship between the F.G.M.F.S. and Potter became closer than before, and an abridged quarterly report from the Central Secretary or Central Committee of the society appeared regularly in the pages of the paper.[15]

At the beginning of 1865 Potter's position was favourable. The *Bee-Hive* was still the official organ of the London Trades Council and in January the National Association of Mineworkers also decided to recognise it as their organ.[16] The First International had also adopted the *Bee-Hive* as its mouthpiece.[17] However, the North Staffordshire iron puddlers' strike made the conflicts between the Junta and Potter increasingly sharp. On the one hand, Potter was a strong advocate of an aggressive and militant policy, as opposed to the conciliatory stance of the Junta. On the other hand, the Junta attempted to subject the militance of the rank and file to their control. On the last day of 1864 the ironmasters gave a fortnight's notice to reduce the wages of the puddlers by 1s a ton, and those of the mill men by 10%.[18] At the expiry of the notice the North Staffordshire men ceased work rather than submit to the reduction. In March a lock-out was imposed throughout south Staffordshire.

As the ironworkers rejected the Earl of Lichfield's offer of arbitration, the London Trades Council gave them no financial aid, and subsequently most 'New Model' trade unions followed the Council's decision. Potter called an 'illegal' meeting independently on 15 March by notice in the *Bee-Hive*, without consulting the council. The meeting was attended by about 250 delegates.[19] At the meeting, after briefly reporting what he had seen in Staffordshire (he went there on glass trade business), Leicester stated that 'the trade with which he was connected would do all in its power to support their brethren in the iron trade'.[20] The F.G.M.F.S. proposed to give £100 from the funds to assist the iron puddlers, in weekly instalments of £10 per week. This proposition secured 1,139 votes without any opposition.[21] Among the total income of the National Association of Iron Workers donated by the various trade unions and individuals (£118 4s 5d), the flint glass makers' donation (£10)[22] was second only to the subscription from the *Bee-Hive* office (£66 2s 4d).

On 29 March 1865 the London Trades Council denounced Potter's action at a special meeting, when Danter, a president of the A.S.E., accused him of being 'a strike jobber'.[23] Immediately, on 4 April, about 200 delegates of the Potter group assembled, and Thomas Connolly of the operative stonemasons criticised the six members of the trades council 'as cowardly and disgraceful in the extreme'.[24] Leicester was absent from this meeting, but on 9 April he wrote to the *Bee-Hive* 'on behalf of the Flint Glass Trade' against the 'brazen-faced slanders of those conspirators who call themselves the "London Trades' Council"'.[25] The lock-out came to an end on 8 April 1865. Throughout this dispute the gulf between the Junta and Potter grew wider than ever. On 4 September the London Trades Council resolved not to keep the *Bee-Hive* as its official organ. The *Workman's Advocate* took its place, although not recognised by formal resolution.[26] Immediately the Stourbridge District of the F.G.M.F.S. wrote to the *Bee-Hive*:

Sir,—In conveying our warm expressions of appreciation for the invaluable services and unflinching and honourable conduct rendered by Mr. Potter to the recent lock out in the iron trade of South and North Staffordshire, and on all occasions where the just interests of the working class are concerned, we wish it to be distinctly understood that, as a section of a trades' union holding shares in the *Beehive*, we totally disagree with the vote of censure passed upon Mr. Potter by the London Trades Council, and consider their conduct reprehensible in moving to injure the circulation of the paper which is really and truly the working man's friend, and which is working wonders in revolutionising the characters, thoughts, actions, and aspirations of that class it so powerfully advocates.[27]

Thus the F.G.M.F.S. became one of the strong opponents of the Junta. This is why the Webbs pushed the union out of sight in chapter V of the *History of Trade Unionism*. If the F.G.M.F.S. was such a leading example of the 'New Spirit and the New Model' in chapter IV, how did it come about that it identified itself with the *Bee-Hive* and George Potter? As already noted, Leicester's activities could not easily be dismissed. But more fundamentally, the conditions for the link of the F.G.M.F.S. with Potter existed in the character of the society. Was the F.G.M.F.S. the same 'New Model' union as the A.S.E. and the A.S.C.J.?

II *From tramp society to 'New Model' union*

Documentary evidence relating to the activities of flint glass makers prior to the reorganisation of the Flint Glass Makers' Friendly Society in 1849 is fragmentary. As early as 1755 glass makers in Newcastle upon Tyne formed their Friendly Society and it survived at least until the turn of the century.[28] In 1800 the contribution was 1s 4d every six weeks.[29] The activities of the society are not known, but its aim was to provide the members with sick and death benefits.[30] The subsequent history of the society is also obsure. It was not until the mid–1830s that a national federation of flint glass makers was established with sufficient strength to challenge the position of the manufacturers. This was a 'tramp' society with 646 members in twenty-five branches throughout England, Scotland and Ireland.[31] Birmingham was the main centre, with 111 members, Dudley being next with fifty-one, and Newcastle third, with fifty.[32] Stourbridge had only twenty-nine members. During a period of a year and a half from December 1835 to July 1837 the total number of tramps was 615, and £352 was spent on them. This constituted 43·7% out of the total expenditure of £805.

It was significant that the purpose of the society was not only to aid tramping. The funds which were expended on at least thirty-two strikes in the same period amounted to £143, 17·7% of the total expenditure. Nonetheless the financial condition of

the society was sound, leaving £124 in hand.[33] The response of
the employers seems to have been aggressive. On 5 December
1837 the flint glass manufacturers of Birmingham and Stourbridge gathered at the Dudley Arms hotel in response to a
circular urging them 'to consider the best means to prevent the
injurious combination of workmen'.[34] They eventually resolved:

That it is the opinion of the meeting that the union formed in 1836 will,
if persevered in, operate very prejudicially to the trade; that the meeting
pledges itself, individually, to express to his workmen their dis-
approbation of all combinations and that he will not take into his
employ any workman who is a member of the Glass Makers' Union.[35]

Under attack by the glass manufacturers, the society appears to
have faded away.

Afterwards the 'powerful'[36] United Flint Glass Makers'
Society was organised in 1844,[37] when 'a marked revival in
Trade Unionism took effect'.[38] The society extended all over the
kingdom. In 1846 the membership was 850, out of which 360
were workmen (42·4%), 372 were servitors (43·8%) and 118
footmakers (13·8%). Although considerable numbers of flint
glass makers seem to have been left unorganised,[39] this association was strong enough for an attempt to be made again in 1847
to establish a national organisation of manufacturers in order to
counter-attack. A circular was issued by an anonymous flint
glass manufacturer in Gloucester to the Flint Glass Manufacturers of the United Kingdom for the purpose of regulating
prices and fixing wages.[40] E. & J. Webb, of Holloway End Glass
Works in Stourbridge, immediately replied:

The time has now arrived, something must be done, to raise prices, and
increase our profits, Wages and Materials being very high. We can only
say that We perfectly concur in your suggestions, and do hope the trade
generally will concede with your views as it is to the interest of one and
all that we should be united, and which is very easily accomplished.[41]

But another firm, the Worsbrodale Glass Works, showed reluctance to accept the proposal:

Glass Masters Meetings have been tried before and the Faithful have
been the dupes of the Faithless . . . We thank you for your letter. But we
fear the results of a Meeting would be similar to previous ones.[42]

The Glass Makers' Society was not crushed.
By this time a new tendency had appeared in Stourbridge and

Birmingham. In both areas 'the men became very dissatisfied with the tramping system and the result was a split in the Old Society'.[43] It is of great importance that the 'self-support' society emerged in Stourbridge and Birmingham, where the most skilled glass makers had become concentrated. Members of both new and old societies went 'side by side for some years, they were closely connected with each other'.[44]

A great strike began in 1848, however, which led both the societies to destruction. It took place at the Five Ways Flint Glass Works of Rice Harris in Birmingham, in July 1848. Harris, one of the manufacturers who had adopted pressed glass production, put some of his blown flint glass apprentices to supply a shortage of men in the pressed glass process. But 'they, after continuing at it for a few days, began to get dissatisfied, and a large number, after giving notice to Mr. Harris on Monday evening that they would not work at press-work any longer, absented themselves, and had not gone near the works since'.[45] Behind it lay the recognition that a would-be skilled blown glass maker could not master the skill if he was employed in pressed glass production.

Harris sued several apprentices for breach of contract and the case was examined at the Public Office in Birmingham on 20 July 1848. W. P. Roberts, a well known solicitor from Manchester and the 'Miners' Attorney General',[46] was engaged on behalf of the defendants. He insisted:

The defence which I have to make is that the work which the lads have been called upon to do is not that which they are bound apprentice to learn. I am instructed that it is totally different, and that to be able to blow well requires more than ordinary skill and practice, whilst pressing requires very little – (hear, hear from the crowd) – so little that any man taken out of the street is able to do it ... If I could succeed in convincing the Bench that the glass-blowing is a distinct business, and the lads were required to do press-work when they ought to be learning blowing, which required a great deal of time and practice bestowed upon it to acquire anything approaching to perfection – then I might show that the lads were justified in refusing to do the work which is set them.[47]

The magistrates eventually dismissed the charge, but the settlement of the strike was protracted. About 100 men besides a number of boys were brought out. Harris imported twenty-six blacklegs from France. The *Morning Chronicle* remarked, 'The

Frenchmen were hooted and pelted in the streets of the town, and rows often occurred. The union offered the Frenchmen 26s per week each, if they would join the strike and undertook to pay their expenses back to France, if they preferred to go; but they all refused'.[48] The society borrowed money from 'private individuals' to enable workmen 'who had sacrificed their places for the good of the trade, to take home 2s on a Saturday night – 2s to support, in many cases, a wife and family'.[49] The funds of both societies were by now exhausted. The strike lasted until March 1849, and the employers eventually succeeded in beating their men. A few months later, in September that year, a Birmingham flint glass maker recalled that 'the funds used in the strike were all dissipated and nothing was left for fighting the battle of the trade'.[50] Thus both societies died out, leaving debts of £88.[51]

In September 1849 the Flint Glass Makers' Friendly Society was reorganised. On 13th–15th of the month the delegates from Warrington, St Helens, Rotherham, Catcliff, York, Hunslet, Dudley, Holly Hill, Dublin, Edinburgh, Tutbury, Longport, Manchester and Birmingham assembled at the house of Mr Deakin, Brown Cow, Ruler Street, Manchester.[52] From their bitter experiences in the previous years there was 'a general consensus of opinion among all the delegates that "Strikes are no good to anybody" for they only starve the men for months and then force them to go back at the employers' terms'.[53] All the delegates 'complain of the very bad state of trade and the continual reductions of wages consequent upon the various districts underselling each other. This chief grievance in every case seems to be that of too many apprentices'.[54]

At the first annual conference, held on 11–12 July 1850 in Birmingham, the same opinions were expressed. It was literally a national conference.[55] The delegates, 'representing near upon 1,000 operatives', assembled 'chiefly with the view of determining on the best course to be pursued in removing the vast amount of surplus labour at present prostrating the manufacture, and as to the necessary steps to be taken to benefit the condition of the workmen generally'.[56] The *Birmingham Mercury* of 13 July 1850 reported:

We are given to understand that the society does not recognise the general necessity of strikes, but prefers a withdrawal and support of such of its members as may have good grounds of complaint. It has also abolished the old tramp system, and substituted for it a general plan of registration, by which vacancies are ascertained and filled, and the unemployed equally distributed in the various markets of their labour. Altogether the glass makers' society appeared to be one of the very best of its kind.

At first sight this appears to be double-talk: 'withdrawal and support of such of its members as may have good grounds of complaint', i.e. provision for strike action. However, the intention was that such strikes should occur seldom, be local in character and subject to central control which would keep them low-key and try to prevent them from growing into the sort of confrontation that had been so disastrous in the past.[57]

The first step in the transition from a loose alliance of separate local clubs to a national organisation was 'the appointment of a seat of government or "general branch"'.[58] The officers of the general branch were charged with the responsibility of conducting the current business of the whole society, and accordingly it became the central authority within it. The seat of government in the F.G.M.F.S. was changed not by simple rotation but by periodical vote of the whole membership. The 1858 rules of the society provided that 'there shall be a Central Secretary elected annually by majority of the vote of the trade'.[59] But it seems likely that the Central Secretary was elected every three years.[60] The rule also provided that the Central Secretary 'shall have power to nominate a Central Committee, in whose hands the executive power of this society shall be vested from year to year'.[61]

Among British trade unions the F.G.M.F.S. was the only one to give the Central Secretary the power of nominating the Central Committee.[62] This system enabled the Secretary to select people with ideas similar to his own for the committee. Consequently it made for a strong policy, and, potentially, it was hardly in conformity with 'primitive democracy'. The only way to prevent arbitrary imposition of the policy of the committee was the election of the Central Secretary. There always was an election: no Central Secretary was ever returned unopposed. The rules of the society did not prohibit the Secretary from being re-elected, but in fact there was no instance of this apart from the election of 1870. Even when, in that year, the existing

Central Secretary, T. J. Wilkinson of Birmingham, declared his willingness to serve another year on the grounds that the government's trade union Bill had not been published as expected, a second candidate, W. H. Packwood of Stourbridge, appeared. The result of the vote was a victory for Wilkinson by the small majority of 121,[63] but he could extend his stay in office only one year. Thus the general branch normally moved every three years, and this worked as rotation *de facto*.

As the activities of the society expanded, and as the secretarial work became more complicated, the institution of a permanent Secretary began to be considered. At the conference of 1871 it was resolved that 'considering the increasing duties devolving upon the Central Secretary and the very great demand upon his time, [we] recommend the trade to consider the propriety of making the office a permanent one'.[64] Soon after, letters favourable to the decision of the conference appeared in the *Magazine*. One writer insisted that:

it is utterly impossible for any Central Secretary who follows his work as a glass-maker to keep such a set of books as is kept by other societies, and are absolutely necessary as a safeguard for the Society's interests, and as such affecting the interest of every one of us individually and collectively . . . In electing a Central Secretary permanently, we should centralize the power of the Society, and if we elected a permanent Central Committee and a central place this would be true.[65]

It was thus proposed that '£2 per week as wages' should be paid to the permanent Secretary.[66]

The centralisation of power in the hands of a permanent secretary would provide efficiency at the cost of 'primitive democracy'. Even the members in favour of a permanent Secretary thought that the office should move from Division to Division after a certain interval.[67] Because they still proposed rotation as a means of securing primitive democracy, the proposal was impracticable and had its contemporary critics. 'Who is to pay for the removing of his wife, family and furniture? He cannot do it out of wages, and it takes a deal of money to take a family from Birmingham to Glasgow'.[68] Opposition also centred on another aspect of the expenses. £2 a week in salary for the Secretary was 'a large item in our expenditure' and 'it is too little if he has devoted his whole time and energy for the benefits of our Society', because 'he could make far more at glass making, if he is anything of a glass maker, and have no responsibility at all'.[69] Thus the post of permanent Secretary was not set up in the F.G.M.F.S., partly because the scale of the society was not so large as the A.S.E., but more substantially because 'primitive democracy' still permeated the union, at least in the third quarter of the century. The flint glass makers may have been suspicious that a professional Secretary would lord it over the ordinary members.

The depth of primitive democratic sentiment in the F.G.M.F.S. before it was superseded by the idea of representative democracy was well reflected by the changing role of the general conference of the society over the period. In the early 1850s the conference was regarded as an important means of enabling delegates from all Districts to discuss and decide future policy. One group of flint glass makers clearly recognised that the holding of the conference was one of the new features (together with publication of the *Magazine*) which distinguished the re-organised F.G.M.F.S. from the tramping society of the pre–1849 period. 'The great safety valve of our present society is the Annual Conference; – although the expense is great, it amply repays back all the cost by the good it does – by the impetus that it gives to our principles'.[70] On the other hand, at the 1849 conference 'the establishment of a monthly *Magazine* for the Trade'[71] was recommended, although it appears that it did not materialise. However, the Birmingham conference in July 1850 decided 'to establish a penny monthly magazine, to disseminate information on all points connected with the manufacture abroad and at home, to uphold the interest of the working men, and to communicate scientific knowledge and information of a nature calculated to improve the morals and elevate the social condition of the general body'.[72] It may be that an attempt was made to implement the decision of the conference immediately. The *Birmingham Mercury* of 13 July 1850 reported that the *Flint Glass Makers Magazine* was a 'well edited monthly paper'. But the monthly *Magazine* was probably ephemeral. It was in September 1850 that the *Flint Glass Makers Magazine* was first published as a quarterly journal.[73] From that year onwards the *Magazine* appeared regularly as 'a powerful engine that Glass-makers have ever called to their assistance in battling with the giant Capital for the rights of Labour'.[74]

It should be admitted, however, that there was another group who feared that both the holding of the conference and the publication of the *Magazine* would undermine the finances of the society. 'One of the Good Old School', a member from Birmingham, called the utility of both into question in 1852:

I think it is a scandalous shame that we should spend £60 and £70 a year for it, specially now that the expenses on the funds are so heavy. Add this expense to the Conference and we have nearly £200 per year thrown away foolishly. In the good old times, our forefathers had neither Conferences nor Magazine and I don't see what we want with them.[75]

Immediately 'one of the New School', of Newcastle, criticised the statement:

He says, our forefathers had no Magazine, no conferences, &c. One good reason why; because they could not. In his good times it would have taken some of the delegates a week each way to have travelled to a conference. A reason why they could not have a Magazine, is, the expense would have been as great for that alone, as both conference and it cost now.[76]

The 'New Model' unionism was not an invention of the Webbs and not a 'historical fiction'.[77] It is clear that contemporary flint glass makers realised the novelty of their union in the early 1850s, or the dispute between the 'Old School' and the 'New School' would hardly have taken place. As the organisation came to be more firmly established by the mid–1850s support for the 'Old School' disappeared.

The conference came to be held, in principle, every three years.[78] The 1858 rules of the society provided that 'a general conference of this society be held every three years; such conference to be movable, the society choosing the next place of meeting. The triennial conference to meet in the early part of the first week in June; in case of emergency the executive to have power of calling a special conference'.[79] The Webbs clearly felt that the conferences were less than all-powerful. 'The delegates came together only for specific and strictly limited purposes. Nor were even these purposes left to be dealt with at their discretion. In all cases that we know of the delegates were bound to decide according to the votes already taken in their respective branches'.[80] In the case of the F.G.M.F.S. many important issues, such as the form of the quarterly report, payments for the unemployed, the introduction of the promissory note during the strike and lock-out of 1858–59, the foundation of the death funds, the benevolent funds and sick funds, were decided outside the conference, by the decision of the Central Secretary or by a vote of members. The *Magazine* played an important role in decision-making. The propositions of the Central Committee or other Districts were communicated through its pages, as also were the results of the votes. Hence in the late 1860s and the early 1870s the usefulness of holding the conference was seriously questioned.

The issue of delegates' expenses for the Edinburgh conference in 1867 became a focal point of opposition to the general conference. As regards the delegates' allowance, the first conference, held in 1849, fixed it as low as 1s a day, on the ground that 'there were no funds to pay more'. The next conference, in 1850, allowed 5s a day.[81] At subsequent conferences the question of allowances was discussed but no alteration was made until the Manchester conference in 1864, when the allowance was advanced to 6s per day. The Edinburgh conference of 1867 revised it upwards once again: 'That every delegate to the general conference shall receive 7s 6d per day for his expenses and 7s 6d per turn during the time the factory is at work where he is employed; but on no account shall any delegate suffer any loss through attending trades conference, and every delegate shall receive second-class fare'.[82] As a result, the 1867 Edinburgh conference cost £324, whilst the one at Manchester in 1864 had cost only £113.[83] The upshot was that the expenditure in 1867 gave rise to a 'great amount of unfavourable criticism and chronic dissatisfaction amongst members of our Society'.[84]

The delegates' train fares became the focus of controversy. Joseph Leicester strongly advocated that the delegates should travel second-class, as most middle class people did until the mid–1870s. He remarked:

Our Society is the richest Society in the world, yet, it is the only Society giving third-class fare to those who are delegated on its business. Men who are used to every comfort at home desire comfort when away from home. Twice in my life I have taken second-class tickets and only charged third-class fare, because I would not be boxed up for a journey of four hundred miles in the third-class carriage.[85]

According to the reminiscences of an old friend, about twenty years earlier, in 1847, Leicester 'had walked thirty miles' to attend the conference, where 'the supper was provided for the delegates at 1s 9d per head, but such was the depth of poverty in which he was placed, that with a full heart and an empty pocket he walked about the streets during the time of supper'.[86] Twenty years later this self-sacrificing spirit was replaced by a more labour-aristocratic consciousness. Leicester continued:

> It must not be forgotten that this rule regarding third-class fare was made when we had no funds, in 1849 . . . but the state of things is gone; the Trade can now afford to make its servants as respectable as other societies, and it is only an act of justice and right which the Conference passed when it put our rules on a footing with other respectable trades.[87]

Criticism of the conference reached its peak in 1870. The Warrington District made a drastic proposal in September of that year that the conference itself should be abolished. The vote was 1,104 for and 447 against. As the Webbs wrote, 'the delegates' meeting became, in fact, superseded by the Referendum'.[88] The leaders of the society seem to have been embarrassed by the decision, although they took the official attitude that 'we neither supported nor opposed the resolution'.[89] They observed that 'the rule clearly states, "That a General Conference be held every three years, if necessary." The proposition means that one shall be held "when necessary"'.[90] They tried to reconcile the contradiction between the rules and the decision. Thereafter every conference came to be held as 'a special conference in case of emergency'. Soon after the decision, a conference was convened in July 1871. Because the Central Committee thought that 'the conference is not the right place at which to fix the rate of pay for delegates'[91] the following proposal was made in advance:

1) Delegates to Conference to receive 7s per day.
2) Deputations who are sent upon the above conditions to other districts 5s per day, but if compelled to stay all night, 6s per day.
3) In both cases second-class railway fare, also an insurance ticket shall be allowed.[92]

The reason for advocating the second-class fare was that 'we always expect them [delegates] to be well dressed; that, and many reasons, convinces us that second-class railway travelling should be allowed'.[93] The proposal was approved and fixed in the 1874 rules of the society.[94]

Such a view derived from the fact that, in the eyes of its

constituents, the F.G.M.F.S. was a union of labour aristocrats. The qualification for membership was laid down by a rule that 'Every man who has served an apprenticeship to Flint Glass Making, and in employment at Flint Glass Making shall be eligible to become a member of this Society, by being proposed and seconded by two members of the Society and paying entrance money'.[95] Takers-in were not eligible. Although apprentices who had served five years (according to the 1858 rule) or six (according to the 1867 and 1874 rule) were admitted, they were entitled to receive benefits only after promotion to journeyman. Apprentices paid the full contributions for one or two years as a preparatory stage to the 'clear' membership. A factory inspector reported in 1879 that 'not infrequently apprentices become "joining members" at the age of 18 or 19, upon payment of a small fee, and take part in the deliberations of the society'.[96] Journeymen footmakers were fully entitled to membership, and they were well organised. According to the national survey undertaken by the society in 1857, 84·3% of 1,100 journeymen employed in fifteen Districts were organised in the society, as were 84·0% of workmen, 80·4% of servitors and 95·4% of footmakers.[97] If we include 201 apprentices, the rate of organisation was 77·4% for servitors and 48·6% for footmakers. It is clear that seven in ten flint glass makers (including apprentices but not takers-in) were members of the society, the degree of organisation gradually diminishing as status in the chairs diminished. As a result the two highest groups in the chairs formed 78·4% of total membership. Of 1,119 members in twenty-one Districts in 1857, 472 (42·1%) were workmen, 406 (36·3%) servitors and 181 (16·2%) footmakers.[98] Although data indicating the degree of organisation in other years are unobtainable, there seem to have been no substantial changes in the composition of the society over the third quarter of the century. In short, the F.G.M.F.S. was a union of labour aristocrats.

III *Financial system of the society and friendly benefits*

William Gillinder, the first Central Secretary of the society, reformed the old financial system by which each District had decided individually on the disposal of its funds. He endeavoured to centralise the funds in the hands of the Central Committee.

Gillinder declared that, 'taking the principle that we are a national society, I hold that as soon as a man has paid his contribution to the society, the money for ever ceases to be his. Under this consideration I hold that money in districts no more belongs to these districts individually, than it does to individuals'.[99] Gillinder issued an account book to every District to record income and expenditure and published them in the *Flint Glass Makers Magazine* in order that all members could see the financial situation. Without doubt this financial reorganisation distinguished the new society from the tramping one of the pre–1849 period.

The effect was remarkable. In October 1853 the society succeeded in banking the first thousand pounds at the Western Bank of Glasgow,[100] and held a meeting at Vauxhall in Birmingham to commemorate the deposit on 7 October 1853, attended by 'upwards of 170 workmen'.[101] Delegates attended from most of the Districts. Gillinder, having taken the chair, 'earnestly hoped that the universal cry would be "Let us have more thousands"'.[102] The *Birmingham Mercury* reported that 'such a gathering had never been witnessed at any of the societies' meetings before, so that the greatest liberality and enthusiasm prevailed'.[103] Since the deposit of the money was an unprecedented event, 'the great difficulty was the establishing of confidence to accomplish the banking of the money'.[104] In fact, Gillinder had been suspected of having run away with it,[105] but after the initial success the suspicion vanished. In September 1854 Benjamin Smart, the second Central Secretary, was able to report that another thousand pounds had been deposited in the Bank of Birmingham. But, soon after, the society met with some financial difficulty as a result of the increased payment of unemployment allowance, so that it was compelled to draw a thousand pounds out. The Central Committee noted in July 1857 that 'we had two years of very dull trade, during which there was expended upwards of £4,000 to the unemployed; and to enable us to meet the demands of the Society, we had to draw £1,000 from our Bankers'.[106] Moreover the suspension of the Western Bank at the end of 1857 made the society's finances even more difficult.[107]

The failure of the Western Bank, followed shortly by the lock-out of 1858–59, produced something of a financial crisis for the union. But recovery was rapid as trade picked up in the 1860s, so much so that the society had banked a thousand pounds by the end of 1860 and another thousand by March 1863.[108] Benjamin Smart contended at the celebration meeting in March 1864 that 'the day was not far distant when they would be able to say that the Flint Glass Society [*sic*] had £20,000 in the bank'.[109] In September that year, when another thousand pounds was deposited at the Stourbridge & Kidderminster Bank, making a total of £4,000, about 250 glass makers assembled at the Corn Exchange to partake of a dinner. Smart stated there that 'it was not generally understood what they were collecting their funds for. The money was collected for defending their rights, and their object was something like that of the volunteers – "defence and not defiance" ... He believed that strikes would continue to occur as long as the present system of trades was carried on.'[110]

It is interesting to note that the flint glass makers habitually compared their funds with those of the A.S.E. to measure the strength of their organisation.[111] In 1861 Alexander Campbell, an old Owenite and an honorary member of the F.G.M.F.S., made a speech at the Edinburgh and Glasgow Flint Glass Makers' yearly meeting in which he explicitly compared the F.G.M.F.S. with the A.S.E. 'Even now the glassmakers as a society were equal to the best organised trades in the kingdom in wealth proportionate to their members, and in intelligence second to none. Take for example the Amalgamated Engineers with their 22,000 members, and their £60,000 capital, and compare their numbers with their money and it will be found that the glassmakers have fully more money in proportion to their members than the engineers'.[112] In July 1866, at the meeting to celebrate the banking of the sixth thousand pounds of its funds, Campbell again stated that the society was 'the best organisation of working-men in the three kingdoms', because 'the funds counted £5 per member as compared with £3 of the A.S.E.'.[113] To flint glass makers the A.S.E. set a target to surpass. In August 1869 T. J. Wilkinson, the Central Secretary, declared that the total of £9,000 banked by the society 'is nearly £6 per paying member, and shows that we rank as the richest trade society in Great Britain, as the Amalgamated Engineers, who are said to be the wealthiest society, have only £2 18s 11d per man in their

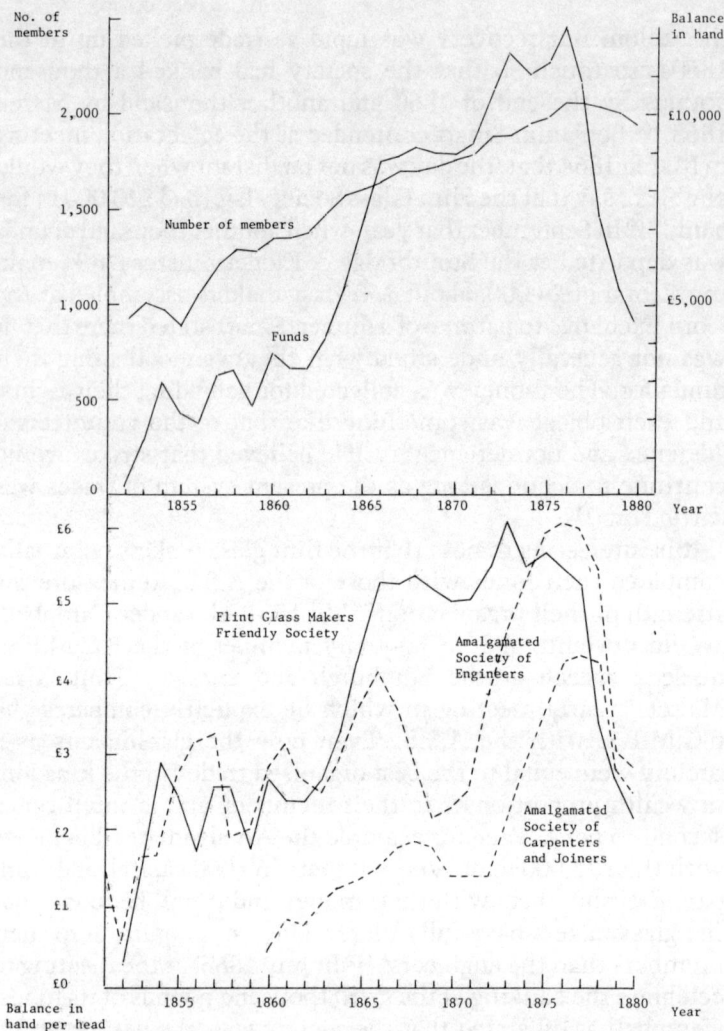

Fig. 3 The funds of the F.G.M.F.S., 1852–80. Source: calculated from S.
Webb, *Flint Glass Makers*, Ms, *op. cit.*, p. 17. For the A.S.E. and
the A.S.C.J., calculated from tables in George Howell, *The
Conflicts of Capital and Labour*, 2nd edn, London, 1890, pp. 497,
517

funds'.[114] As fig. 3 shows, in the period between 1863 and 1874
the F.G.M.F.S. surpassed the A.S.E. in terms of funds *per
capita*.[115] In 1876 the balance in hand of the F.G.M.F.S. reached

a peak, amounting to £12,264, but in terms of funds *per capita* it was surpassed by the A.S.E., which had over £6 *per capita*. Consequently the glass makers' claims of this kind disappeared from the *Magazine* in the mid–1870s.

It is hardly surprising that, with the accumulation of funds, the F.G.M.F.S. came to stress friendly society rather than trade union functions. Especially important was the unemployment allowance, a vital new substitutionary measure to combat the problem of the unemployed after the abolition of the tramping system at the Manchester conference in 1849. However, the old tramping system was not instantly abolished by the decision. In times of depression signs of a resurgence of tramping appeared. In 1852 there was word that 'men in the various districts are beginning to talk of going on tramp'[116] and in 1855 the Central Secretary gave instructions to 'stop the allowance of men who go on tramps'.[117] It was not until 1857 that the 'roll system' was established throughout the society. Under it, when any of the members fell out of work, the society's factory secretary was obliged to inform the District secretary, who 'shall immediately write to the Central Secretary for an unemployed certificate, and request the Central Secretary to place the man or men upon the unemployed roll, likewise making a correct statement of the abilities of the unemployed men'.[118] The Central Secretary should 'keep a roll or list of the unemployed, with their respective abilities, and the situations they are capable of filling'.[119] No unemployed member who was not so listed was entitled to receive the unemployment allowance. Thus the Central Secretary was able to see the state of employment throughout the trade. On the other hand, the District secretary, who kept a list of the unemployed of each District, was empowered to supply the men required in his own District on the principle of 'the longest on the roll having the first claims'.[120] This system was explained by T. J. Wilkinson before the Royal Commission on Trade Unions in 1868:

If there is anyone wanted in that manufactory, and if the employer just informs the factory secretary that he wants such and such a man, he immediately applies to the district secretary to see if there is a man upon the roll competent to take the situation. This is done simply to facilitate the obtaining of the man required.[121]

If there was no one in the District on the roll or none qualified to fill the situation, the District secretary should write to the Central Secretary, who would supply the men from other Districts. Consequently the employers had little or no power to employ their own men. The system gave a factory inspector the impression that the duty of the Central Secretary was 'to move about the members of the Union as if they were chessmen, from square to square and so to fill any vacancies occurring in different districts, taking care at the same time ever to strengthen the rate of wages'.[122] When Lloyd was asked by the Royal Commission on Trade Unions in 1868 whether he had the power to control the labour market, he answered, 'No.'[123] T. J. Wilkinson did not deny that such a control of labour was working:

Question. If you have a man that can supply that labour, the employer must take the man you offer?
Wilkinson. Well, we consider he ought to do so; we do not make it an imperative duty always that he should do so.[124]

Thus a 'chessman' was sent to the new situation and received an allowance from the society according to the distance of the removal.[125] If the employers refused the men sent by the society, a strike was unavoidable. In fact as will be shown later, one of the causes of the great strike and lock-out in 1858–59 was just such a refusal.[126]

In 1853 Gillinder was forced to change the allowance from 7s 6d to 4s 6d for a workman and a servitor and from 5s to 3s for a footmaker, and appealed to the members that 'it is in slack times that our previous societies have fallen to pieces, and left the members individually at the mercy of their oppressors'.[127] Although Gillinder was called 'Dictator' as a result, the society solved the financial crisis and survived. In August 1854 a new rule was adopted. Workman and servitor were to receive the sums of 10s per week for the first three months, 8s for the second three months, 6s for the next six months, and 4s for the following six months. Footmakers received two-thirds of these amounts. This rate was basically fixed in the rule of 1858. Changes in the rate of unemployment allowance thereafter are shown in table 4:1. If the member had been working in the glass trade and had subscribed the appropriate amounts for more than two years, he was entitled to receive the rate in the table when he lost his job.[128] But if he lost it through drink or neglect of duty or if he left 'without first consulting and getting the consent of the men in the factory he works in, and the District Officers', he was not entitled to receive the allowance.[129] If he left because of 'oppression' he enjoyed preference on the roll and received higher allowance than the ordinary unemployment allowance if the District committee and the Central Committee sanctioned it. According to the 1858 rule, he was entitled to 15s a week for the first six months and 10s for the next six months, then came under the unemployment rule.[130]

TABLE 4:1 Scale of unemployment allowance of the F.G.M.F.S and the A.S.C.J. (per week)

F.G.M.F.S.				A.S.C.J.	
The Rule of 1858		The Rule of 1867 and 1874		The Rule of 1866	
For 4 months	10s	For 13 weeks	12s	For 12 weeks	10s
4 „	8s	13 „	10s	6 „	6s
8 „	6s	26 „	8s		
14 „	5s	26 „	6s		
12 „	2s 6d	26 „	5s		
Thereafter superannuated allowance					

Notes
(a) The rate of allowance of the F.G.M.F.S. was that of workmen and servitors. Footmakers were paid two-thirds of the allowance.
(b) Sick allowance was the same scale as unemployment allowance in the rule of 1867 and 1874.
Source. Rules and Regulations of the F.G.M.F.S., 1858, 1867 and 1874. For the A.S.C.J., the 1866 rule book of the A.S.C.J.; quoted in C. G. Hanson, 'Craft unions welfare benefits, and the case for trade union law reform, 1867–75', *Economic History Review*, 2nd ser., XXVIII, 1975, p. 249.

What proportion did the unemployment allowance constitute out of the total expenditure of the F.G.M.F.S.? Not surprisingly it varied from year to year, largely according to movements of the trade cycle. The average percentages in every five years are shown in table 4:2. As the table shows, the proportion of the expenditure for the unemployed out of the society's total expenditure tended to decrease, from 76·9% in the early 1850s to 38·0% in the first half of the 1870s. It suggests that the financial burden of unemployment allowance in the early years of the society gradually diminished as the flint glass trade became

TABLE 4:2 Expenditure of the unemployment allowance of the F.G.M.F.S. between 1852 and 1881

Year	Average expenditure for the unemployed*		Average allowance per unemployed member	
	%		s	d
1852–54	76·9		39	2
1855–59	68·7†		54	9†
1860–64	59·9		51	3
1865–69	54·6		67	0
1870–74	38·0		61	5
1875–79	56·8		78	4
1880–81	62·2		52	5

Notes
* Out of the society's total expenditure.
† Does not include the effects of the strike and lock-out of 1858–59.
Source. Calculated from the Quarterly Report of the F.G.M.F.S., *Flint Glass Makers Magazine*, I–XI.

prosperous after 1860, in spite of the fact that the average amount of the allowance per unemployed member did not decrease. However, in the late 1870s expenditure on unemploy-

TABLE 4:3 Regional variations in the unemployment rate among flint glass makers in five districts between 1853 and 1881 (%)

Year	Stour-bridge	Rother-ham	Birming-ham	Man-chester	New-castle	All Districts
1853–54	6·9	6·1	5·5	6·6	9·2	10·5
1855–59	6·0	1·6	13·4	12·9	22·5	12·7
1860–64	8·1	8·2	9·3	7·7	17·1	9·8
1865–69	4·3	3·5	8·6	8·4	17·8	8·9
1870–74	3·0	0·8	8·6	13·3	17·2	8·5
1875–79	9·3	11·0	8·4	21·4	26·2	15·0
1880–81	10·8	35·9	10·4	20·8	35·8	18·2

Notes
(a) A glass maker who received unemployment allowance from the society at any time during these three months between June and August is counted as unemployed in the year, irrespective of the duration of his receipt of the allowance.
(b) The rate of unemployment allowance recipients in the year (%) is given as: number of unemployment allowance recipients in the society or District divided by the number of members in the society or District × 100.
Source. Calculated from a list of the recipients of unemployment allowance in the Quarterly Report of the F.G.M.F.S., from 1853 to 1881, in *Flint Glass Makers Magazine*, I–XI.

TABLE 4:4 Frequency and length of unemployment among flint glass makers in Stourbridge and Newcastle between 1871 and 1881 (%)

	Frequency			Longest period	
No. of times	Stourbridge	Newcastle	Period (months)	Stourbridge	Newcastle
1	65·1	47·2	1– 4	35·4	55·3
2	19·5	22·6	5– 9	19·5	14·5
3	9·8	15·1	10–14	11·8	6·9
4	3·6	5·0	15–19	8·2	6·3
5	1·0	3·8	20–24	7·7	5·1
6	0·5	1·9	25–29	10·2	6·3
7	0·5	4·4	30–34	3·1	2·5
8	0·5	0·0	35–39	3·1	2·5
			40–44	0·5	0·6
			45–49	0·0	0·0
			50–	0·5	0·0
Total (N)	195	159	*Total* (N)	195	159

Notes
(a) A glass maker who received the unemployment allowance from the society for more than a week is regarded as unemployed in the month.
(b) When the glass maker experienced unemployment more than twice, the longest period is chosen.
(c) The period is June 1871 to August 1881.
Source. Calculated from the list of those receiving unemployment allowance in the Quarterly Report of the F.G.M.F.S., in *Flint Glass Makers Magazine* from 1871 to 1881.

ment increased again, and in the early 1880s it became over 60 per cent of total expenditure.

Regional variations in the rate of those in receipt of unemployment allowance in five areas between 1853 and 1881 are shown in table 4:3. Stourbridge flint glass makers suffered less than those in other districts. Rotherham showed the same tendency as Stourbridge until the late 1870s, when unemployment suddenly increased. In contrast, Newcastle had almost always higher than average rates in the society as a whole over the same period. Particularly during the whole period of the depression in the late 1870s and the early 1880s, the proportion of unemployment allowance recipients in Newcastle remained double or three times (sometimes four times) higher than in Stourbridge. This difference stemmed from the fact that Stourbridge glass of high quality was relatively strong in the markets and less

TABLE 4:5 The scale of superannuation of the F.G.M.F.S. (per week)

		F.G.M.F.S. Rule of 1867		Rule of 1874	
Rule of 1858					
If a member for:					
10 years	2s 6d	10 years	3s	10 years	2s 6d
15 „	3s	13 „	4s	15 „	3s
20 „	3s 6d	16 „	5s	18 „	4s
30 „	4s	19 „	6s	21 „	6s
and upwards		22 „	7s	24 „	7s
		25 „	8s	and upwards	
		and upwards			

	A.S.E. Rule of 1864		A.S.C.J. Rule of 1866	
If a member for:				
18 years	7s	12 years	5s	
25 „	8s	18 „	7s	
30 „	9s	25 „	8s	

Source. Rules and Regulations of the F.G.M.F.S., 1858, 1867, 1874; the 1864 rule book of the A.S.E. and the 1866 rule book of the A.S.C.J., quoted by Hanson, 'Craft unions, welfare benefits, and the case for trade union law reform, 1867–75', p. 249.

influenced by the downturn of trade. Birmingham and Manchester lie between Stourbridge and Newcastle, moving around the average for the society between 1855 and 1872. But after 1873 Manchester began to exceed the average, and during the depression it reached around 20 per cent. Since the Manchester District was expanding rapidly in the 1870s, the high proportion

TABLE 4:6 Number of superannuated in the F.G.M.F.S., 1852–80

Year	No.
1852	3
1855	23
1860	21
1865	49
1870	55
1875	98
1880	144

Note. The number is that of the third quarter in that year.
Source. Quarterly Report of the F.G.M.F.S., in *Flint Glass Makers Magazine*, I–X.

of unemployment allowance recipients in the area significantly increased the number in the society generally. More important, as table 4:4 suggests, when the Stourbridge men were once unemployed the period of unemployment tended to be more prolonged than at Newcastle, for example. In Stourbridge, glass makers who received the unemployment allowance for less than nine months formed 54·9% of total allowance recipients in the area, while in Newcastle they formed nearly 70%. It is surprising that even in Stourbridge some 45% of the unemployed were unemployed for more than ten months and 7·2% of those were out of work for more than two years. During such long periods they were dependent on the unemployment allowances.

Superannuation allowance was another important benefit. Any member of society, 'incapacitated from earning a livelihood by his trade, through age, accident, or inability' was able to receive the allowance 'for the remainder of his life'.[131] Since the retirement age was not fixed, glass makers in good health probably preferred to go on working rather than retire on an allowance of 2s 6d to 8s. The scale of superannuation is shown in table 4:5. As already suggested when looking at the whole working life of the glass makers, they were more likely to enjoy a high standard of living after the age of fifty. As table 4:6 shows, the number of glass makers dependent on superannuation was small in the early history of the society. But, as time went by, the number of members entitled to receive the allowance increased and in 1875 nearly 100 and in 1880 144 men received it. This was obviously a burden upon the society's resources, and the Central Committee proposed in 1879 to reduce the two highest scales of 6s and 7s to 5s and 6s, and the proposition was accepted.[132] Thus after March 1879 no member received more than 6s per week.

Sick allowance began to be paid in 1867 after several years of discussion. In November 1861 the Central Committee proposed the setting up of the allowance:

We are aware that a vast majority are in other sick and benefit societies — Oddfellows, Foresters, &c. — but we think if the subject was taken into consideration and some plan drawn up, it would be seen that a sick society, in connection with our present society, would be less expensive and more beneficial to us as a body.[133]

Again in June 1864 the *Flint Glass Makers Magazine* published a leading article, 'Shall we have a trades' sick club?', in which it was stated that 'we are fully aware that most of our districts have sick clubs established, but these are not of such a sound, permanent character as we desire'.[134] The rate of sick allowance was the same as the unemployment allowance in 1867 but soon after it was reduced slightly.[135] It was finally stopped in September 1880 under the burden of increasing unemployment allowance caused by the depression.

The death fund rounded off the society's benefit functions. In the 1858 rule the death fund was separated from the general fund. All members of the society were eligible to become members of the death fund by paying 3d each to every death that occurred.[136] So, on the death of any member of the society, his widow (or his nearest relative) received the sum of 3d per member. The money was collected by the District secretary and forwarded to the Central Secretary, who supplied the widow with £5. According to the 1867 rule, on the death of any member his widow (or nearest relative) was able to receive the sum of £10, and on the death of a member's lawful wife the member was eligible to receive £10 from the general fund.[137] In the 1874 rule it was revised as follows:

On the death of every Workman, Servitor or Footmaker, paying full contribution, if a paying member one year, the sum of £5 shall be paid to his widow or friends towards defraying his funeral expenses; two years and upwards, £10; and on the death of a member's lawful wife, if a paying member one year, £3; two years and upwards, £6; and these payments to be paid for one wife only.[138]

Between September 1858 and May 1882 594 widows (or relatives) received the death allowance on the death of glass makers in the society as a whole.[139]

A wide range of friendly benefits was an important feature of the 'New Model' unions. The A.S.E. and the A.S.C.J. had the full range of benefits: funeral, sickness, superannuation, accident, unemployment donation and strike pay. In 1869 Boilermakers and Iron Shipwrights, Ironfounders, Steam Engine Makers and Operative Stonemasons also had the full range of benefits.[140] Some other unions had some but not full benefits. The F.G.M.F.S. had almost full friendly benefits and death funds other than accident benefits. Strike pay was not abolished but absorbed into the unemployment allowance.[141] The rates of payment of the F.G.M.F.S. were approximately the same as those of the A.S.E. and the A.S.C.J., although, as the table shows, there were small differences. For the unemployment allowance the F.G.M.F.S. paid a slightly higher rate over a longer period than the A.S.C.J. So far as superannuation was concerned, both the A.S.E. and the A.S.C.J. paid slightly higher rates, but before they were eligible to receive the allowance members of the A.S.E. and the A.S.C.J. needed to have had a much greater length of membership (eighteen and twelve years respectively) than those of the F.G.M.F.S. (ten years). More than that, in the A.S.E. the minimum age of entitlement to the benefit was fixed at fifty. Thus it is clear that the F.G.M.F.S. was very much a 'New Model' union so far as friendly benefits were concerned. When both the A.S.E. and the A.S.C.J. were in substantial deficit as a result of payment of friendly benefits in the 1860s,[142] the F.G.M.F.S. was able to continue paying benefits to its members. The glass makers' larger accumulated funds were clearly the key factor.

IV *The problem of amalgamation*

As already noted, the F.G.M.F.S. was not an 'Amalgamated' union. In this point it differed greatly from the A.S.E. or the A.S.C.J. The United Flint Glass Cutters' Society was established in 1844; when the preceding tramping society 'almost broke down for want of funds there were so many on the road that they could not all be supported'.[143] As an unemployment benefit society it was more defensible against the manufacturers' attack. On 12 November 1845 the meeting of the Master Flint Glass Cutters in Stourbridge and Birmingham pledged itself not to employ any glass cutter who 'has left his work in consequence of a strike having taken place either on account of prices or any other pretext, and who does not produce a written discharge from his last employer'.[144] But the union survived. Even in 1848, when the membership decreased to 500 and the funds were not merely exhausted but the society was deeply in debt,[145] it survived. Thus flint glass makers and cutters had their own unions. They never amalgamated. Why not?

Since glass cutters were often working in the same premises as flint glass makers, and even if they were in different premises the processes of glass making and cutting were related to each other, there seemed a possibility of amalgamation between the two unions. As a matter of fact, however, the relationship was complicated. An observer from the A.S.E. at the conference of the flint glass makers in 1852 found that 'the glass cutters have hitherto held aloof from the other departments of the trade, or rather that the trade has been arbitrarily divided in society into two bodies who, instead of co-operating with each other, have viewed each other with mutual distrust, and unfriendly feeling has prevailed between them'.[146] 'Unfriendly feeling' was also observed by J. E. White, the chief commissioner of the Children's Employment Commission. He reported in 1865 that 'Flint Glass Makers are a set as distinct even from flint glass cutters, though in most cases working in the same manufactory, as if they were engaged in totally distinct manufactures'.[147]

An amalgamation between glass makers and cutters was seriously considered in 1873. The proposal originated in Manchester. On 6 January 1873 both the committee of the Manchester branch of the Glass Cutters' Society and the Central Committee of the F.G.M.F.S. issued an appeal to both societies. J. Rudge, the Central Secretary of the F.G.M.F.S., said in his address:

As a great deal of the work made is for cutting, and we are generally employed on the same premises, by the proposed Amalgamation we should be better able to act together, coupled with the fact that we are all working for one object, namely to ameliorate our condition as working-men. On these grounds, we can not see any reason why we should remain disunited, as at present; and if any prejudice exists on either side, let it be at once removed for ever.[148]

C. Warburton, secretary of the Manchester branch of the Cutters' Society, remarked that 'there are few trades whose interests are more closely connected than ours. We are both engaged in branches of workmanship depending on each other . . . Then let our cry be "Amalgamation".'[149] Clearly the engineers' strike on Tyneside, begun in 1871, had an impact. Warburton continued:

When the Smiths, Mechanics, and Engineers were in separate Societies, they were easily beaten and broken up and the men scattered about the country, when they dared to stand out against oppression and tyranny . . . What a noble battle they fought last year at Tyneside! . . . By the firmness of the men, the Tyneside employers now give both the nine hours and an advance of wages too.[150]

Continuous discussions took place among the members of the
F.G.M.F.S. for nearly a year. But the proposal met strong opposition and ended without concrete results.

The difficulty was threefold. In the first place the interrelated
production process in flint glass making and cutting was vital.
The glass makers' fear was simply that, if glass makers went on
strike, cutters would lose their jobs as a result of having nothing
to cut. So if the societies amalgamated, glass makers would be
under an obligation to give financial support not only to their
own members but to the cutters. If the cutters went on strike,
however, it would not be necessary for them to support the glass
makers, who would be able to continue to work without glass
cutters. This seemed to put glass makers at a great disadvantage.
They had experienced both cases in the past in 1858–59 and
1865–66.

The process of evolution at the time of the flint glass makers'
strike in 1858–59 will be fully described in chapter five, but it is
necessary here to give some account of the problem relating to
contacts with glass cutters. The strike which took place in
October 1858 in Stourbridge was a glass makers' problem. The
glass cutters had never declared a strike but they were necessarily involved in it and locked out, because they had no glass to
cut. In December the *Brierley Hill Advertiser* reported that 'the
glass cutters are sadly interfered with, and their employment
shortened, by the blowers not supplying them with the customary amount of material to operate upon'.[151]

The glass cutters' loss of work and wages was felt by them to
be unreasonable. In December 1858 Idas Ogle, a glass cutter of
the Mills Stewart & Webb factory in Wordsley, claimed for £3
under the Master and Servant Acts because although no strike
had been declared he and his colleagues had been discharged on
28 November. On that day he was told that 'there was no more
work for him in consequence of the glass-blowers having ceased
to work'.[152] A man who appeared for the defendants insisted
that 'the law never contemplated that when the master had no
work through the glass-blowers having struck, the employers
should pay the cutters as though they were at work'.[153]

In Birmingham the glass cutters were still working in mid-
January 1859, despite the increasing shortage of glass to be cut.
The *Birmingham Journal* gave a warning, however, that if both

glass manufacturers and glass makers failed to settle the dispute immediately the result would be disastrous, for 'though at the present time the cutters have not ceased working, they will shortly be compelled to do so for want of material. Thus a large body of men, who really are not involved in the disagreement, will be deprived of the means of earning their daily bread, and the result will be deplorable.'[154]

By the end of January the shortage of glass for cutting had become critical. The financial crisis worsened. The total balance in hand was only £700.[155] At the beginning of February the Cutters' Society appealed from Birmingham to the various trades and the public for assistance. After reporting that the society was paying the unemployment allowance of 10s a head weekly to 300 cutters, the appeal ran: 'this number will soon be greatly increased, as there are a number of the employers, who, having no dispute with the glass cutters, are keeping the men employed to cut up what stock they have on hand; this, you will be well aware, will soon be exhausted, unless a settlement with the glass blowers is effected'.[156]

The F.G.M.F.S. showed little concern for the glass cutters' plight, contending that 'the battle solely belonged to the glass makers and their employers, and that our Society could not be held responsible for the conduct of the employers towards the glass cutters'.[157] The F.G.M.F.S. 'deeply regretted the unavoidable circumstances, but to share our funds with them, or what was collected from kindred Societies, was to waste our ammunition and play into the enemy's hands. It was our business to go on with the battle to the end, as best we could, and afterwards consider what was best to be done for the sister Society.'[158] It is scarcely surprising that the experience worsened relationships between makers and cutters. As W. H. Packwood recalled twenty years later, in 1878, it began to bear 'the semblance of a strike within a strike, or our Society against the employers and the glass cutters, and the employers against both'.[159] The cutters had to act independently. It was not until March that a joint circular was issued in the name of the glass makers' society and the glass cutters' society. After that day donations from other trade societies came to be divided between the two, but the financial loss to the glass cutters had been severe.[160]

After the strike the financial state of the Cutters' Society improved. In February 1864 the society had £2,210 and its half-yearly report boasted of being 'one of the best trade societies in the United Kingdom'.[161] In 1865 it was organising more than 1,100, equivalent to some two-thirds of all the glass cutters, of which there were some 1,400 to 1,500, in the kingdom.[162] But the glass cutters' own strike in 1865–66 changed the situation. The strike began in July 1865 in Dudley, near Stourbridge, and over 200 cutters were thrown out of work. According to the appeal issued by August William Doody,[163] General Secretary of the Glass Cutters, the cause of it was that 'Two men who had formerly been active members of our society, and staunch advocates for our apprentice law, started as small out-door masters, or sweaters, and immediately broke through all restrictions'.[164] The strike continued over fifty weeks, ending in defeat for the men in July 1866.[165] Flint glass makers were not involved in the dispute, having 'no strike at present in their trade',[166] because the disruption in cutting did little harm to glass making itself. The situation was totally different from that of the glass makers' strike in 1858–59, when cutters were necessarily involved in the glass makers' strike. Therefore James Cuthbertson, District secretary in Glasgow of the F.G.M.F.S., wrote in September 1873 that 'amalgamation with the Cutters would do no good, but rather a deal of harm, inasmuch as they could not keep us when on strike or lock-out, because, they would have to support their own men: whereas if they went on strike, we would have to support them for God knows how long, for I don't know'.[167]

The second difficulty of amalgamation concerned the difference in the accumulated funds of the two bodies. During the cutters' strike of 1865–66 gifts and loans from outside amounted to £882. The members of the society were paid 2s a week for twenty-seven weeks, 3s for four weeks, and 4s for seventeen weeks. But expenditure during the strike amounted to £9,486,[168] so that the Cutters' Society was in a critical condition. As table 4:7 shows, membership began to decrease after 1866, and in 1870 the financial crisis deepened. It was not until 1871 that funds began to accumulate again. By the time the amalgamation was proposed in 1873 the F.G.M.F.S. had banked about £8,000, while the Cutters' Society had only £2,660. Naturally this made flint glass makers reluctant to merge.

TABLE 4:7 Membership and finance of the Glass Cutters' Society between 1864 and 1885

Year	No. of branches	Member-ship	Balance in hand	Year	No. of branches	Member-ship	Balance in hand
1864	20	1,066	£2,639	1875	19	1,226	£5,391
1865	20	1,133	3,719	1876	19	1,223	6,362
1866	20	1,159	631	1877	21	1,203	4,083
1867	21	1,024	106	1878	21	1,176	1,252
1868	20	886	116	1879	21	1,000	228
1869	19	877	171	1880	19	976	231
1870	19	915	74	1881	19	925	356
1871	19	865	497	1882	19	956	757
1872	20	1,119	1,879	1883	19	853	568
1873	20	1,123	2,599	1884	19	824	718
1874	18	1,212	3,854	1885	19	803	808

Source. S. Webb, *Flint Glass Cutters, Ms, op. cit.*, p. 357.

The difference in the effective strength of the two bodies was another factor. To glass makers who were proud of their firmly established apprentice restrictions, the failure of the glass cutters to maintain control over apprenticeship after the disastrous strike seemed an irreparable weakness. J. Husselbee, a Dudley flint glass maker, wrote in October 1872 that since the glass cutters' strike of 1865–66 'cutters' apprentice law has been almost wholly disregarded by every employer. A few yards from where I write, so near that I can almost hear the groaning of its wheels, is a cutting shop crowded with apprentices, with only one solitary unionist among them; and yet your apprentice law of 1844 allows one apprentice to every five men.'[169]

Because of these difficulties amalgamation failed. It is noteworthy that the proposal had originated in Manchester, where artisan consciousness was wearing relatively thin as a result of the rapid expansion of flint glass manufacture, particularly after the 1860s. On the other hand, opposition occurred in the West Midlands and Scotland, where organisation and traditional artisan consciousness remained strong and reproduced itself among flint glass makers. Stourbridge and Birmingham were strong financial supporters of the glass cutters on strike in 1865–66, but they never agreed to amalgamation with them, because amalgamation would have damaged their own interests.

The flint glass makers might also have joined with the bottle makers. The F.G.M.F.S. included a Yorkshire Bottle Section.

But the F.G.M.F.S., which was dominated by the skilled glass makers, had rather complex relations with the Bottle Section. The section decided its own policy independently of the executive of the society, so that the complexity was twofold: the executive sometimes supported the policy decided by the Bottle Section, sometimes not. Conflict appeared when the Bottle Section attempted to amalgamate with the London flint bottle makers. Support appeared when the Bottle Section found itself in dispute with the ordinary bottle makers in Yorkshire.

Whereas blown flint glass makers in the West Midlands and other areas were competing with pressed glass makers in the Newcastle area, the great competitor of the Yorkshire flint bottle makers was London. The London flint bottle makers were producing cheaper products than the Yorkshiremen. As the *Flint Glass Makers Magazine* stated in 1875, 'the London Bottle Trade will always be a source of anxiety to the bottle workers in our trade. They work with the same kind of tools, same moulds, and make the same class of bottles that are made in Yorkshire, and could, with a little forebearance and practice, master the better class of work and yet we have no control over their operations.'[170] The London men had established their own trade union – The Glass Bottle Makers' and Blowers' Society of London (hereinafter referred to as the London Society) on 27 April 1874.[171] The members were 'originally cribmen who were looked down upon and despised by the factory men'.[172] There had been 'a little public house club' among them, which was 'never properly managed, nor able to exert much influence over the trade, and it had financially collapsed about 1868–70'.[173] In 1875 the reorganised London Society had a membership of about 200 but fell away during the next year or two until it was reduced to about 160.[174]

Hence, there existed three societies in the London glass trade in the mid–1870s, and they were in conflict with one another. The Yorkshire flint bottle makers in the F.G.M.F.S. wished to amalgamate with the London Society so as to diminish competition. At the half-yearly county meeting of the Bottle Section on 19 June 1875 it was resolved that 'this meeting thinks it highly desirable that an Amalgamation should take place between this and the London Flint Bottle Makers' Society'.[175] It was also requested that the Central Secretary of the F.G.M.F.S.

should take immediate steps to convene a meeting of the representatives of the two societies because 'it would prove beneficial to the trade in general'.[176] Nonetheless other Districts of the F.G.M.F.S. opposed the amalgamation, declaring that 'the London bottle makers would hang as a dead weight round the neck of our Society'.[177] Other Districts already felt that the Yorkshire Bottle Section itself was 'a dead weight in the Society'. As a result the Central Secretary merely recommended 'moral amalgamation' which aimed only 'to keep back men from going to work in each other's District to your mutual injury'.[178] On the other hand, G. Rose, secretary to the London Society, was for a short time 'desirous for an understanding to be agreed upon between the two bodies'.[179] But, soon after, he came to realise that the F.G.M.F.S. as a whole was reluctant to amalgamate. He wrote to the F.G.M.F.S. in February 1877 of 'how the members of the Flint Glass Makers' Society sympathize with us; they take every opportunity to sneer and scoff at our endeavours to elevate ourselves'.[180] In the event, the amalgamation did not take place.

The executive of the F.G.M.F.S. supported its Yorkshire bottle makers when a dispute between the section and the Yorkshire Bottle Makers' Society took place in 1877. After the dissolution of the amalgamated society, the Glass Bottle Makers of Yorkshire United Trade Protection Society was reorganised in 1860.[181] From 1862 to 1865 it was merely a kind of federation of the various districts, with Castleford at the centre. In 1865 an executive committee was established and Castleford was appointed the governing branch with power to deal with disputes.[182] From that year onwards membership increased. Three years later, in February 1868, the total membership was 646, in ten branches.[183] In 1870 membership was 792, in 1875 1,120, in 1880 1,001, and in 1885 it reached 1,522.[184]

Since the *flint* bottle makers in Yorkshire were not organised by the Protection Society but by the F.G.M.F.S. a complicated dispute took place. The Bottle Section of the F.G.M.F.S. also expanded rapidly in the 1870s, and in 1875 the section had a membership of 280 in eight branches,[185] about one in fifty of all organised bottle makers in Yorkshire. From the viewpoint of commodity markets, flint bottle makers and table flint glass makers had no common interests. On the other hand, it was extremely difficult to define the real difference between the type of work done by flint bottle makers and ordinary bottle makers. The ordinary bottle makers made bottles for the general market such as wines, mineral waters, and large medical bottles, while the flint bottle makers concentrated on medical bottles, usually small ones.

It had long been a custom in the bottle trade that any earnings above those gained by the tantum should be placed in the coffers of the society.[186] In 1877 the bottle makers in Sykes MacVay & Co.'s factory at Castleford put on a 'tantum' of £2 per hole per week. The employers declared that 'if the tantum was not taken off they should have to get hands elsewhere to come to work'.[187] The council of the Yorkshire Bottle Society was of the opinion that the tantum should be removed,[188] but the workmen refused and were immediately discharged. The employers tried to open the bottle house by employing *flint* bottle glass makers, and began to negotiate with the F.G.M.F.S. On 9 April 1877 the council of the Yorkshire Bottle Society opened a correspondence with the F.G.M.F.S. and in about a fortnight it became apparent that preparations were being made for the flint bottle makers to start one of the bottle houses.[189] Although the *Quarterly Report of the Glass Bottle Makers of Yorkshire United Trade Protection Society* related these affairs in great detail, the *Flint Glass Makers Magazine* did not comment on the negotiations with the Yorkshire Bottle Society at all, probably because the F.G.M.F.S. thought it was dishonourable behaviour for them. The F.G.M.F.S. tried to conceal from its members the dispute with the Yorkshire Bottle Society, but by chance a secret letter from Hargreaves, secretary to the Hunslet District of the F.G.M.F.S., to R. Sykes was revealed in the *Magazine* by MacHenry, a 'sole manager' of Sykes MacVay & Co.[190] Probably personal rivalry for the position of manager in the company between Hargreaves and MacHenry led to the letter's publication. The upshot was that it became public knowledge that the District secretary had applied for a position in the firm which Sykes was about to start. He had to acknowledge that he had written the letter, and said, 'When the offer was made me of the situation as shop manager, I felt desirous to improve my position.'[191]

On 5 May the council of the Yorkshire Bottle Society convened a special delegate meeting at Normanton. It was resolved that 'the central secretary communicate with the Flint Glass Makers' Society, and ask them if they will meet a deputation to consider the subject'.[192] The council appointed representatives to meet the delegates from the F.G.M.F.S. and on 12 May delegates from both societies met at Castleford and discussed the problem for seven hours.[193] At the meeting 'the glass bottle hands demanded from the glass makers a definite statement as to what they considered their proper work. Nothing came of the conference. There is really no distinct line of demarcation it would be impossible to make one.'[194] Thus the conflict between the two societies came to a head. The central secretary of the Yorkshire Bottle Society wrote on 17 May that 'our society has to fight not only the Masters' Association and the men of the North of England District who have come to Thornhill and Conisbro', but also *the National Flint Glass Makers' Society*'.[195]

By this time some flint glass makers had started to work in one of the bottle houses. According to Greenwood, general secretary of the Bottle Society, 'the Flint hands say they are justified in starting the houses which are changed for them, and that they shall work them and make any kind of Bottles they can'.[196] The Bottle Society was thus forced to agree at a special delegate meeting in Normanton on 14 July that the tantum would be removed 'unconditionally'.[197] But the situation was worse than had been expected. Sykes MacVay & Co. 'would not engage to take all the men back who had been discharged when it stopped'.[198] Every bottle maker 'condemned the Flint hands for taking their trade from them'.[199] Without the flint glass makers' intervention, bottle makers would have not been so easily deprived of their traditional 'tantum'. Flint glass makers clung to their own customs, but paid little attention to those in the kindred society. The executive of the F.G.M.F.S. authorised the right of the members of the Bottle Section to play the role of blackleg. This was an extreme example of the exclusiveness of the F.G.M.F.S. Hardly any sign of sympathy with the less skilled can be found, however closely the production process required them to work together.

In many important respects the F.G.M.F.S was a 'New Model' union, except in one highly significant respect. It resembled the

A.S.E. or the A.S.C.J. organisationally in that it was a national
union with a Central Committee and Central Secretary, and
actuarially in that it stood for high contributions and high
benefits, unemployment allowance, superannuated allowance,
sick and death benefits, all of which were secured by the growing
funds of the society. In the 1860s these funds *per capita* sometimes amounted to twice those of the A.S.E. It was these firmly
established benefits which completed the transformation from
old tramp society to 'New Model' union. Strategically the society
insisted upon 'Defence, not Defiance' and stressed its policies
respecting the restriction of apprenticeship, promotion control,
regulation of labour mobility between areas of slack and full
employment, limitation of production, encouragement of
emigration and co-operative production, all aimed at creating a
permanent scarcity of skilled labour in order to keep wages high.
This was a decisive transition 'from custom to calculation'.
Hence, the Webbs' use of the F.G.M.F.S. as an example of a 'New
Model' union. Certainly co-operative production was thought of
as 'a means of absorbing the unemployed' among flint glass
makers in the early 1850s and was revived again in the mid–
1860s, but the glass makers thought it too risky.[200]

An emigration scheme guided by doctrines of orthodox political economy was also discussed in the early 1850s, as shown by
a leading article entitled 'Emigration as a means to an end' in the
Flint Glass Makers Magazine.[201] Gillinder, the first Central
Secretary, planned that £1,000 'would send fifty men out of our
surplus labour every year'[202] to Australia with £20 a head. He
himself resigned as Secretary in 1854 in order to emigrate to
America.[203] But few followed him. In the period between 1852
and 1881 only fifty-nine glass makers emigrated (twenty-seven
for America, eleven to Australia and twenty-one to unknown
destinations).[204] About half of them had emigrated by 1856. In
comparison to other trade unions which encouraged emigration
in the third quarter of the century, the number of emigrants
from the F.G.M.F.S. was very small.[205] It is therefore misleading
to regard the society as enthusiastic emigrators by citing the
policies often described in the *Flint Glass Makers Magazine*, as
the Webbs have done. What the Webbs did not do was count the
actual number of emigrants.

Moreover, the way in which the Webbs dealt with the F.G.M.

F.S. was a trifle unscrupulous: they left the union out of consideration in the case of Potter *v.* the Junta. From the Webbs' point of view the F.G.M.F.S. ought to have supported the Junta. This chapter has shown how deeply the F.G.M.F.S. was connected with Potter's group. The riddle can be solved in terms of the personal relations between Potter and Joseph Leicester. The importance of Leicester's activities in linking the F.G.M.F.S. with the national movement has been described, but his activities must not be overestimated. It is important to try to explain, in terms of the nature and structure of the F.G.M.F.S. itself, why he was so effective in support of Potter. The F.G.M.F.S. had relatively few members compared with the engineers or the carpenters. Glass makers could persuade themselves that they had no need of full-time officials like Allan or Applegarth. Its constitution 'enshrined the principles of "primitive democracy"'. In this sense it was a disturbing hybrid placed between the traditions of localism and the requirements of the new national unions. The Webbs themselves appear to have failed to recognise this hybrid so far as their typology was concerned. The fact that the F.G.M.F.S. supported not the Junta but Potter prevented the glass makers from having any contacts with the First International.

Notes

1 Webb, *History of Trade Unionism*, p. 181.
2 The Webbs nicknamed a group in the London Trades Council the 'Junta', consisting of William Allan (the A.S.E.), Robert Applegarth (the A.S.C.J.), Daniel Guile (the Ironfounders), Edwin Coulson (the Bricklayers) and George Odger (the Ladies' Shoemakers). For Allan see J. B. Jefferys, *The Story of the Engineers, 1800–1945*, London, 1946, *passim*. For Applegarth see A. W. Humphrey, *Robert Applegarth. Trade Unionist, Educationist, Reformer*, Manchester and London, 1913, and A. Briggs, *Victorian People*, London, 1954, chapter VII. For Odger see D. R. Moberg, 'George Odger and the English Working Class Movement: 1860–1877', Ph.D. thesis, London University, 1953. For Guile see H. J. Fyrth and H. Collins, *The Foundry Workers*, Manchester, 1959, chapter III.
3 Harrison, *Before the Socialists*, p. 6. Rothstein stereotyped the Webbs' view, and maintained that in the second half of the nineteenth century English labour leaders such as Applegarth 'diverted the Labour movement from revolutionary to opportunist, from proletarian to middle class, from political to trade union lines'

(T. Rothstein, *From Chartism to Labourism*, London, 1929, pp. 194–5). On the other hand Selig Perlman wrote that 'the "Junta period", in which the labor leaders of Britain so inspired the public with confidence in the essential soundness and moderation of their movement, weathered all sorts of storms, and turned the very attacks by enemies into promising opportunities, [this] is perhaps the most notable chapter in world labor history' (S. Perlman, *A Theory of the Labor Movement*, New York, 1928, p. 129).

4 G. D. H. Cole, 'Some notes on British trade unionism in the third quarter of the nineteenth century', *International Review of Social History*, II, 1937, reprinted in E. M. Carus-Wilson (ed.), *Essays in Economic History*, vol. III, London, 1962, p. 202.

5 *Ibid.*, p. 203.

6 *Ibid.*, p. 205.

7 *Ibid.*, p. 205.

8 *Ibid.*, p. 206.

9 Webb, *History of Trade Unionism*, chapter IV, 'The New Spirit and the New Model' (1843–60), and chapter V, 'The Junta and their allies'.

10 S. Coltham, 'George Potter, the Junta, and the *Bee-Hive*', *International Review of Social History*, new ser., IX, 1964, pp. 392–3. See also S. Coltham, 'The *Bee-Hive* newspaper; its origin and early struggles', in A. Briggs and J. Saville (ed.), *Essays in Labour History*, vol. I, London, 1960, pp. 174–204.

11 *Flint Glass Makers Magazine*, V, p. 145.

12 *Ibid.*, V, p. 237, and *Bee-Hive*, 26 March 1864.

13 *Ibid.*, V, p. 206.

14 *Ibid.*, V, p. 145.

15 The first article about the F.G.M.F.S. in the *Bee-Hive* appeared in the issue of 13 June 1863. As to Joseph Leicester, see Brian Harrison, *Dictionary of British Temperance Biography*, published by the Society for the Study of Labour History, 1973, p. 78; id., *Drink and the Victorians*, London, 1971, p. 309; P. T. Winskill, *The Temperance Movement and its Workers*, vol. II, London, 1891, pp. 259–60; H. Gosling, *Up and Down Stream*, London, 1927, p. 11; Powell, *Glass-making in England*, pp. 136–7; F. M. Leventhal, *Respectable Radical. George Howell and Victorian Working Class Politics*, London 1971, p. 151. Leicester's career is described in T. Matsumura, 'The Flint Glass Makers in the Classic Age of the Labour Aristocracy, 1850–80', Ph.D. thesis, University of Warwick, 1976, pp. 286–91.

16 Coltham, 'George Potter, the Junta, and the *Bee-Hive*', p. 402.

17 This was decided on 22 November 1864 (*ibid.*, p. 396).

18 The proceedings of the strike are elaborately described in the *Bee-Hive*, 11 March 1865.

19 *Bee-Hive*, 18 March 1865.

20 *Ibid.*

21 *Flint Glass Makers Magazine*, V, p. 451.

22 'Balance-sheet of the Iron Workers' dispute', published by the Executive Council of the National Association of Iron Workers, in *Bee-Hive*, 28 June 1865.

23 *Mr Potter and the London Trades' Council*, 1865, p. 2. In the Webbs' eyes Danter was 'the outspoken president of the Amalgamated Engineers' (*History of Trade Unionism*, p. 255).

24 *Bee-Hive*, 8 April 1865.

25 *Ibid.*, 15 April 1865.

26 Coltham, 'George Potter, the Junta and the *Bee-Hive*', p. 413.

27 *Bee-Hive*, 16 September 1865.

28 *Articles, Laws, and Rules of the Glass-Makers' Friendly Society, held at the House of Mr. William Wilson*, Newcastle upon Tyne, 1800 (British Library). This rule book tells us that the friendly society began on 15 November 1755.

29 *Ibid.*, provision IV. A new member had to pay, at his entrance, 2*s* 9*d* and nobody above the age of thirty-five was, on principle, accepted. Also 'No Pitman, Collier, Sinker, or Waterman to be admitted this Society' (provision XXIV) and 'If any member of this shall enter into any other society, he shall be expelled and excluded from all benefits, allowances, and advantages' (provision XXIII).

30 *Ibid., passim.*

31 *An Account of the Receipts and Expenditure of the Glass Makers' Friendly Society, from December 30 1835 to July 28 1837*, 1837 (Brierley Hill Library).

32 The other branches with more than ten members in 1837 were: Edinburgh (forty-seven), St Helens (forty-five), Manchester (forty-one), London (thirty-eight), Deptford (thirty-five), Dublin (twenty-eight), Belfast (nineteen), Bristol (seventeen), Warrington (seventeen), South Shields (sixteen), Cork (sixteen), York (twelve), Plymouth (twelve), Longport (twelve) and Greenock (eleven) (*An Account of Receipts and Expenditure of the Glass Makers' Friendly Society*, 1837, op. cit.).

33 *Ibid.*

34 *Pottery Gazette*, 1 November 1880. At the meeting there were present Thomas Hawkes, M.P., Isaac Badger, Thomas Budger, Gammon (Birmingham), Green (Birmingham), Harris (Birmingham), Shakespeare (Birmingham), Greathead, Richardson (Stourbridge), Stevens (Stourbridge), Davis (Stourbridge) and Wheeley (Stourbridge).

35 *Ibid.*

36 Webb, *History of Trade Unionism*, p. 181.

37 G. Lushington, 'An account of the strike of the Flint Glass Makers in 1858–9', in National Association for the Promotion of Social Science, *Trades' Societies and Strikes*, London, 1860, p. 105.

38 Webb, *History of Trade Unionism*, p. 181.

39 The Worshipful Company of Glass Sellers of London, *Essays on the Glass Trade in England*, London, 1883, p. 13.

40 The circular does not exist but six replies—from the Holyrood Flint Glass Works, Edinburgh (Mr Ford); the Holloway End Glass Works, Stourbridge (E. & J. Webb); the Haverton Hill Glass Works, Haverton Hill; the Phoenix Flint & Bottle Glass Works, Bristol; the Worsbrodale Glass Works (Wood & Perkes) and the Grazebrook Glass Works, Stourbridge—are preserved in the Brierley Hill Library.

41 *A letter from E. J. Webb of Stourbridge*, dated 31 March 1847, Ms (Brierley Hill Library).

42 *A letter from Worsbrodale Glass Works*, dated 3 April 1847, Ms (Brierley Hill Library).

43 S. Webb, *Flint Glass Makers*, Ms (Webb Trade Union Collection, Section A, vol. XLIII, 1), p. 238. The date of the split in the old society is not specified.

44 *Ibid.*

45 *Birmingham Journal*, 22 July 1848.

46 For W. P. Roberts see Webb, *History of Trade Unionism*, pp. 182–3, and E. Welbourne, *The Miners' Unions of Northumberland and Durham*, Cambridge, 1923, pp. 66–72, 78, 142–5.

47 *Birmingham Journal*, 22 July 1848.

48 *Morning Chronicle*, 23 December 1850.

49 *Flint Glass Makers Magazine*, I, pp. 79–80. William Gillinder, 'An Appeal for the Birmingham Debt, dated 8 March 1851'.

50 The statement of the Birmingham delegate at the conference of the F.G.M.F.S. held in September 1849, in Webb, *Flint Glass Makers*, Ms, *op. cit.*, p. 228.

51 Whereas the total income for the Five Ways strike was £1,408 12*s* 3½*d*, the total outlay was £1,496 12*s* 5*d* (*Flint Glass Makers Magazine*, I, p. 80).

52 Webb, *Flint Glass Makers*, Ms, *op. cit.*, p. 228.

53 *Ibid.*, p. 227.

54 *Ibid.*, p. 226.

55 The conference was attended by delegates from London, Edinburgh, Dublin, Birmingham, Manchester, Glasgow, York, Bristol, Belfast, Newcastle upon Tyne, Waterford, St Helens, Warrington, Tutbury, Longport, Rotherham, Catcliffe, Haverton Hill, Dudley, Stourbridge, Wordsley, Hunslet and Worsbrodale (*Birmingham Journal*, 13 July 1850).

56 *Ibid.*

57 See a letter on 'The Evil Consequences of Strikes', in *Flint Glass Makers Magazine*, July 1850, quoted in Webb, *History of Trade Unionism*, pp. 199–200; 'As man after man leaves, and no one [comes] to supply their place, then it is that the proud and haughty spirit of the oppressor is brought down, and he feels the power he cannot see.'

58 Webb, *Industrial Democracy*, p. 12.

59 *Rules and Regulations of the F.G.M.F.S., 1858*, rule III.

60 *Royal Commission on Trade Unions*, 10th Report, 1867–68, p. 32, q. 18641.

61 *Rules and Regulations of the F.G.M.F.S.*, 1857, rule III.

62 This rule survived until 1893, when it was modified, in so far that seven members were elected, the Central Secretary nominating four from the district in which he resided. The Webbs paid special attention to this nomination system. They wrote, 'the only Trade Union in which this example still prevails is that of the Flint Glass Makers, where the rules until lately gave the Secretary "the power to nominate a central committee" (open to the objection of the trade), in whose hands the executive power of the society shall be vested from year to year' (Webb, *Industrial Democracy*, p. 8, n. 2).

63 *Flint Glass Makers Magazine*, VI, p. 868.

64 *Ibid.*, VI, p. 1151.

65 *Ibid.*, VI, p. 1164. The writer's name is not given.

66 The Central Secretary of the society was paid a salary of £20 per annum by the 1858 rule, £30 by the 1867 rule, and £50 by the 1874 rule.

67 *Flint Glass Makers Magazine*, VI, p. 1164.

68 *Ibid.*, VII, pp. 167–8.

69 *Ibid.*

70 *Ibid.*, I, p. 129.

71 Webb, *Flint Glass Makers*, Ms, *op. cit.*, p. 229.

72 *Morning Chronicle*, 23 December 1850.

73 Although the Webbs wrote that the *Magazine* was an octavo monthly of ninety-six pages (*History of Trade Unionism*, p. 197), it was not a monthly one.

74 *Flint Glass Makers Magazine*, I, p. 1.

75 *Ibid.*, I, p. 231. According to the first quarterly report of the society ending September 1852, 1,000 copies of the *Magazine* (vol. I, No. 13) printed cost £4 10s, which was 4·3% of the total expenditure of the Central Committee in that period (£105 13s).

76 *Flint Glass Makers Magazine*, I. p. 248.

77 Allen, 'Abstract of "a methodological criticism of the Webbs as trade union historians"', p. 5.

78 After the inaugural conference in 1849 the triennial conferences were held in Stourbridge in 1852, in Glasgow in 1855, in London in June 1858, in Birmingham in December 1858 (especially for the long strike), in Manchester both in 1861 and in 1864, in Edinburgh in 1867, and in Manchester in July–August 1871.

79 *Rules and Regulations of the F.G.M.F.S.*, 1858, rule XLIV.

80 Webb, *Industrial Democracy*, p. 19.

81 *Flint Glass Makers Magazine*, VI, p. 67. The 1858 rule of the society provided 5s per day (rule XXVII).

82 *Rules and Regulations of the F.G.M.F.S.*, 1867, rule XXII.

83 The costs of other earlier conferences were Glasgow (1855), £107; London (1858), £119; Birmingham (1858), £51, and Manchester (1861), £66 (*Flint Glass Makers Magazine*, VI, p. 68).

84 *Ibid.*, VI, p. 68.

85 *Ibid.*, VI, p. 284.

86 *Ibid.*, VI, p. 924; a reminiscence of J. Roberts in 1870, when the testimonial to Joseph Leicester was given. Roberts was a secretary to the Testimonial Fund.

87 *Ibid.*, VI, p. 284.

88 Webb, *Industrial Democracy*, p. 21.

89 *Flint Glass Makers Magazine*, VI, p. 1057.

90 *Ibid.*, VI, p. 1057.

91 *Ibid.*, VI, pp. 1087–8.

92 *Ibid.*, VI, p. 1081.

93 *Ibid.*

94 *Rules and Regulations of the F.G.M.F.S., 1874*, rule XXXIX.

95 *Rules and Regulations of the F.G.M.F.S. 1858*, rule 1. The entrance money was to be paid according to age in the case of workmen and servitors in 1858, probably because when they grew older the possibility of retirement and sickness increased. The scales in the 1858 rule and the 1859 rule were as follows (brackets show those in the 1867 and the 1874 rule). Under twenty-one years old, 7s 6d (10s); under twenty-five, 10s (20s); under thirty, 15s (30s); under thirty-five, 20s (40s); under forty, 50s (60s); under forty-five, 40s (80s). All above the age of forty-five were 'to be sent around the trade for approval; their entrance money not to be under £3 nor more than £5' (*The 1858 rule*, rule 1).

96 *Factory Inspectors' Report ending October 31 1879*, 1880, p. 31.

97 Concerning the number of glass makers employed, see chapter one, n. 59. The number of members is taken from 'Names of the Members of the F.G.M.F.S.' for the year ending 31 December 1857; in *Flint Glass Makers Magazine*, III, pp. 228–43.

98 *Ibid.*, III, pp. 228–43.

99 *Ibid.*, I, p. 311.

100 The rules of the society provided that 'when the surplus moneys in the various districts amount to the sum of one thousand pounds the whole shall be banked in the names of six trustees to be chosen by a majority of the members of this society, who shall likewise choose the bank and the locality that it shall be banked in' (*Rules and Regulations of the F.G.M.F.S., 1858*, rule XXXIX).

101 *Birmingham Journal*, 8 October 1853.

102 *Ibid.*

103 *Birmingham Mercury*, 8 October 1853.

104 *Flint Glass Makers Magazine*, II, p. 38; Gillinder's address, dated 17 August 1854.

105 Gillinder recalled at the farewell party before his emigration in 1864 that 'when I took the office, I found there was £116 in debt, and yet they boasted of what they had done. I know that my measures were not popular, and I was denounced as a second Napoleon ... I knew that if I proposed to have a fund of one thousand pounds, it would be said I wanted to run away with it, and it was said so' (*ibid.*, II, pp. 107–8).

106 *Ibid.*, II, p. 546.

107 *Ibid.*, III, p. 109.
108 *Ibid.*, IV, pp. 265, 686.
109 *Bee-Hive*, 12 March 1864.
110 *Stourbridge Observer*, 10 September 1864.
111 The A.S.E. had devoted its attention to the strengthening of its own organisation after the defeat of the strike in 1852, and membership figures grew from a bare 9,737 in 1852 to 33,007 in 1866, while funds in the same period increased from £7,103 to £138,113 (Jefferys, *The Story of the Engineers*, p. 75).
112 *Flint Glass Makers Magazine*, IV, p. 305. For Alexander Campbell see W. H. Marwick, *Alexander Campbell*, Glasgow, 1963. Although many historians have followed the Webbs in regarding Campbell as 'the virtual founder of the Glasgow Trades Council' (*History of Trade Unionism*, pp. 251–2, n. 1; see Thomas Johnston, *The History of the Working Classes in Scotland*, Glasgow, 1929, p. 385), he was only 'a reporter for the *Sentinel*, in which capacity he was given the right to speak but not to vote' (W. H. Marwick, 'Scottish social pioneers, VI: Alexander Campbell', *Scottish Educational Journal*, 24 February 1932, p. 261). The flint glass makers affiliated were entitled to send two members to the council (*Glasgow Sentinel*, 24 December 1859). However, the peculiar pattern of working hours in flint glass making made it impossible to send the two every Wednesday night. So the F.G.M.F.S. chose Alexander Campbell as a representative 'though not members of their own body' (*ibid.*) The friction between the F.G.M.F.S. and the Glasgow Trades Council which took place when he was accepted by the society as an honorary member is described in T. Matsumura, 'The Flint Glass Makers in the Classic Age of the Labour Aristocracy, 1850–80', Ph.D. thesis, *op. cit.*, pp. 291–7, and W. H. Fraser, 'Trades Councils in England and Scotland, 1858–1897', Ph.D. thesis, University of Sussex, 1967, pp. 28–9. See also W. H. Fraser, *Trade Unions and Society. The Struggle for Acceptance, 1850–1880*, London, 1974, p. 198.
113 *Flint Glass Makers Magazine*, V, p. 720.
114 *Bee-Hive*, 21 August 1869.
115 The F.G.M.F.S. surpassed the A.S.C.J. in terms of funds *per capita* between 1860 and 1877.
116 *Flint Glass Makers Magazine*, I, p. 260.
117 *Ibid.*, II, p. 190.
118 *Rules and Regulations of the F.G.M.F.S., 1858*, rule VI.
119 *Ibid.*, rule VI.
120 *Ibid.*, rule IX.
121 *Royal Commission on Trade Unions*, 10th Report, 1867–68, p. 33. q. 18662.
122 *Factory Inspectors' Report, ending October 31 1879*, 1880, p. 32.
123 *Royal Commission on Trade Unions*, 10th Report, 1867–68, p. 25, q. 18446.
124 *Ibid.*, p, 32, q. 18647.

125 According to the rule of the Society, 'any unemployed member sent to a situation not more than 50 miles from the district he is in, shall receive 2s 6d. and third-class fare; above 50 miles, 4s; above 150 miles 5s; above 200 miles 6s' (*Rules and Regulations of the F.G.M.F.S., 1867*, rule XIII).

126 This roll system lasted at least until the beginning of the present century. E. A. Pratt wrote in 1904 that 'almost, if not quite, as incredible is the fact that in the flint-glass trade an employer is not allowed to choose his own employees. If he did so the whole body of men would be withdrawn, and his works stopped. When a flint-glass employer wants an additional hand he must write to the district secretary of the men's union and ask him to send him one' (Pratt, *Trade Unionism and British Industry*, p. 99).

127 *Flint Glass Makers Magazine*, I, p. 259.

128 *Rules and Regulations of the F.G.M.F.S., 1858*, rule XXXIV. Those who had paid twelve months were entitled to half the unemployment allowance (*ibid.*).

129 *Ibid.*, rules XXIX and XXX.

130 *Ibid.*, rule XIX. According to the 1874 rule, in this case, he was entitled to receive 15s per week for the six months and came under the first scale of unemployment allowance (rule XXV).

131 *Rules and Regulations of the F.G.M.F.S., 1858*, rule XXII. Under the 1867 rule 4s per week was paid as superannuation allowance if he became incapable of working at the glass trade by an accident, and if in the society for more than ten years (rule XIV).

132 *Flint Glass Makers Magazine*, IX, p. 828.

133 *Ibid.*, IV, p. 398.

134 *Ibid.*, V, p. 246.

135 *Royal Commission on Trade Unions*, 10th Report, 1867–68, p. 33, q. 18684, T. J. Wilkinson's statement. 'It is reduced to 9s for 13 weeks, 7s 6d for 13 weeks, 6s for 26 weeks, 5s for 26 weeks, 4s for 26 weeks and 2s per week as a superannuation allowance as long as they are ill' (*ibid.*).

136 Rules for Death Fund, in *Rules and Regulations of the F.G.M.F.S., 1858*, rule II.

137 *Rules and Regulations of the F.G.M.G.S., 1867*, rule XV.

138 *Rules and Regulations of the F.G.M.F.S., 1874*, rule XXX–1.

139 Compiled from the Quarterly Report of the Death Fund, published in the *Flint Glass Makers Magazine* in the period concerned. The main causes of death of flint glass makers were: consumption 10·9%, bronchitis 11·7%, phithisis 7·2%, heart 5·0% and natural decay 4·7% (17·3% of the total deaths did not have a cause of death) (calculated from the Quarterly Report, *ibid.*). In Stourbridge ninety-five widows (or relatives) received the death benefit on their husband's death and seventy-eight glass makers did so on their wife's death in the same period.

140 C. G. Hanson, 'Craft unions, welfare benefits, and the case for trade union law reform, 1867–75', *Economic History Review*, 2nd. ser., XXVIII, 1975, p. 248, table I.

141 See below, p.130.
142 Hanson, 'Craft unions, welfare benefits, and the case for trade union law reform', pp. 252–3.
143 Webb, *Questionnaire for the Glass Cutters' Society*, p. 367.
144 *Report of a Meeting of Master Cutters in 1845* (leaflet), (Stourbridge *Reference Library*). This leaflet is introduced in Sandilands, 'The History of the Midland Glass Industry', M.Com. thesis, *op. cit.*, p. 248.
145 *Bee-Hive*, 18 February 1865: 'The Half-Yearly Report of the Glass Cutters Society'.
146 The *Operative*, 1852, p. 447.
147 *Children's Employment Commission*, 4th Report, 1865, p. 203, q. 176.
148 *Flint Glass Makers Magazine*, VII, p. 271.
149 *Ibid.*, VII, pp. 272–3.
150 *Ibid.*, VII, p. 273.
151 *Brierley Hill Advertiser*, 24 December 1858.
152 *Ibid.*, 24 December 1858.
153 *Ibid.*, 26 February 1859.
154 *Birmingham Journal*, 15 January 1859.
155 *Bee-Hive*, 18 February 1865.
156 *Reynolds's Newspaper*, 6 February 1859.
157 *Flint Glass Makers Magazine*, IX, p. 455.
158 *Ibid.*
159 *Ibid.* W. H. Packwood recalled in 1878, 'We still have a very vivid recollection of the turbulent and unhappy ending of the first amalgamated meeting [date not specified], that met, at the "Little Pig Inn", for the sake of giving strength and unity to the principles of the strike and lock-out. The meeting broke up in confusion, lights were extinguished, threats were used; and no wonder, when it was a question of living with these men; their cry was for bread and the salvation of their Society, not principles, as they were not called upon to sacrifice any' (*ibid.*).
160 The Cutters' Society received donations from other trade societies which amounted to about £50 as gifts and £340 as loans (*Flint Glass Makers Magazine*, III, p. 618), but the expenditure of the society for the first half of 1859 amounted to £2,612, mainly to support the unemployed, varying between 300 and 370 from January to April of 1859 (*Bee-Hive*, 18 February 1865).
161 *Bee-Hive*, 20 February 1864.
162 *Ibid.*, 5 August 1865.
163 William Doody of Birmingham was probably the permanent general secretary of the Glass Cutters' Society. The *United Kingdom First Annual Trades' Directory*, published in February 1861, indicates that Doody was general secretary, and it was he that gave a report as general secretary of the Glass Cutters' Union for the limitation of apprentices at the second Trades Union Congress, held in 1869 (*Bee-Hive*, 28 August 1869).

164 *Bee-Hive*, 5 August 1865, and Webb, *Flint Glass Cutters*, Ms, *op. cit.*, p. 354.

165 Eric Hopkins writes that the strike continued for eight months, ('An anatomy of strikes in the Stourbridge glass industry, 1850–1914', *Midland History*, II, 1973–74, p. 25), but this seems to be an error. Sidney Webb was more accurate when writing that 'in the strike and lock-out of 1865 £9,500 was spent in this struggle which lasted 12 months and ended in defeat' (Webb, *Flint Glass Cutters*, Ms, *op. cit.*, p. 361).

166 *Bee-Hive*, 14 October 1865. The statement of Benjamin Smart of Glasgow, the Central Secretary of the F.G.M.F.S. at the time.

167 *Flint Glass Makers Magazine*, VII, p. 476.

168 *Bee-Hive*, 29 December 1866: 'A Balance Sheet of the Gifts and Loans from Trades' Societies and Friends in Great Britain, Ireland and America', and George Potter, 'Strikes and lock-outs, from the workman's point of view', *Contemporary Review*, XV, August 1870, p. 549.

169 *Flint Glass Makers Magazine*, VII, p. 463.

170 *Ibid.*, VIII, p. 210.

171 *Rules of the London Glass Blowers' Trade Society, 1875*, 1875 (Webb Trade Union Collection, Section C, vol. XLII, 4), p. 1.

172 S. Webb, *Glass Blowers*, Ms. (Webb Trade Union Collection, Section A, vol. XLIII, 2), p. 260.

173 *Ibid.*, p. 257.

174 *Ibid.* In 1877 the London Society organised eighteen bottle houses out of twenty-two or twenty-three in London (*Flint Glass Makers Magazine*, VIII, p. 942).

175 *Flint Glass Makers Magazine*, VIII, p. 275.

176 *Ibid.*, VIII, p. 275.

177 *Ibid.*, VIII, p. 211.

178 *Ibid.*, VIII, p. 733.

179 *Ibid.*, VIII, p. 722–3.

180 *Ibid.*, VIII, p. 942.

181 *Manchester Guardian*, 3 June 1868. The report of J. Wild, a representative of the Yorkshire Bottle Makers' Society, read at the first Trades Union Congress. The history of this society is written in the preface of *Rules of the Glass Bottle Makers of Yorkshire United Trade Protection Society, 1906*, 1906. See also Brundage, 'The Glass Bottle Makers of Yorkshire', M.A. thesis, *op. cit.*, chapter II, pp. 32–58.

182 Webb, *Flint Bottle Makers*, Ms, *op. cit.*, p. 275.

183 The *Bee-Hive* of 8 May 1869 reported that the number of members was about 720.

184 Webb, *History of Trade Unionism*, pp. 746–7.

185 See appendix.

186 The 'tantum' was a limitation of individual output fixed by the society. They were not allowed to exceed it. If they did, that amount of money was paid into the funds of the society. See Webb,

Industrial Democracy, p. 447, and Brundage, 'The Glass Bottle Makers of Yorkshire', M.A. thesis, *op. cit.*, p. 45.

187 *The Quarterly Report of the Glass Bottle Makers of Yorkshire United Trade Protection Society, ending November 12 1877*, No. XLVIII, p. 210.

188 *Ibid.*

189 *Ibid.*

190 *Flint Glass Makers Magazine*, IX, p. 22. The letter was dated 22 April 1877.

191 *Ibid.*, IX, p. 134.

192 *The Quarterly Report of the Glass Bottle Makers of Yorkshire United Trade Protection Society, ending November 12 1877, op. cit.*, pp. 211–12.

193 *Ibid.*

194 S. Webb, *Questionnaire for the Yorkshire Bottle Makers' Protection Society* (Webb Trade Union Collection, Section A, vol. XLIII, 3), p. 263.

195 *The Quarterly Report of the Glass Bottle Makers of Yorkshire United Trade Protection Society, ending November 1877, op. cit.*, p. 214. My emphasis.

196 *Ibid.*, p. 215.

197 *Ibid.*, p. 220.

198 *Ibid.*, pp. 222–3.

199 *Ibid.*, p. 223.

200 For co-operative production planned by the F.G.M.F.S. see T. Matsumura, 'The Flint Glass Makers in the Classic Age of the Labour Aristocracy, 1850–80', Ph. D. thesis, *op. cit.*, pp. 272–84.

201 *Flint Glass Makers Magazine*, II, p. 1 (in 1854). See Webb, *History of Trade Unionism*, p. 201, n. 1.

202 *Flint Glass Makers Magazine*, II, p. 2.

203 After leaving England with his family, Gillinder started the Franklin Glass Company in Philadelphia in 1861 and began making pressed glass in 1863 (A. C. Revi, *American Pressed Glass and Figure Bottles*, New York, 1964, p. 163, and MacKearin, *American Glass*, p. 601). Thus the skilled artisan in blown flint glass-making in England, who had opposed pressed glass-making, turned successful pressed glass manufacturer in America. This was an example of the social elevation of a labour aristocrat from a 'Staunch trade's Unionist' to an 'honorable and good employer' (Gillinder's obituary in *Flint Glass Makers Magazine*, VI, p. 1085. He died on 22 February 1871 at the age of forty-nine).

204 Compiled from the Quarterly Report (Districts) of the F.G.M.F.S., in *Flint Glass Makers Magazine*, I–IX.

205 Whereas the Ironfounders' Society, one of the most ardent unions in favour of emigration, spent £4,700 on it between 1854 and 1874, the F.G.M.F.S. spent only £306 between 1852 and 1874. (For the figures of glass makers, calculated from the Quarterly Report (Districts) of the F.G.M.F.S.) Emigration undertaken by the

F.G.M.F.S. is discussed in terms of the Erickson *v.* Clements debate (C. Erickson, 'The encouragement of emigration by British trade unions, 1850–1900', *Population Studies*, III, 1949—50, and R. V. Clements, 'Trade unions and emigration, 1840–80', *Population Studies*, IX, 1955) in T. Matsumura, 'The Flint Glass Makers in the Classic Age of the Labour Aristocracy, 1850–80', Ph.D. thesis, *op. cit.*, pp. 260–71.

Chapter five

The great strike and lock-out of 1858–59

The Webbs wrote that the *Flint Glass Makers Magazine* between 1850 and 1855 was full of denunciations of strikes and from this drew support for their view that the 'New Model' unionism was opposed to them. They also pointed out that 'in 1854 the Flint Glass Makers, on the proposition of the Central Committee, abolished the allowance of "strike-money" by a vote of the whole of the members'.[1] As already shown, the F.G.M.F.S. sought to avoid strikes, particularly in the early 1850s. Yet the society was far from ready to abandon the strike weapon. When the editor of the *Flint Glass Makers Magazine* appealed for the abolition of 'strike-money' and stated that 'we believe that strikes have been the bane of Trades Unions' (only this part is quoted by the Webbs),[2] he added, 'It must not be thought from the above that we have abandoned the idea of strikes in all cases; we know that in some cases they cannot be avoided.'[3] The context of these comments by the Central Committee was not a proposal for the abolition of the strike money but the proposal that 'so long as the unemployed allowance continues at ten shillings per week, the unemployed allowance and the strike allowance be alike', viz. the strike allowance was to continue to be paid like the unemployed allowance. It is clear that the Webbs' interpretation of 'strike-money' in 1854 was misleading. In fact flint glass makers often went on strike in the 1850s and a great strike took place in 1858–59.

The great strike and lock-out began in 1858 and lasted six months. Equivalent conflicts among engineers in 1852 and among builders in 1859–60 have attracted much attention from historians, but the flint glass makers' has been relatively neglected in spite of arousing a good deal of contemporary interest.[4]

Early in October 1858, at the Stevens & Williams factory in

Stourbridge, the employers proposed that one of the apprentices should be taken on as a journeyman footmaker at something less than 14s (nominal wages) per week,[5] disregarding the rules and regulations of the society, which only four months before had been revised and ratified at a conference in London. The London conference of 15–19 June 1858 'deeply' regretted that 'the wages of journeymen footmakers are in general so low, and agree that the trade shall not supply footmakers for less wages than fourteen shillings per week and one shilling and twopence per move, and that each district adopt such measures as will insure the desired effect'.[6] On 12 October, on the refusal of the employer, twenty-two men gave fourteen days' notice to leave in accordance with the decision of the Stourbridge District of the society. They all left on 23 October. Three days later the following leaflet was issued and sent to other flint glass manufacturers.

Brierley Hill Glass Works
October 26th, 1858

Dear Sir,
  In consequence of our refusal to submit to the dictation of the Glass Makers in our employ, the undermentioned have signified their intention of not recommencing work until we comply with their demands, we shall be obliged by your not employing them, as it is the interest of the Trade generally to support us in resisting such tyrannical proceedings.
We are,
Yours respectfully,
Stevens and Williams[7]

This circular listed the names of nine discharged workmen, nine servitors and four footmakers.
  Simultaneously another dispute took place as Grazebrook's Audnam Glass Works in Stourbridge, where there were four apprentices to nine chairs. The London conference had made more stringent rules with regard to apprentices so as to regulate the 'supply of labour', prescribing that 'no more than one apprentice be allowed to three chairs, two to five, and so on in proportion; and every one put on shall be bound an apprentice—Note—No journeyman footmaker must be discharged to make room for an apprentice.'[8] This meant one apprentice beyond the number of the rule already in the glass factory. M. & W. Graze-

brook proposed to take on another, a fifth apprentice. It seems likely that Grazebrook's refused to take on the man who had been sent from Edinburgh by the society and attempted to employ another.[9] When the men refused to agree, the Grazebrooks gave notice to all the men that 'they would not fill any more metal, unless the men consented for the lad to be put on'. Grazebrook's found it necessary to ask for external aid against the society and issued a circular on 16 October, declaring that 'the following men, having formed a combination to stop our glass works, and dictate their own rules, have all been discharged by us, and we shall be obliged by your not employing them, and feel sure that it is the interest of the glass trade to support us'.[10] On 23 October, when the notice expired, the discharged men proposed terms to the employers for reengagement, but 'Mr. J. Grazebrook replied, "He had made his arrangement; he would have no society men, and meant to pursue a different system in future."'[11] Thus the men in two factories, amounting to about fifty altogether, were out[12] and received their first strike allowance of 15s from the society on 30 October.[13]

Grazebrook's sued five of their workmen, 'for that on the 25th day of October last they deserted their service without the consent of their masters, and without any lawful excuse'.[14] On 15 November 1858 the Wordsley petty sessions examined the case. During cross-examination it was disclosed that the two circulars had been issued. The Bench decided that, 'from what appeared in the document, which they considered had been published indiscreetly and without forethought, there was no case against the defendant, and accordingly dismissed the charge'.[15] The employers' claim that it was illegal to give the notices on Wednesday was also rejected. It appeared to be a considerable setback for the employer. 'The result of the investigation seemed to give considerable satisfaction to the men and their friends, who on leaving the Court gave a loud and hearty cheer.'[16]

The society's members were militant and firmly united. On the following day, 16 November, the Central Committee ratified the proposition by the Stourbridge District that both the committee and the District 'shall be allowed to take what measures they may think best and most expedient in the present struggle; and that, should it be necessary, they shall be allowed to draw out two or four factories or the whole of the district on strike, and shall receive the allowance stated in Rule 19'.

On the other hand, the flint glass manufacturers who received the circulars from Grazebrook's and Stevens & Williams supported the two employers by refusing to employ the discharged workers. According to Joseph Leicester, 'the masters sent round a printed circular all over the kingdom, asking other masters not to employ those men who had struck on their establishments, and when they applied for work in other towns, that printed circular was thrust in their faces, and they were refused'.[17] The manufacturers also supplied the two glass factories with the plain goods for the glass cutters to work up at lower than market prices when the two factories began to experience some difficulty in getting them, early in November. But glass cutters were gradually involved in this dispute, because of the shortage of glass.

On 1 November the manufacturers held a meeting at the Talbot Hotel, Stourbridge, to organise their own defence association[18] The meeting was attended by fifteen glass manufacturers from Stourbridge, Dudley and Birmingham. Thus the Flint Glass Manufacturers' Defence Association came into being. At a meeting at Dudley on 15 November the name was changed to the Midland Association of Flint Glass Manufacturers and George Green, of Brettell Lane, Stourbridge, was appointed secretary, with a salary of £120 a year.[19] George Lloyd, of the Lloyd & Summerfield factory in Birmingham, was appointed chairman and William Walker, of the Heath Glass Factory, of Stourbridge, treasurer. The circular issued on the following day stated:

The recent attempts to enforce the view of the Glass Makers' Society in two of the manufactories of this district, upon grounds wholly untenable, and, if carried out, destructive to the liberty of the manufacturer in the employment of labour, have compelled the proprietors to appeal to the sympathy of the trade in supporting them in resisting those attempts and they have resulted in the formation of an association of the glass masters in the districts of Birmingham, Stourbridge, and Dudley.[20]

The association succeeded in organising about nineteen or twenty glass manufacturers in Birmingham, Dudley and Stourbridge.[21] Originally it was intended to be temporary, for 'the defence of the members against any unjust interference (more especially in the form of strikes) on the part of the men employed either of their own movement, or in concert or combination with other, for the purpose of coercing their employers'.[22] But after the strike the association continued as a negotiator with the F.G.M.F.S.

On 4 December 1858 the glass makers held a general meeting of the society in the Corn Exchange in Stourbridge, attended by upwards of 250 men connected with the glass trade.[23] Delegates from Birmingham, Manchester, Dudley and York were also present. It was agreed that 'the hands still employed at the other glass works should be allowed to go "out" as soon as they thought fit'[24] and that the usual subscription would be doubled; to rise from 1s to 2s per week for Workmen and Servitors, from 8d to 1s 4d for Footmakers, and from 4d to 8d for Apprentices'.[25] Certainly the high contribution became a burden to the glass makers. But 'in many districts the men offered to pay the levy which was fixed, even if it amounted to half their wages'.[26] By 7 December the workers of five factories in Stourbridge, including the Grazebrook and Stevens & Williams factories, were locked out.[27]

On 18 December the society held a meeting in the Corn Exchange again, at which about 600 glass makers attended. Deputations from London, Warrington, Birmingham and Dudley were present.[28] It was announced that 'four other factories of glass makers had received notice, and that in consequence of the other hands at the other five factories (previously 'out') being at play, four factories of glass-cutters had received notice'.[29]

This notice was an organisationally planned attack by the manufacturers' association. On 14 December the Midland Association held a meeting, attended by four Lancashire glass manufacturers, who were beginning to found their own association following the Midlands' example.[30] Deputations from the Midlands and Lancashire induced all the employers in Yorkshire, Northumberland and Scotland to lock their men out, with the avowed intent of extinguishing the society. Those who attended the meeting were prepared to give the notice and planned to do so on the very day the society would be holding a meeting. George Lloyd wrote to J. D. Bacchus, a Birmingham glass manufacturer, on 17 December:

I do not doubt your co-operation, but it is most important that the notices should be simultaneous and in the same form of words and a printed form has been adopted and distributed and the Secretary has directly sent forms to your works. It is also important that the notices should be given tomorrow, for the men intend holding a meeting tomorrow at Stourbridge, and with great exertion to make it important if not triumphant.[31]

Thus more factories stopped working. As the *Brierley Hill Advertiser* reported, 'the unfortunate differences between the employers and employed in the glass trade are as far from settlement as ever'.[32]

TABLE 5:1 Numbers of society men locked out and unemployed during the strike and lock-out of 1858-59

	Totals of 16 Districts	Stour- bridge	Birming- ham	Man- chester	Edin- burgh	New- castle	Rother- ham
1858							
September	87	7	19	6	6	21	2
October	95	8	19	8	5	17	9
November	134	57	19	2	5	20	4
December	143	77	16	6	4	17	2
1859							
January	595	185	134	125	4	19	0
February	670	180	124	124	22	17	0
March	612	171	96	109	20	29	0
April	560	176	92	119	1	20	0
May	113	27	20	9	0	12	0
No. of members	1,142	273	274	138	40	93	50

Notes

(*a*) The first week each month is chosen, except January 1859, when the second week is chosen, because the lock out was declared at the beginning of January.

(*b*) Membership of the Districts as at August 1858. The total membership of all twenty-two Districts of the society was 1,270.

Source. A list of the recipients of unemployment allowance in the Quarterly Report of the F.G.M.F.S., in *Flint Glass Makers Magazine, III, passim.*

At the turn of the year the conflict became a national one. The glass makers held a general conference on 31 December 1858 and 1 January 1859 at Birmingham at which were present about thirty delegates from Stourbridge, Birmingham, Dublin,

Dudley, Edinburgh, Glasgow, London, Longport, Manchester, Newcastle, St Helens, Warrington, York and Rotherham.[33] The conference resolved to modify the society's rules, revised at the London conference, so as to conciliate the masters. One of the modifications was to loosen apprentice restriction to one apprentice to two chairs. The other was to adopt the old standard rule of minimum wages in the trade: 22s a week for workmen, 16s 6d for servitors and 12s for footmakers. However, these conciliatory propositions were rejected by the association. Instead, on the second day of the conference, more than 500 men, including non-society men from seventeen factories in Stourbridge, Dudley and Birmingham, were locked out. Only two factories in Stourbridge and four in Birmingham were working.[34] The *Flint Glass Makers Magazine* wrote that other Districts followed the Midlands 'as the lock-out mania spread, or as the other employers were brought under the influence of the newly organised Association of the Midlands Employers'.[35] As a result nearly 600 members of the society were unemployed in the second week of January. The lock-out spread to Manchester, Warrington, and St Helens,[36] but, as table 5:1 suggests, the men in other Districts seem not to have been affected. It was in mid-February that men in Glasgow and Edinburgh were locked out.[37] Irrespective of the resolution at the society's general conference, the association had decided to lock the men in the Midlands out. George Lloyd wrote to J. D. Bacchus on 30 December that it was necessary to suspend the works

in order to impress upon the men the firm determination of the Employers of resisting their encroachments. If we hesitate to give way now, they will renew their attacks where it will be much more difficult for us to resist them . . . As matters stand at this moment, whatever may be the result of the men's meeting, a suspension for three weeks is inevitable, on account of the time necessary for holding meetings.[38]

The employers found in the depression of the time an opportunity for breaking the society. George Lloyd continued:

We are now tolerably unanimous, and when trade is better, then will spring up motives which will destoy much of our courage and the men will have more strength and more resolution in proportion to our weakness. There could not possibly be more favourable an opportunity of vindicating our rights as Masters, and if lost now, it may be long ere another offers, and our freedom will be lost.[39]

Therefore, George Lloyd replied to a copy of the modified rules of the Society, which was sent to every employer in the country,

I am compelled to state, after the fullest consideration, that the alterations proposed leave the rules essentially the same in meaning and effect, so that there is no ground afforded me for submitting them to the consideration of the association.[40]

The *Midland Advertiser* wrote an article critical of the employers. 'The workmen evince a conciliatory spirit, and have actually revised their rules in order to meet the employers something like half way. We cannot, however, say so much for the masters. They have locked the men out, and do not seem willing to resume operations except on terms of an unconditional surrender.'[41] On 8 January a large meeting of the society took place in Dudley in order to consider Lloyd's letter. Various speakers 'showed their surprise and indignation that employers should wish to change their Trade Union into a merely provident society.'[42] Although a deputation saw the manufacturers the following day, it met with no response. The lock-out was as strict as ever. After 8 January the subscriptions of members of the society rose to 5s for workman and servitor, 3s 4d for footmaker and 1s 8d for apprentice.[43]

Three days later, on 13 January, a leaflet by 'the Women's Glass Washers' Friendly Society' was circulated.[44] It was a parody. Each of six surnames that appeared at the end of the leaflet, with the forename feminised, was that of a member of the Central Committee, all of them Stourbridge men. The leaflet parodied the causes and evolution of the strike.

We regret being obligated to appeal to you for assistance, at the present time, to enable us to thwart the intentions of our Mistresses, who have joined themselves together for the express purpose of destroying our union . . . The origin of the dispute was, that [at] a certain Hotel in Sturbrig, a girl wanted fourteen pence per day, which was we vow and declare the average wages other Land-ladies in the locality were paying; this request was refused by the Landlady . . . Another Lady in Sturbrig requested us to send for a servant (very polite of her wasn't it?) and we did, from Glasgow, and when she arrived she refused to engage her, and demanded a little girl to be set on to fill the vacancy; and because we would not agree to this (though perhaps the little girl could have done the work), they gave us fourteen days' notice to leave and each of the landlords sent copies of a printed circular (we should like to know who pays for the printing) to every other Landlord requesting them not to take into service any whose names they then sent, and the consequence is that we are refused employment everywhere . . . But our mistresses finding that we were firm, and that they had no chance of success, called a meeting and formed themselves into an association whose first action was to lock out several hundred women . . . Their second action was to send deputations to Lancashire and Scotland (with one solitary exception) also to lock us out.[45]

The leaflet ended with the request that 'all communications to be addressed and subscriptions received by Josephina Woolley,[46] Sturbrig, Worcestershire.' Although its author has not been identified, his purpose was clear enough. By comparing the skilled glass makers to unskilled working women he intended to ridicule them and remind them of the risk which they ran of forfeiting their respectability. Apparently in the eyes of 'respectable society' to be reduced to the level of a working woman was the last word in absurdity and humiliation.

In mid–January the dispute took a new turn. The manufacturers, meeting at the Queen's Hotel, Birmingham, on 18 January, decided to continue the lock-out and to enforce the following 'document':

In re-entering your employment, we agree to give up the Glassmakers' Society, as now constituted. We declare we will not interfere with your management or right to employ labour as may be required by you in your works, nor contribute funds to any society that shall have this effect, as long as we remain in your employment.[47]

It was so obnoxious that the *Midland Advertiser* reported that 'if carried out to the letter it would reduce the men to the position of the merest slave'.[48] From that day onwards the conflict between the society and the association revolved round this 'document'.

It was also at this time that the glass makers began to draw support from other trade unions. On 27 January a meeting of delegates from all the trades of London was held at the Bell Inn, Old Bailey.[49] Woolley from the F.G.M.F.S. and Doody from the Glass Cutters' Society attended to explain the nature of the dispute with their employers. A resolution was passed that 'their case was one worthy of support, the delegates pledging themselves to use their best exertions to render assistance'.[50] A committee of five was appointed for that purpose and met every Thursday at the Bell to collect funds for the locked-out men.[51] William Burn, an old Chartist who 'was in 1859 in very distressed circumstances, but had for twenty-seven years devoted his main strength to the Trade Union Movement', [52] was appointed secretary of the 'Bell Inn Committee'.

On 8 March the society held a meeting in Birmingham which delegates from Stourbridge, Birmingham, Manchester, Warrington and other Districts attended. It passed a more conciliatory resolution which confirmed that 'any master may have any member he prefers, by telling the secretary or any of his men whom he desires to have'.[53] However, the association resolved at its meeting on 14 March to enforce a second 'document'. This was softer in tone than the first, in the sense that the declaration that men should not subscribe to any union was withdrawn, but it still had the following provision: 'I will not attempt, by myself or through others, to interfere with your freedom in the management of your works, more especially in reference to the engagement of the men or number of apprentices whom you choose to employ.'[54] Hence the society ordered members not to sign:

This bond is the same in spirit as the other, excepting that they have omitted "NOR CONTRIBUTE FUNDS TO ANY SOCIETY THAT SHALL HAVE THE EFFECT." But why have they left out this favourite sentence? Simply because public opinion has cried out in ten thousand voices, Shame! Shame! yes, and by the same power will the present "BOND" die a natural death.[55]

Without any agreement between the society and the association, however, some works in Scotland, Lancashire and Birmingham had reopened by the beginning of March 'on the same conditions at which they left off. The men in these districts have gained all they required, the masters having given way.'[56] In March the number of workers returning to work gradually increased, but late in that month about 560 men were still out. Lloyd still insisted upon the document as the terms upon which the men should resume,[57] but 'the men seemed determined not to abandon their society'.[58] On the other hand, on 31 March the manufacturers decided, at a meeting in Birmingham, to settle the dispute by giving up the attempt to enforce their 'yellow dog contract', as the Americans call it. The exhaustion of the Association's defence fund partly accounts for the compromise. By this time about £848 had been spent on fourteen factories.[59]

On 1 April the society learned of the compromise from the association; the executive immediately held a meeting at Stourbridge and accepted the manufacturers' invitation to meet on 4 April at Dudley. The society had also exhausted its funds, and welcomed the compromise.[60] W. H. Packwood of Stourbridge recalled in 1878 that W. A. Siverwright of Tutbury, a modifier of the newly adopted laws, and Packwood 'talked matters over, and came to the conclusion and felt a relief that the end of the struggle was so close at hand. We rose early, it was a lovely spring and clear morning, everything seems gay, the leaves were putting forth new life . . . We arrived in Dudley in time to take part in the meeting.'[61] At 10 a.m. on 4 April the meeting between the association and the society to terminate the strike and lock-out began.[62] 'Very little discussion took place, and as if by mutual consent, the meeting at once resolved itself into a formal character, the business principally being transacted between the Chairman and the C.S.'[63]

The revised rule resolved upon at the meeting of the society on 8 March was agreed in principle. Fourteen shillings a week was granted to footmakers. The apprentice rule was modified from one apprentice to three chairs to one apprentice to two chairs, a gain on the employers' part.[64] It was also agreed that 'if masters engaged a non-society man the society men should object to work with him, and that our society will support men for so doing'.[65] In this way the F.G.M.F.S. ended the struggle with an almost complete victory, although some concessions were made. Its success was exceptional among the trade union disputes which occurred in the 1850s, most of which were outright defeats for the men, or were settled upon far less favourable terms.

The explanation for this success can be found in circumstances on both sides of the glass trade. First, the unity of the glass makers was important. For six months during the strike they had been united behind the Stourbridge District. The 'traitors' whose names were printed in the *Magazine* at the end of the strike were few and far between: only six in Stourbridge and twenty-one in Birmingham.[66] Certainly the fact that the Central Committee was in Stourbridge at that time served to widen a local strike into a nation-wide one and attracted the support of other Districts. The Central Committee wrote in July 1859 that:

Unfaithfulness and desertion we have had in a small degree, but the great mass of our lock-outs have remained firm and unshaken to the end; but, perhaps the greatest heroism and firmness had been displayed by the men of Grazebrook's and Stevens and Williams' who were out about twelve or fourteen weeks before the general lock-out took place, and about six or eight weeks after all others had begun again; to these men belong the special thanks of the trade, as they have exhibited a continued firmness and resolution not to betray the society, for a period of thirty weeks.[67]

It is noteworthy that the most skilled Stourbridge men fought most militantly until the end of the strike.

Second, the support given by other trade unions cannot be ignored. The 'Bell Inn Committee' played an important role in collecting donations and loans, which amounted to over £400.[68] American glass makers donated £75. Money collected by Districts of the society amounted to £575, so about £1,000 was received altogether. Workers and shopkeepers in Stourbridge and its vicinity also supported the glass makers and cutters. The Stourbridge District received donations of £30 from the Tin Plate Workers' Society of Wolverhampton, £16 from 'Various Subscriptions', £10 from Stourbridge shopkeepers and £105 from elsewhere, totalling £161.[69] The society never lowered the amount of unemployment allowance during the struggle, but after 8 January 1859 payments had been made two-thirds in cash and one-third on promissory notes issued by the society. The promissory notes meant debt for the members, and it amounted to £2,000 at the end of the strike. Although the *Brierley Hill Advertiser* reported on 9 April that 'notwithstanding the thousands that have been expended in the present strike, the position of the Glass-makers' Society is very good, and their resources were far from exhausted',[70] the society certainly ran into difficulty.

However, it was rapidly overcome. On 3 December a dinner party was held at Stourbridge Town Hall 'in commemoration of the termination of the first, and it is to be hoped the last lock-out in the flint glass trade; but more especially for the celebration of the entire liquidation of the debt of £2,000 due to the members of our Society'.[71] When in July 1860 W. Woolley, the Central Secretary, was presented with a testimonial at a party held at Aston Hall, Birmingham, he said that 'there was a total balance on the 26th May of £2,068 0s. 11d., so that they occupied almost precisely the same position as they did prior to the memorable 'lock-out' . . . At present there was an excellent feeling subsisting and he trusted that by mutual conciliation it would not be impaired.'[72]

The manufacturers for their part organised a few local associations in the Midlands, Lancashire and Scotland but failed to establish a national body corresponding in strength to the F.G.M.F.S. Before the Royal Commission on Trade Unions of 1868, in reply to Lord Elcho, who asked that 'as the Glasgow shipbuilders have done, would not such a combination of capitalists be able to control the combination of working men?', Lloyd explained the reason for a reluctance to establish a national body among the manufacturers:

There would be this objection probably in the first instance in proposing such a thing, that the master glassmakers are scattered over the kingdom at large intervals, consequently communication with one another would be difficult, in order to regulate by frequent meetings their affairs. Between London and Glasgow and Edinburgh there are dotted about districts in which the glass trade is being carried on; and again there is a variation in the amount of produce as well as in the value of labour in different districts; more produce is allowed to take place in the North than in the South or in the Midland districts, that is to say, the Scottish and Lancashire masters are, I may say, permitted to produce more, consequently to have an advantage over the Midland and Southern houses.[73]

Accordingly, the negotiations during the strike took place mainly between the *national* F.G.M.F.S. and the *Midland* manufacturers' association.

Finally, the significance of the flint glass makers' struggle in the history of the labour movement as a whole is noteworthy. Part of the dispute's significance lay in its relation to the builders' strike, which began a few months later. In July 1859 Trollope of Pimlico, one of the largest firms in London, dismissed the mason who had headed a deputation demanding the nine-hour day. The London lodges ordered the men in the firm to go on strike, and the masters immediately replied with a general lock-out. Every large builder in London closed his shop within a fortnight and 24,000 men were put on the streets. The Central Master Builders' Association drafted a document.[74] It seems likely that the flint glass makers' successful rejection of the 'document' a few months earlier encouraged the locked-out builders. When a meeting of the amalgamated building trades of London was held at St Martins Hall on 17 September 1859 against the obnoxious document, the F.G.M.F.S. sent Joseph Leicester to the meeting. *Reynolds's Newspaper* of 1859 reported:

> He [Leicester] had come from the battle-field where the glass-blowers had battled for thirteen weeks, and had received the sympathy and assistance of other trades in the country. The result had been that they had gained a complete victory over their masters; other trades societies came forward to assist them in the struggle, and now they had their trade society to assist those that wanted assistance and to lift the arm of the weak against their oppressors. (Cheers)[75]

Following the experience of the flint glass makers' lock-out, the 'Bell Inn Committee' was re-formed in London to collect funds for the locked-out builders.[76] This time not only in London but in many industrial cities 'Trades Committees' were formed. Glasgow and Manchester sent £800 each and Liverpool over £500. An enormous amount was subscribed by the A.S.E., £3,100. As R. W. Postgate wrote, 'such a subscription had never been heard of before, and its moral effect in encouraging the men and flabbergasting the employers helped very greatly in defeating the attack'.[77] The F.G.M.F.S. had set up 'Benevolent Funds' after the strike to render 'aid to the members of other trades who have been oppressed in return for the donations given by various trade unions during the strike'. For the locked-out builders the F.G.M.F.S. subscribed £145 17s,[78] even though their financial position had not fully recovered as a consequence of their own strike. Altogether the subscriptions given to the builders' society amounted to £23,165.[79] On 18 May 1860 a delegate meeting was called to establish the London Trades Council to combat the weakness of the 'Bell Inn Committee' and Burn became one of its founders.[80] The flint glass makers' dispute, with its far-reaching consequences for subsequent labour history, at least indirectly paved the way for the formation of the London Trades Council.

Notes

1 Webb, *History of Trade Unionism*, p. 199.
2 *Ibid.*
3 *Flint Glass Makers Magazine*, II, pp. 145–6.

4 An account of the strike of the flint glass makers in 1858–59 was given by Godfrey Lushington, at the fourth annual meeting of the Association for the Promotion of Social Science in 1860: Lushington, 'An Account of the Strike of the Flint Glass Makers'. Jacob Waley referred to the strike in 'On strikes and combinations, with reference to wages and the conditions of labour', *Journal of the Statistical Society*, XXX, Part I, March 1867, p. 16. (H. Martineau), 'Secret organisation of trades', *Edinburgh Review*, CX, October 1859, also referred to the strike (pp. 539–40). George Howell described this strike in *Labour Legislation. Labour Movement and Labour Leaders*, London, 1902, pp. 120–2, but his description relies entirely on Lushington's account. The Webbs referred only briefly to the strike (*History of Trade Unionism*, pp. 228, 230). The first attempt to investigate it was Sandilands, 'The History of the Midland Glass Industry', M.Com. thesis, *op. cit.*, chapter VIII, pp. 71–5. George Barnsby's research on the strike is inaccurate; he traced the strike only until December 1858 and writes 'the result is not recorded' (George Barnsby, 'The Working Class Movement in the Black Country, 1815 to 1867, M.A. thesis, University of Birmingham, 1965, p. 338, and *id.*, *The Working Class Movement in the Black Country 1750 to 1867*, Wolverhampton, 1977, p. 169). Eric Hopkins's paper, 'An anatomy of strikes in the Stourbridge glass industry, 1850–1914', *op. cit.*, is the most valuable attempt to analyse the strike. Since the publication of the *Flint Glass Makers Magazine* was stopped for nearly nine months during most of the period of the strike, the *Magazine* included few articles on it. But a later series of articles on reminiscences of the strike in the *Magazine*, VIII and IX (1878), are informative. The newspaper which most continuously reported the strike was the *Birmingham Daily Post*, controlled by the radical editor, John Thackray Bunce (A. Briggs, *History of Birmingham*, vol. II, London, 1952, p. 102).

5 The name of the man was probably William Wild, who receive 13*s* weekly nominal wage (eleven moves) and 1*s* per move for an extra (wages book of Stevens & Williams).

6 Minutes of Conference (June 1858), Resolution 3; in *Rules and Regulations of the F.G.M.F.S., 1858*, p. 18.

7 The circular is preserved in the Stevens & Williams archives. It is also reprinted in Lushington, 'An Account of the Strike of the Flint Glass Makers', pp. 106–7 (the reprint of Lushington does not contain the name of the firm and the date is inaccurate), and partly in Guttery, *From Broad-glass to Cut Crystal*, p. 130.

8 *Rules and Regulations of the F.G.M.F.S., 1858*, rule XLV.

9 *Royal Commission on Trade Unions*, 10th Report, 1867–68, p. 32, q. 18644, Thomas Wilkinson's statement, and *ibid.*, p. 20, q. 18315, George Lloyd's statement.

10 Lushington, 'An Account of the Strike of the Flint Glass Makers', p. 106.

11 *Brierley Hill Advertiser*, 20 November 1858. The quotation was

from the statement given by John Grazebrook of the Audnam Glass Works, at the petty sessions held on 15 November 1858.

12 Lushington, 'An Account of the Strike of the Flint Glass Makers', p. 106. In the Stevens & Williams factory twenty-two men were out of work, but twelve footmakers and takers-in continued to be paid during the strike (Wages Book of Stevens & Williams).

13 *Flint Glass Makers Magazine*, VIII, p. 838.

14 *Brierley Hill Advertiser*, 20 November 1858.

15 *Ibid.*

16 *Ibid.*

17 *Reynolds's Newspaper*, 18 September 1859. Joseph Leicester's speech at the Builders' meeting held on 17 September 1859 in support of the locked-out builders.

18 Haden, *The Stourbridge Glass Industry*, p. 30.

19 *Ibid.*

20 The circular is printed in the *Birmingham Daily Post*, 6 January 1859, and also in Lushington, 'An Account of the Strike of the Flint Glass Makers', pp. 107–8. Accompanying the circular the extracts from the *Rules and Regulations of the F.G.M.F.S., 1858* were circulated as *The Real Cause of the Strike* (*ibid.*, pp. 110–11).

21 In Stourbridge and Dudley almost all manufacturers belonged to the association except Richardson's factory. In Birmingham half the glass factories belonged to the association (*Royal Commission on Trade Unions*, 10th Report, 1867–68, p. 24, q. 18436).

22 *Birmingham Daily Post*, 6 January 1859. George Lloyd remarked that 'the Association when first established was intended to be only temporary, we only contemplated defending ourselves through the strike' (*Royal Commission on Trade Unions*, 10th Report, 1867–68, p. 22, q. 18380). Each member firm subscribed £100 to the 'Defence Fund' established to assist firms affected by disputes, and a further sum of £10 a year, payable quarterly (*ibid.*, p. 22, qq. 18376–9).

23 *Birmingham Daily Post*, 7 December 1858.

24 *Ibid.*

25 Lushington, 'An Account of the Strike of the Flint Glass Makers', p. 113.

26 *Brierley Hill Advertiser*, 24 December 1858.

27 *Ibid.* In mid-December, however, Stevens & Williams began to work three of their nine chairs. Three workmen (Isiah Scriven, William Scriven and John Scriven) and a servitor (Thomas Scriven) returned to work (Wages Book of Stevens & Williams, week ending 18th December 1858). All of them were condemned as 'Traitors' by the F.G.M.F.S. They worked intensively, nineteen moves to twenty-three moves a week, and earned respectively 68s, 68s, 48s and 39s in January 1859. After the end of the strike all of them remained in the same factory, although expelled from the society.

28 *Brierley Hill Advertiser*, 24 December 1858.

29 *Ibid.*

30 Letter from G. Lloyd to J. D. Bacchus, dated 17 December 1858, Ms,

in *Letters, Accounts, Documents, etc. relating to the Union Glass Works, Dartmouth Street, Birmingham 1817–1882* (Birmingham Reference Library).

31 *Ibid.*

32 *Brierley Hill Advertiser*, 24 December 1858.

33 *Birmingham Daily Post*, 3 January 1859.

34 *Flint Glass Makers Magazine*, VIII, p. 937, and Lushington, 'An Account of the Strike of the Flint Glass Makers', p. 109. Lushington wrote that 'only seven factories were left working in the Stourbridge and Birmingham Districts' (*ibid.*, p. 109). William Smith, a Birmingham manufacturer, was one of those who did not suspend his works. George Lloyd 'had seen Sir William Smith, who is in favour of the position taken by the Association, though he is not prepared to give notice of suspending his works' (Letter from George Lloyd to J. D. Bacchus, dated 30 December 1858, Ms, in *Letter, Accounts, Documents, etc. relating to the Union Glass Works, op. cit.*).

35 *Flint Glass Makers Magazine*, VIII, p. 937.

36 According to the Quarterly Report of the society, in Manchester 120 out of 138 men, in Warrington forty-eight out of fifty-three men and in St Helens twenty-one out of thirty-five men were locked out.

37 In Edinburgh and Leith the men were locked out on 19 February 1859, and a deputation of the F.G.M.F.S. appealed to the Edinburgh Trades Council on 1 March 1859 (I. MacDougall (ed.), *The Minutes of Edinburgh Trades Council, 1859–1873*, Edinburgh, 1968, pp. 4–5). It seems likely that in other Districts such as Newcastle and Rotherham the lock-out was not applied.

38 Letter from George Lloyd to J. D. Bacchus, dated 30 December 1858, Ms, *op. cit.*

39 *Ibid.*

40 *Birmingham Daily Post*, 7 January 1859.

41 *Midland Advertiser and Birmingham Times*, 8 January 1859.

42 *Brierley Hill Advertiser*, 15 January 1859.

43 Lushington, 'An Account of the Strike of the Flint Glass Makers', p. 113. These high subscriptions continued till mid-May 1859, more than a month after the end of the strike.

44 One copy of the leaflet, 'The Glass Washers' Lockout, an Appeal to the Servant Girls of the United Kingdom on Behalf of the Flint Glass Washers' Friendly Society Fellow Working Girls, Sturbrig [*sic*], January 13th 1859', is preserved in the Brierley Hill Public Library and another is lodged in the files of *Letters, Accounts, Documents, etc. relating to the Union Glass Works, op. cit.*

45 The content of the leaflet is reprinted in full in *Bulletin of the Society for the Study of Labour History*, XXVIII, spring 1974, pp. 16–17.

46 'Josephina Woolley of Sturbrig' was the feminised name of the Central Secretary, Joseph Woolley of Stourbridge.

47 *Birmingham Daily Post*, 20 January 1859.

48 *Midland Advertiser and Birmingham Times*, 22 January 1859.

49 *Reynolds's Newspaper*, 30 January 1859.
50 *Ibid.*, 30 January 1859.
51 *Ibid.*, 6 and 13 February 1859.
52 R. W. Postgate, *The Builders' History*, London, 1923, p. 249. William Burn (or Burns) had been a Chartist and one of the delegates from the counties of Forfar and Aberdeen to the National Convention of the Industrious Classes (J. West, *A History of the Chartist Movement*, London, 1920, pp. 121, 139, 277). In 1848, together with other London Chartists, he was brought to trial (R. G. Gammage, *History of the Chartist Movement, 1837–1854*, 1894 edn, Newcastle, p. 338).
53 *Brierley Hill Advertiser*, 9 March 1859. Lushington wrote that the meeting was held on 11 March ('An Account of the Strike of the Flint Glass Makers', p. 112).
54 *Flint Glass Makers Magazine*, IX, p. 573.
55 *Ibid.*
56 *Globe*, 22 March 1859. The quotation is Joseph Leicester's article.
57 *Birmingham Daily Post*, 28 March 1859.
58 *Brierley Hill Advertiser*, 2 April 1859.
59 Lloyd & Summerfield of Birmingham received £134 17s from the Defence Fund. The defence money which each factory received is given in Haden, *The Stourbridge Glass Industry*, p. 31.
60 The leading article, 'The lock-out and its lessons', in the *Flint Glass Makers Magazine* remarked in January 1860 that 'since this time last year we have expended about £8,000, which is about the cost of the strike and lock-out to us. The loss to the employers, though only about twenty-six in number, has been estimated to be at least £10,000 or £12,000. The loss to ourselves, in wages, must have been about £4,000' (*Flint Glass Makers Magazine*, III, p. 547).
61 *Ibid.*, IX, pp. 665–6.
62 *Brierley Hill Advertiser*, 9 April 1859, and *Birmingham Journal*, 9 April 1859.
63 *Flint Glass Makers Magazine*, IX, p. 666.
64 *Rules and Regulations of the F.G.M.F.S., revised and corrected in April 1859* provided that 'no more than one apprentice be allowed to two chairs, and so on in proportion, and all allowances given for young footmakers to be decided by the masters and men in each district' (rule XXI).
65 *Ibid.*
66 *Flint Glass Makers Magazine*, III, p. 424.
67 *Ibid.*, IV, p. 416.
68 The Central Secretary of the society remarked in his address on 16 July 1859 that 'the report of the London trade's committee for our lock-out, just received, shows that more than £400 was raised, in gifts and loans, for our help, but the secretary, Mr. Burns, who was requested to act in that capacity, is now outlawed by the employers of London', and appealed to the members of the society to give him financial aid (*ibid.*, III, p. 419). Burns was then made general

secretary of the new Brickmakers' Society (see Postgate, *The Builders' History*, pp. 249–50, and Fraser, *Trade Unions and Society, op cit.*, p. 211).

69 *Flint Glass Makers Magazine*, III, pp. 542–5.
70 *Brierley Hill Advertiser*, 9 April 1859.
71 *Flint Glass Makers Magazine*, III, p. 618.
72 *Brierley Hill Advertiser*, 7 July 1860.
73 *Royal Commission cn Trade Unions*, 10th report, 1867–68, p. 25, q. 18448.
74 Postgate, *The Builders' History*, pp. 171–2. For the builders' strike see R. Price, *Masters, Unions and Men. Work Control and the Rise of Labour, 1830–1914*, Cambridge, 1980, pp. 45–50.
75 *Reynolds's Newspaper*, 18 September 1859.
76 A continuity between the 'Bell Inn Committee' established for supporting the flint glass makers in January 1859 and the re-formed committee is stressed in Fraser, 'Trades Councils in England and Scotland, 1858–1897', Ph.D. thesis, op cit., p. 35.
77 Postgate, *The Builders' History*, p. 176.
78 'Balance-sheet of the Conference of the Building Trades', in *Trades and Societies*, pp. 73–4. The biggest three Districts of the F.G.M.F.S., Manchester, Stourbridge and Birmingham, subscribed respectively £30, £27 8s 4d and £22 17s 6d (*Flint Glass Makers Magazine*, IV, p. 41).
79 'Balance-sheet of the Conference of the Building Trades', *ibid*.
80 Burn was one of the first seven executive committee members of the London Trades Council elected on 10 July 1860 (J. Jacobs and G. K. Tate, *London Trades Council*, London, 1950, p. 5).

Chapter six

Flint glass makers in the local community

The process of stratification in social relationships in the local community was complicated, but it is important if one is to deepen understanding of the social dimension of the labour aristocracy. We must pass, therefore, from trades to communities. As a local community Stourbridge is an obvious choice, for it produced flint glass of the highest quality and had the greatest concentration of the best skilled craftsmen in Britain. The Stourbridge glass makers, with a long and deeply rooted craft tradition, maintained the strictest apprenticeship and promotion regulations. As we have seen, they pursued the defence of their rights and privileges with the utmost militancy. Fortunately, the Stourbridge flint glass trade is survived by a rich collection of primary sources. This chapter analyses the recruitment of flint glass makers to the trade and then marriage patterns and housing conditions. The final discussion looks at social gatherings and local politics and assesses the role of the flint glass makers in both.

Stourbridge had eleven glass factories in 1861, most of them located outside Stourbridge town. 'Stourbridge' encompassed three different areas. As a 'District or Union' it contained three sub-districts: (1) Halesowen, (2) Stourbridge and (3) Kingswinford. As a sub-district it had six parishes or townships: (1) Stourbridge town, (2) Lye, (3) Wollaston, (4) Wollescote, (5) Upper Swinford and (6) Amblecote. The number of glass workers shown in table 6:1 includes Stourbridge town, Wollaston, Upper Swinford, Amblecote (in the census enumerators' books of 1861, R.G. 9 —, No. 383: 2065, 2066, 2068), Wordsley and Brierley Hill (No. 383: 2069–74). From Stourbridge (sub-district) Wollescote and Lye were omitted, as almost no glass workers were found there. Instead, Wordsley and Brierley Hill from

from Kingswinford were included, because these two areas had a large number of glass workers. The table shows that, out of 1,032 people in the glass trade, 366 lived in Wordsley (35·5%) and 271 in Amblecote (26·3%). Both adjoining areas constituted 61·8% of the total number. Stourbridge town and Upper Swinford had only 11·7% and 4·9% respectively.

It can be assumed that this six-area investigation covers

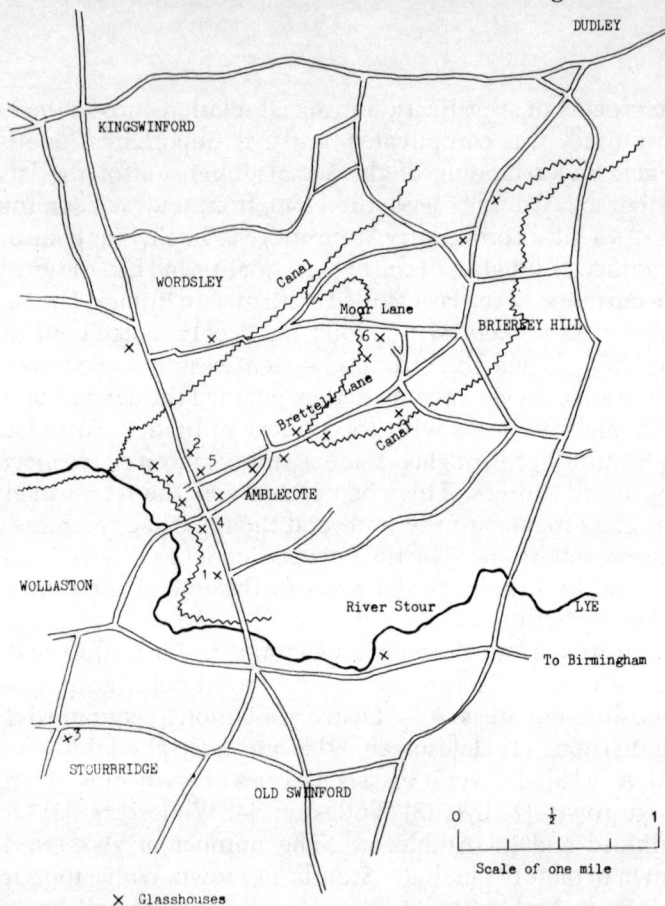

Fig. 4 Glassworks in Stourbridge. *1* Holloway End, *2* Audnam, *3* The Heath, *4* Coalbournbrook, *5* The Dial, *6* Moor Lane

TABLE 6:1 Number of glass workers and manufacturers in Stourbridge in 1861

	Stour-bridge town	Wollas-ton	Upper Swin-ford	Amble-cote	Words-ley	Brierley Hill	Total
Glass maker	47	31	23	107 (58) (98*)	135	46	389
Glass cutter	54	74	12	98 (58) (90*)	166	28	432
Glass engraver	4	1	0	6 (6) (16*)	12	4	27
Other workers in the glass trade	9	11	9	55 (53) (34*)	47	33	164
Glass manufacturer	1	0	7	5 (5) (9*)	6	1	20
Totals	115	117	51	271 (180) (247*)	366	112	1,032
Houses	1,800	418	570	531 (402) (568*)			
Population	8,783	2,041	2,749	2,613 (2,053) (2,771*)			
No. of glass workers & mfrs per 100 of the population	1·31	5·73	1·86	10·37 (8·78) (8·91*)			

Note. The number in brackets is that in 1851 in Amblecote and the asterisked number in brackets is that in 1871 in the area.
Source. Census Enumerators' Books of 1861, Stourbridge.

almost all glass workers engaged in the so-called Stourbridge glass industry. Eric Hopkins's data, showing that there were 409 glass workers in Stourbridge in 1851, does not include those in Wordsley and Brierley Hill, but is confined to the sub-district of Stourbridge.[1] His figures are comparable with those in Stourbridge town, Wollaston, Upper Swinford and Amblecote in my figures, totalling 541 glass workers in 1861. We can therefore assume that the number of glass workers in Stourbridge (sub-district) increased from 409 in 1851 to 541 in 1861. In Amblecote alone the number of glass workers rose from 180 in 1851 to 271 in 1861 and to 247 in 1871.

The analysis of the social dimension in local communities

should not be isolated from that in the trades themselves. In a small town like Stourbridge the superiority of glass makers in the 'economic' sphere was more directly reflected in social life than in big cities like London and Edinburgh. An enquiry into recruitment of the labour force clearly suggests this state of affairs. The first problem concerning recruitment is to what extent the glass makers and cutters were recruited from Stourbridge and its vicinity and to what extent from other regions. According to the census enumerators' books of 1861, the birthplace of 90% of 389 glass makers in Stourbridge was Staffordshire, Worcestershire, Warwickshire or Shropshire. Nine per cent came from other parts of England, 0·2% from abroad. The birthplace was not necessarily the place from which they migrated but it provides a useful indicator. On the other hand, the birthplace of 78·9% of 341 glass cutters in Stourbridge was one of the above four counties. 11·4% came from other parts of England, 1·4% from Scotland, 8·1% from Ireland and 0·2% from foreign countries. Clearly a larger proportion of glass cutters originated from outside these four counties. It is notable that 8·1% of glass cutters came from Ireland, probably as a result of the decay of the Irish glass cutting industry in the first half of the nineteenth century.

The second, more important problem about recruitment is to what extent flint glass makers were 'self-recruited' from glass makers' families. The census enumerators' books of 1861 for Stourbridge again provide some information. The books record the occupation of the father and that of his child, if both of them were in work and if they lived in the same household. It is thus possible to pair them to show occupational continuity in the year 1861. The results are shown in table 6:2. Both rows and columns are meaningful. Rows show the parental occupation of glass makers, glass cutters and other glass workers, and suggest where glass workers were recruited from. Columns show the child's occupation and therefore suggest recruitment for the next generation. (This includes not only sons but daughters, although only a few daughters got jobs.)

The most interesting fact to emerge is that there was a surprisingly strong barrier to recruitment between glass makers and glass cutters, and that more than half the glass makers were recruited from other trades' families. Rows in the table indicate

TABLE 6:2 Occupational continuity between fathers and children in Stourbridge, 1861 (percentages in brackets)

Occupation of child	Occupation of father				
	Glass maker	Glass cutter	Other jobs in the glass trade	Other trade	Total
Glass maker	37 (29·6)	6 (4·8)	10 (8·0)	72 (57·6)	125 (100·0)
Glass cutter	3 (2·3)	44 (34·4)	6 (4·7)	75 (58·6)	128 (100·0)
Other jobs in the glass trade	14 (15·4)	10 (11·0)	13 (14·3)	54 (59·3)	91 (100·0)
Other trade	31	33	24	–	(88)
Total (N)	85	93	53	(201)	–

Source. Census Enumerators' Books of 1861, Stourbridge.

that, out of 125 young glass makers, there were thirty-seven (29·6%) with parents also employed in glass making. Seventy-two glass makers (57·6%) had parents in other trades. But only six glass makers (4·8%) came from glass cutters' families. Similarly, out of 128 young glass cutters, forty-four (34·4%) were recruited from glass cutters' families, but only three cutters (2·3%) came from glass makers' families. It is clear that both in glass making and in cutting there was a fairly high degree of 'self-recruitment', but there was little 'inter-recruitment' between glass makers' and glass cutters' families.

It should be admitted, however, that the information obtainable from the census enumerators' books has considerable limitations, because when children formed their own households after marriage, or when their children were too young to be employed as workers, the occupational continuity between parents and children cannot be traced. Marriage registers enable historians to overcome these limitations to some extent. The registers record the occupation of the father of the groom as well as that of the groom himself so that it is possible to trace the occupation of parents and children even in the separate households, although the occupations of boys before marriage cannot be discovered. The results obtained from the marriage registers in the four churches in Stourbridge are set out in table 6:3. Rows and columns have the same meaning as in table 6:2. Here again the high degree of 'self-recruitment' among both glass makers and cutters is clearly revealed: 61·0% of glass makers and 33·6% of glass cutters were self-recruited. Much higher percentages of glass makers are self-recruited in the table 6:3 than was indicated by the census enumerators' books. The discrepancy has been discussed in chapter III, in connection with the issue of promotion prospects. In contrast, we can find again that inter-recruitment between glass makers and cutters was rare: only 8·1% of glass makers were recruited from glass cutters' families, and only 9·2% of glass cutters from glass makers' families. It is thus clear that in Stourbridge glass makers and glass cutters are distinct groups in terms of occupational continuity and that many sons came to flint glass making from families in other trades but about half of them seem to have left as a result of not being apprenticed. The other half remained as apprentices in flint glass making.

It should be added to the recruitment argument that the flint glass factory did not employ Poor Law apprentices. The Board of Guardians of the Stourbridge Union reported that, out of a total of 140 Poor Law apprentices between 1846 and the early 1880s, nobody was apprenticed to glass-making.[2]

In an attempt to estimate social distance within the working class, several social historians have used marriage records. Foster used marriage certificates in Northampton, Oldham and South Shields for 1846–56 and made it clear that the frequency of marriage between labourer and craft families was 70%–80%

TABLE 6:3 Occupational continuity between fathers and children in Stourbridge, 1850–85 (percentages in brackets)

Occupation of son	Occupation of father				
	Glass maker	Glass cutter	Other jobs in the glass trade	Other trade	Total
Glass maker	75 (61·0)	10 (8·1)	3 (2·4)	35 (28·5)	123 (100·0)
Glass cutter	14 (9·2)	51 (33·6)	5 (3·3)	82 (53·9)	152 (100·0)
Other jobs in the glass trade	0 (0·0)	4 (25·0)	3 (18·8)	9 (56·3)	16 (100·0)
Other trade	26	25	8	–	(59)
Total (N)	115	90	19	(126)	–

Source. Marriage registers in Stourbridge. See p. 79, n. 52.

TABLE 6:4 Occupational relations in marriages in Stourbridge, 1850–85, (a) Groom (%)

Father of bride	Groom			
	Glass maker		Glass cutter	
Glassworker	20·3		23·0	
Glass maker		12·2		14·5
Glass cutter		6·5		8·5
Other glassworker		1·6		0·0
Skilled worker	24·4		27·0	
		6·5 (Ironworker)		5·9 (Ironworker)
		3·3 (Shoemaker)		3·3 (Carpenter and joiner)
		3·3 (Chandler)		2·6 (Bricklayer)
		3·3 (Engineer)		2·0 (Engineer)
		1·6 (Bricklayer)		2·0 (Shoemaker)
Semi-skilled worker	30·1		23·0	
		6·5 (Miner)		5·3 (Miner)
		4·1 (Boatman)		2·6 (Nailer)
		3·3 (Nailer)		1·3 (Chainmaker)
		3·3 (Blacksmith)		1·3 (Boatman)
		1·6 (Potter)		1·3 (Furnaceman)
Unskilled worker	13·8		13·2	
		10·6 (Labourer)		7·9 (Labourer)
Retailer	2·4		6·5	
Non-manual worker	0·8		2·0	
Manufacturer	1·6		1·3	
Farmer	4·1		3·3	
No occupation	0·8		0·0	
Unknown	1·7		0·7	
Total cases (N)	123		152	

Source. Marriage registers in Stourbridge. See p. 79, n. 52.

of the expected number of marriages between these groups in the three towns, although there were slight regional differences.[3] Crossick's analysis of marriage in Kentish London took the occupational relations of the *father of the groom* and the *father of the bride* in the two periods 1851–53 and 1873–75. The picture is of a substantial degree of 'closed' marriage. The chances of a bridegroom from a skilled working-class background marrying into the skilled working-class or non-manual strata ranged between 60% and 70% in the 1850s, and was generally even higher in the 1870s. In contrast, the chance of marrying into those strata was only half as great for someone of labouring background (29% and 36% for each period). The greater likelihood was of marriage into the unskilled working class. In detail in the 1850s, shipbuilding workers, watermen and lighter-men, engineering and metal craftsmen and tailors had the lowest marriage contact with unskilled groups, all with well under 20%. They are followed by building crafts, small metal workers and shoemakers.[4] Thus social distance between skilled and unskilled workers is clearly revealed. Gray examined the occupational relations between the *groom* and the *father of the bride* in Edinburgh in both 1865 and 1869: 'in all the skilled trades but one (the iron moulders) a third or more married the daughters of other skilled workers; similarly, the daughters of semi- and unskilled workers account for the largest single cate-gory of the brides of building labourers and carters'.[5]

In this chapter an attempt has been made to discover the occupational relationship both between the groom and the father of the bride and between the father of the groom and the father of the bride. The data relating to glass makers and cutters in Stourbridge were obtained from the marriage certificates in four churches from 1850 to 1885. The results shown in table 6:4 suggest almost the same marriage pattern as that described by Gray and Crossick.[6] Glass makers marrying into unskilled families formed only about 15% of the total. On the other hand, 20·3% of glass makers married glass makers' daughters. If we include other skilled workers, then at least 43% of glass makers married daughters of the skilled. The same tendency can also be found in the occupational relations between fathers of the groom and the bride (table 6:5). When the groom was a glass maker the father of the bride was more likely to be a glass maker also than when a glass maker's son married the daughter of a glass maker.

But the difference was relatively small. It is important to understand that occupational relations in marriage were much looser than occupationally hereditary relations between fathers and sons. As already shown, 61·0% of glass makers in the marriage registers came from glass makers' families and 65·2% of glass makers' sons became glass makers. There was also a strong barrier in labour-force recruitment between glass makers and cutters. But, so far as marital relations were concerned, the

TABLE 6:5 Occupational relations in marriages in Stourbridge, 1850–85, (b) Father of groom (%)

Father of bride	Father of groom			
	Glass maker		Glass cutter	
Glassworker	13.9		18.9	
Glass maker	8.7		8.9	
Glass cutter	1.7		10.0	
Other glassworker	3.5		0.0	
Skilled worker	28.7		25.6	
		12.2 (Ironworker)		7.8 (Ironworker)
		3.5 (Plasterer)		4.4 (Carpenter and joiner)
		3.5 (Engineer)		2.2 (Shoemaker)
		3.5 (Shoemaker)		1.1 (Bricklayer)
Semi-skilled worker	16.0		27.7	
		7.8 (Miner)		5.6 (Nailer)
		3.5 (Blacksmith)		4.4 (Miner)
		2.6 (Boatman)		2.2 (Chainmaker)
		2.6 (Ironworker, semi-skilled)		2.2 (Furnaceman)
		2.6 (Nailer)		2.2 (Blacksmith)
Unskilled worker	20.9		13.3	
		7.0 (Labourer)		8.9 (Labourer)
Retailer	5.2		6.7	
Non-manual worker	0.9		0.0	
Manufacturer	1.8		1.1	
Farmer	2.6		5.6	
No occupation	0.0		0.0	
Unknown	0.0		1.1	
Total cases (N)	115		90	

Source. Marriage registers in Stourbridge.

barrier seems to have been small: 6.5% of glass makers married daughters of glass cutters and 14.5% of glass cutters married daughters of glass makers. If we use social distance from labourers in marriage as a measure of the relative positions of glass makers and cutters in the local community, then we find the glass makers and cutters on a similar plane. So we can see that, passing from trades to community, the demarcation between the skilled flint glass makers and the unskilled becomes clearer, while the difference between glass makers and cutters tends to lessen. They emerge as 'glass workers' in the community.

Similarly, there do not seem to have been any large differences in housing conditions between glass makers and cutters. Glass makers' houses in Stourbridge 'generally have a bit of garden attached to them, which can be made to produce a good share of vegetables that will materially assist in the sustenance of a family'.[7] Certainly they lived in better-quality working-class houses in Amblecote in great numbers and not in the slum properties in the older parts of the town of Stourbridge or in the outlying townships of Lye and Wollescote, where the nail makers were concentrated. However, only a few glass makers owned their own houses. Table 6:6 is obtained from the rate book of 1861, Amblecote in Stourbridge. Since the rate book does not indicate occupations, the census enumerators' books of 1861 were used to identify glass makers and cutters in the rate book. For workmen a membership list of the F.G.M.F.S. is also used in identification. The table shows that in Amblecote, out of forty glass makers identified, only two owned their houses and out of forty-five glass cutters only three did so.[8] Others rented their house.[9] About 55% of glass makers in Amblecote in 1861 lived in houses rated between £4 and £6. No large differences in the ratable value of the property rented between glass makers, cutters and all other inhabitants can be found. An

TABLE 6:6 Housing of glass workers in Amblecote, Stourbridge, in 1861 (%)

Ratable value	Glass maker	(Workman)	Glass cutter	All households
£2—	0·0	0·0	0·0	2·0
£3—	7·5	0·0	4·4	9·7
£4—	27·5	13·4	20·0	24·6
£5—	27·5	50·0	28·9	24·4
£6—	17·5	21·4	15·6	13·9
£7—	15·0	7·1	4·4	4·8
£8—	2·5	0·0	8·9	5·2
£9—	0·0	0·0	2·2	1·8
£10—	2·5	7·1	15·6	13·6
Totals identified (N)	40	14	45	505

Note. Factories and other estates except dwellings are excluded from the table.
Source. Rate book in Amblecote, 1861.

examination of the marriage pattern and housing conditions suggests that *socially* there was little or no difference between glass makers and cutters, although both were demarcated from the unskilled workers in the local community. Both glass makers and cutters emerged as superior groups in the local community, and the difference between them at the point of production seems to have vanished. This fact can be further illustrated by looking at public festivities in Stourbridge.

Festivities and public gatherings were a form of activity which became frequent among trade unionists after the mid-nineteenth century. They provided an opportunity to demonstrate the relative standing of workers in the local community. In Stourbridge after 1860 annual gatherings were held under the auspices of the F.G.M.F.S. They normally attracted between 8,000 and 10,000 people, and after 1865 'during the day special trains ran from Wolverhampton and other stations and deposited their freights of passengers at Haley Station'.[10] By that time the picnic had come to be fixed in the minds of the inhabitants as a great event. The *Brierley Hill Advertiser* wrote that 'for some time past this pic-nic was looked forward to, as being the great pic-nic of the season. A Monday was chosen as usual.'[11] Schools had to be closed. At the Wordsley school on 13 July 1863 'a very low attendance in consequence of a Pic-nic in Prestwood Park – Held by the Glass makers for the benefit of the funds of the Society. The boys had a holiday in the afternoon.'[12] On the same day St Thomas Boys' School in Stourbridge also 'gave the boys half a holiday in consequence of the glass makers' Pic-nic'.[13]

It is important to note that glass makers and cutters co-operated during these celebrations. For instance, at the festival held in 1865 glass makers and cutters, numbering about 800, formed a procession, each carrying some specimen of the trade as was usual. There were many flags and banners with the mottos like 'Prosperity to our employers, and success to the glass trade', 'To the memory of Cobden, Gladstone and the franchise'.[14] The mottos are useful indications of the glass makers' political standpoint – Liberalism – and their attitude towards the employers – co-operation. In the park, quoits, archery, cricket and dancing were popular entertainments, and 'hundreds of specimens of the most artistic workmanship in glass' carried during the procession were exhibited there. Glass manufacturers also exhibited products to demonstrate the high quality of their factories. This festival helped conceal 'unfriendly feelings' between glass makers and cutters and even between glass makers and manufacturers. The common interest in the prosperity of the industry was emphasised.

Finally, the way in which the flint glass makers were related to political movements should be examined. In the reform movement the Stourbridge flint glass makers took the local initiative. The Stourbridge branch of the League was established on 17 September 1866. Until the demonstration at Birmingham on 27 August 1866 the Reform League had not penetrated the Black Country. On that day a crowd of 20,000 gathered to hear Bright declare that he had no fear of manhood suffrage. The demonstration was jointly organised by the Birmingham League and the Liberal Association and supported by trade unions, including the Birmingham Trades Council, and temperance, benefit and friendly societies.[15] It was obviously large. 'Never in the history of England has there taken place a demonstration equal to that which was witnessed in Birmingham on Monday. The voice of the Midland Counties has been heard upon the Reform Question and it has given forth no uncertain sound.'[16] Stourbridge was represented by about five hundred people 'of whom some three hundred were glass makers. There is no political association at Stourbridge, and as there had been no active organisation, there were no bands or banners. The leaders were Messrs. Woolley, W. Packwood, Jukes J. Blurton, G. Lichfield and J. Chance.'[17] Thus a majority of flint glass makers in Stourbridge took part in the demonstration, and because of the lack of political organisation in the town the leaders of the flint glass makers' union led glass makers to the demonstration.

The success of the Birmingham demonstration stimulated the spread of branches into neighbouring counties. One was formed in Wednesbury only three days after the demonstration and by the end of September it counted 200 members. By this time the Wolverhampton Working Men's Liberal Association had affiliated to the Birmingham League and other branches were formed in Walsall, Great Bridge, Brierley Hill and Willenhall in the last months of 1866.[18] By the turn of the year the Reform League was firmly established as the vehicle of working-class reform agitation in the Black Country. Because neither the

Reform Union nor any organisation comparable in attitude and status with the London Working Men's Association developed into a body of any importance in the Black Country, there were no tensions in the early months of 1867 between the League and the Union or between the League and militant trade unions of the George Potter type.[19]

On 17 September 1866, when the Stourbridge branch of the League was established, there was a large attendance, most of the trades in the neighbourhood being represented. Flint glass makers took the initiative in organising the branch. Joseph Woolley, whom we have met before, 'warmly commended the ballot as the best remedy yet propounded for venality and corrupt practices at elections, and contended that it should form an indispensable part of any Reform Bill worthy the acceptance of the people'.[20] W. H. Packwood earnestly advocated a move to connect the meeting with the League, stating that 'the glass makers' society of this district had unanimously passed a resolution in favour of supporting the Reform League, and promising to join in large numbers, this branch on those conditions'.[21] The resolution to establish a branch of the League in the area was unanimously adopted. Akroyd was elected president of the branch, Packwood treasurer and Woolley secretary.[22] Four days later, on 21 September, George Howell, secretary of the Reform League, sent a letter to Woolley, informing him that fifty membership cards for the League would be sent to Stourbridge and that 'if you are a branch of the League you keep two thirds of the subscription for local agitation and expenses'.[23] On 30 September the Stourbridge branch sent £1 13s 4d to the Reform League.[24]

The committee of the Stourbridge branch held weekly meetings and enrolled from twenty to thirty members each night, among whom 'were the names of several gentlemen occupying respectable positions, and tradesmen, but the bulk belonged to the elite of the working classes'.[25] In November that year membership reached 137.[26] On 29 October the first monthly meeting of the branch was held at Wollaston school room, but the attendance was 'rather small'. Packwood argued that 'It was the duty of all who were anxious for Reform to join the League at once. The conservative reformer and the manhood suffrage reformer were welcome, and free to advocate their view on reform — each in his own peculiar manner.'[27] In July 1867 the Midland Department had 9,074 enrolled members in thirty-seven branches,[28] and the General Committee of the Midland Department consisted of sixty-two delegates. W. H. Packwood of Stourbridge not only continued to be secretary of the Stourbridge branch of the League but one of the members of the General Committee of the Midland Department.[29]

This suggests that flint glass makers' support for Potter was by no means absolute. Since the F.G.M.F.S. was associated with Potter's group, it supported the London Working Men's Association in London. Industrially Potter could appeal beyond London. Politically he could not or at least did not. Thus the F.G.M.F.S. in Stourbridge, together with that in Birmingham, supported not Potter's association but the League, probably because the association was only weakly organised in the Black Country. It is not without significance that the most skilled flint glass makers in Stourbridge took the initiative in organising the local branch of the League.

Notes

1 Eric Hopkins, 'Working conditions in Victorian Stourbridge', *International Review of Social History*, new ser., XIX, 1974, p. 403.

2 *Register of Apprentices, Bound or assigned by the Board of Guardians of the Stourbridge Union* (Staffordshire County Record Office). 'Stourbridge' in the register covered Kingswinford, the town of Stourbridge and Lye. The main apprentices bound by the Board of Guardians were chainmakers (twenty-one boys), boot and shoemakers (sixteen boys), nailers (eight boys), bricklayers (seven boys), spademakers (six boys), tailors (six boys) and blacksmiths (five boys).

3 Foster, *Class Struggle and the Industrial Revolution*, pp. 126–7.

4 Crossick, *An Artisan Elite in Victorian Society*, pp. 121–7.

5 Gray, *The Labour Aristocracy in Victorian Edinburgh*, p. 111.

6 Beside the major occupations shown in tables 6:4 and 6:5, the skilled workers include bookbinder, builder, boilermaker, cabinet-maker, compositor, sawyer, slater, printer, watchmaker, wheelwright and so on. The less skilled workers include button maker, crate maker, currier, gas stoker, miller, waterman and so on. The unskilled workers include gamekeeper, gardener, stone cutter, lock-keeper, waggoner, tile cutter, packer and so on.

7 *Flint Glass Makers Magazine*, IX, p. 28.

8 Rate Book of Amblecote in 1861, (Staffordshire County Record Office).

9 The rents of working men's dwelling in Stourbridge were 4s in 1877 (*Flint Glass Makers Magazine*, IX, p. 28).

10 *Stourbridge Observer*, 5 August 1865. Advertisement for the picnic appeared in *Brierley Hill Advertiser*, 29 July 1865.
11 *Brierley Hill Advertiser*, 5 August 1865.
12 Log Book of Wordsley School, vol. I, 13 July 1863, Ms (Staffordshire County Record Office).
13 Log Book of St. Thomas Boys School, Stourbridge, vol. I, 13 July 1863, Ms (Worcestershire County Record Office). On 17 July 1863 it was recorded that 'the attendance has not been so good this week owing to the Glassmakers' Pic Nic on Monday'.
14 *Stourbridge Observer*, 5 August 1865, and *Brierley Hill Advertiser*, 5 August 1865.
15 A. D. Bell, 'The Reform League from its Origins to 1867', D.Phil. thesis, Oxford University, 1961, p. 245, and F. E. Gillespie, *Labour and Politics in England, 1850–1867*, Durham, N.C., 1927, p. 270.
16 *Brierley Hill Advertiser*, 1 September 1866.
17 *Birmingham Journal*, 1 September 1866, and *Saturday Evening Post* (Birmingham), 1 September 1866.
18 Eric Taylor, 'The Working Class Movement in the Black Country, 1863–1914', Ph.D. thesis, University of Keele, 1973, chapter X, particularly pp. 361–9. For a list of provincial branches of the League in the Black Country, see Bell, 'The Reform League from its Origins to 1867', D.Phil. thesis, *op. cit.*, pp. 245–6. The Stourbridge branch does not appear in Bell's lists.
19 Taylor, *op. cit.*
20 *Brierley Hill Advertiser*, 22 September 1866, and *Stourbridge Observer*, 22 September 1866.
21 *Ibid.*
22 *Ibid.*
23 Howell's Letter Book, vol. I, p. 369 (Howell Collection).
24 Reform League Cash-Book, p. 13 (Howell Collection). After that day until the collapse of the League, no subscriptions from the Stourbridge branch can be found in the Reform League cash book.
25 *Brierley Hill Advertiser*, 3 November 1866.
26 *Ibid.*
27 *Ibid.*
28 *Reform League — List of Departments and Branches*, 1867 (Howell Collection). The Reform League had seven departments with 315 branches in July 1867.
29 *National Reform League Midland Department, 2nd Annual Report*, July 1867 (Howell Collection). T. J. Wilkinson came from the F.G.M.F.S. branch of Birmingham.

Conclusion

After I had completed most of my own research Charles More's valuable work, *Skill and the English Working Class, 1870–1914*, appeared. Even if More does not reveal the dialectic between 'skill' as manual dexterity and social ascription, he establishes the possibility of it. After analysing the acquisition of skill by labour aristocrats through the serving of apprenticeship in many industries, he refers to the growth of non-apprenticed skilled work. 'Because such work did away with the "closed" entry method of apprenticeship, and substituted training extending over a longer period, often well into adult life, it created a large class of workers who, although they might be classed and paid as semi-skilled, could expect with greater or lesser degrees of confidence to become skilled. The existence of this class of worker, although it is obvious enough, seems to have gone largely unremarked by historians.' 'One exception is Matsumura, who identified such a group among the flint glass workers, and who makes the valuable point, based on this observation, that membership of the labour aristocracy might depend on what period of his life-cycle a worker was in.'[1] Certainly I point out that it is in the lifetime experience, especially changes in wages, that distinguished the labour aristocracy from the lower orders. I have explained that the labour aristocracy was not simply a group of high wage-earners, although they were, but there was a high degree of occupational continuity over generations. They were an aristocracy of labour who inherited their fathers' skills in almost a literal sense and could expect steadily rising wages in their lifetime. Therefore not all flint glass makers belonged to the labour aristocracy. Most of the workmen and servitors would be counted as members, but not footmakers or takers-in. Foot-makers could be regarded as semi-skilled, but not as non-apprenticed skilled workers. Because of strict craft regulation preservation, there was no growth of semi-skilled workers in blown flint glass-making. It took place in pressed glass-making.

Yet there is a problem as to what extent the rise in wages of flint glass makers over a lifetime and the high degree of occupational continuity between generations can be generalised as characteristic in the *classic age* of the labour aristocracy as a whole. More complains that

unfortunately the flint glass workers are a bad example from which to generalise, because very few, if any, other workers, combined apprenticeship with seniority rules; it would be quite wrong to take the glassmakers' example to mean that most ex-apprentices had to continue as semi-skilled workers for a number of years after their apprenticeship, as the glass makers did; in many cases time-served workers earned the full rate immediately their apprenticeship ended, and in other cases they served for two or three years, not more, as improvers.[2]

As to promotion, More offers sketchy evidence. The skilled grades in spinning and in the iron, steel and tinplate industries were usually recruited by the promotion of less skilled workers. In spinning promotion was virtually guaranteed, while in milling large numbers of labourers were needed and not all could achieve promotion. In chemicals probably only a minority rose above the ranks of the semi-skilled. In cotton spinning, where there was no apprenticeship, the spinners were recruited from among piecers. Those who did not become spinners were obliged to seek other occupations, but did not necessarily become labourers. Yet whether flint glass makers are 'a bad example' or not cannot be determined without tracing the wage curve of other kinds of workers. Since wage data across a working lifetime in other industries have hardly been carefully preserved,[3] the problem remains unsolved.

It is important not simply to indicate, as More does, that 'the growth of non-apprenticed skilled work diluted the labour aristocracy',[4] but clarify the relationships between the labour aristocracy and semi-skilled and unskilled workers. What I have attempted in this book is the analysis of blown flint glass makers' attitudes towards glass cutters, bottle makers and pressed glass makers. At the workshop level, the attitudes of workmen and servitors towards footmakers and takers-in were the crucial ones. The celebrated 'superior' and often exploitative attitude of the labour aristocrat was prevalent in flint glass making. Takers-in were confined to auxiliary tasks. So far as boys' work was concerned, glass makers took the same line as the manufacturers. The most notable instance occurred when there was an attempt to raise the age limit to thirteen in 1875. The glass makers, like the manufacturers, opposed it strongly, because the proposed Bill would do 'a serious injury to the trade, as much as it creates very great inconvenience to the men'.[5] On this subject there was common ground between the glass makers and the manufacturers. So the *Flint Glass Makers Magazine* wrote of the evidence given by the manufacturers to the Factory and Workshops Acts Commission that 'our thanks are due to the Manufacturers, who so earnestly and consistently interested themselves in arresting a revolution of our trade, which if it had succeeded, would, in our opinion, have proved most disastrous in its consequences.'[6]

Consequently the flint glass makers, who thought of themselves as a monolithic group, tended to conceal the stratification between the groups in the chairs, despite the fact that the stratification itself provided the basic economic process of formation of a labour aristocracy. That such stratification existed, however, is illustrated by the Children's Employment Commission of 1865, which vividly described the worst working conditions, the ill treatment and the lack of education among takers-in in flint glass factories. But the *Magazine* tried to gloss over the report. It elaborated on the poor educational attainments of other types of glass workers: ' . . . from the published report of the bottle branch and sheet and crown branches deplorable as our conditions are as regards education, we have no hesitation in saying the boys at our trade would in general have shown a more respectable appearance than those examined in the above branches'.[7] Thus even their boys in the flint glass trade were described as a 'respectable' group distinguishable from those in other branches of the glass trade.

It is also too simplistic to suppose that privilege or unprivilege at work corresponded directly to status in the local community. The stratification within 'chairs' and even the difference between glass makers and cutters at the point of production seems to have diminished in social activities at public gatherings and festivities. Men stood as glass *workers* and consequently as a superior group in a small town where glass-making was the principal industry.

All working-class experience was 'local', but, particularly when national trade unions were established after the middle of the century, some (but not all) working men saw their local experiences in the context of national ones. As members of the local branch of the union, they tended to be involved in the national issues of the time. In the movement against the Master and Servant Acts one sees most clearly how contingencies of the governing branch of the union affected participation in national movements. The breaking of the contract of service by a workman was, by the Acts, a criminal offence, and the workman was to be punished by imprisonment or a fine.[8] Apart from the fact that, as with other working men, flint glass makers occasionally suffered under the Acts,[9] two accidents helped to connect the glass makers' union with the national movement against the law.

The headquarters of the F.G.M.F.S. was in Glasgow between 1863 and 1866, from where the movement against the law sprang in February 1863, because the law was most oppressive in Scotland. Benjamin Smart of Glasgow served as the Central Secretary of the society. Alexander Campbell, as an honorary member, attended many relevant meetings as its representative. Chance played its part in the flint glass makers' involvement in the struggle against the Acts and chance explained why that involvement was so short-lived. Once the amended Act of 1867 passed,[10] the F.G.M.F.S. lost interest in further agitation.

The flint glass makers took part not only in the movement against the Master and Servant Acts but in the agitation for parliamentary reform and educational reform in the 1860s. They financially helped workers on strike in other industries. They even helped the glass cutters when they went on strike in 1865. However, all this is one side of the coin, which shows class consciousness. The other side implies exclusiveness and self-interest. As already shown, to protect their organisation and its accumulated fund they never amalgamated with cutters or bottle makers or pressed glass makers. Similarly they never affiliated to the local trades council until its debt was paid. Since the F.G.M.F.S. supported George Potter's group, it played an important role in the early stage of the Trades Union Congress.

T. J. Wilkinson, the Birmingham flint glass maker, was given 'the higher honour' as president at the second Congress of 1869, and the Congress itself was successful, but the Birmingham Trades Council, the organiser of the Congress of 1869, was left in debt. 'It was not until September 1870 that the amount of rent (five pounds) of the Congress meeting room was paid,'[11] so that the F.G.M.F.S. of Birmingham did not affiliate to the trades council until September 1870.[12] The affiliation of the wealthy New Model-type union was welcomed: 'It is always darkest before the dawn and soon the dawn could be seen approaching. It was at this period that the Flint Glass Makers' Society became affiliated.'[13]

The question whether the labour aristocracy was 'progressive' or 'conservative' and whether there was a continuity in the world of labour between the second and third quarters of the nineteenth century cannot be solved by concentrating on one small group of workers. Probably which side of the coin appeared stronger depended on complex factors such as the trade situation, regional variety, the period and the question with which the workers were involved. It is contended here that in the labour process they were the most conservative towards any change of the existing ways, so that at the point of production there tended to be a continuity between before and after mid-century. But politically discontinuity appeared sharply. Politically the labour aristocracy might in certain circumstances have played a progressive role in the third quarter of the century.

Notes

1 Charles More, *Skill and the English Working Class, 1870–1914*, London, 1980, p. 232.
2 *Ibid.*
3 The lifetime wage curves of engineers, carpenters, compositors, railway signalmen, railway platelayers and dockside labourers are shown in J. A. Spender, *The State and Pensions in Old Age*, London, 1892, pp. 25–45, but places and dates of these trends are not identified.
4 More, *Skill and the English Working Class*, p. 231.
5 *Royal Commission on Factory and Workshops Acts*, 1876, vol. II, p. 455, q. 9201.
6 *Flint Glass Makers Magazine*, VIII, pp. 333–4. When it became clear in 1877 that the Factory and Workshops Bill would prohibit the

employment at night of young persons under fourteen years of age in glass-making, a joint deputation consisting of three each from the glass makers and manufacturers tried to persuade the Home Secretary to stop the Bill (*Capital and Labour*, 6 June 1877).

7 *Flint Glass Makers Magazine*, V, p. 591. As to the educational attainments of takers-in in the flint glass trade, see J. B. Jeffery (ed.), *Labour's Formative Years, 1849–1879*, London, 1948, p. 157.

8 See D. Simon, 'Master and servant', in J. Saville (ed.), *Democracy and the Labour Movement*, London, 1954, pp. 160–200.

9 One of the worst cases revealed was that of Thomas O'Brien, a flint glass maker (servitor) of Glasgow. After giving his fortnight's notice to quit, according to the rules of the trade, he left Glasgow and got a job in Manchester. Thereafter the employers 'made an application, according to the Act, got a warrant, sent a criminal officer from Glasgow to Manchester, took him away from his work in Manchester, carried him, without any information on the warrant, across all the counties between Manchester and Glasgow, and brought him to trial' (*Select Committee on Master and Servant*, 1866 (P.P. XIII), p. 16). The case was noted by Alexander Campbell on 30 July 1866.

10 The amended Act of 1867 was 'the first positive success of the Trade Unions in the legislative field' (Webb, *History of Trade Unionism*, p. 253), but, as G. D. H. Cole pointed out, the Act still left the master and workman unequal parties, by retaining the criminal taint attached to breach of contract by a 'servant' (G. D. H. Cole and A. W. Filson (ed.), *British Working Class Movements. Select Documents, 1789–1875*, London, 1951, pp. 552–3).

11 *A Historical Sketch of the Birmingham Trades Council, 1860–1926*, Birmingham, 1927, pp. 7–8.

12 Birmingham Trades Council Minute Book, vol. I (1867–73), 2 September 1870.

13 *A Historical Sketch of the Birmingham Trades Council*, op. cit., p. 8.

Appendix
Membership of the F.G.M.F.S., 1852–81

Source. The following three tables were compiled from the *Quarterly Report of the F.G.M.S.*, in *Flint Glass Makers Magazine*, I–XI.

Note. Members are those of the third quarter (June – August) in every year.

District	1852	1853	1854	1855	1856	1857	1858	1859	1860	1861
Barnsley	–	–	–	–	–	–	–	–	–	–
Bathgate	–	–	–	–	–	–	–	–	–	–
Belfast	19	22	21	18	14	12	9	8	4	4
Birmingham	186	194	193	181	210	259	274	256	256	261
Bolton	–	–	–	8	12	9	12	14	14	16
Bristol	6	6	6	6	11	11	12	8	7	7
Castleford	–	–	–	–	–	–	–	–	–	–
Catcliff	12	18	17	11	12	12	14	14	12	–
Dublin	21	21	11	15	13	18	16	18	17	16
Dudley	32	35	42	36	38	43	49	36	29	27
Edinburgh	25	17	19	26	25	40	40	40	49	72
Glasgow	48	58	54	53	60	59	67	53	55	53
Haverton Hill	8	11	10	11	5	2	3	1	–	–
Hunslet	–	–	–	–	–	–	–	–	33	28
Kilnhurst	–	–	–	–	–	–	–	–	–	8
Knottingley	–	–	–	–	–	–	–	–	–	–
Leith Walk	12	13	14	13	13	–	–	–	–	–
London	73	45	27	28	32	31	40	41	33	35
Longport	–	6	7	7	9	10	10	9	11	20
Manchester	79	71	87	76	70	102	120	157	147	163
Newcastle	76	85	72	62	81	84	93	100	108	102
Newton	–	–	–	–	–	–	–	–	–	–
Rotherham	22	23	29	33	47	38	50	50	50	77
Shelton	–	–	–	–	–	–	–	22	27	26
South Shields	–	–	32	36	19	16	12	11	–	–
St. Helens	53	73	52	22	45	41	35	34	22	45
Stourbridge	137	133	200	153	221	259	273	286	287	276
Swinton	–	–	–	–	–	12	–	–	–	–
Tutbury	24	24	24	23	24	24	23	23	22	21
Warrington	31	37	50	43	45	34	53	56	58	56
Wordsbrodale	12	11	10	11	10	10	12	19	20	14
York	61	36	43	40	41	48	53	62	39	42
Totals	937	939	1,020	912	1,057	1,174	1,270	1,318	1,300	1,369

District	1862	1863	1864	1865	1866	1867	1868	1869	1870	1871
Barnsley	–	–	–	–	–	–	–	–	–	–
Bathgate	–	–	–	–	17	21	17	16	22	21
Belfast	5	2	1	5	2	2	–	–	–	–
Birmingham	265	279	291	297	293	299	304	318	334	340
Bolton	18	22	25	28	31	8	9	11	8	12
Bristol	9	9	8	13	9	8	10	–	3	4
Castleford	–	–	–	–	–	–	–	–	–	–
Catcliff	–	–	–	–	–	–	–	–	–	–
Dublin	15	21	24	25	24	26	25	23	23	19
Dudley	29	24	24	26	27	28	30	26	22	26
Edinburgh	59	64	70	71	54	70	82	88	67	72
Glasgow	53	56	62	70	68	85	79	87	86	76
Haverton Hill	–	–	–	–	–	–	–	–	–	–
Hunslet	31	26	48	41	50	58	46	50	51	48
Kilnhurst	8	8	7	21	23	22	19	20	18	19
Knottingley	–	–	–	–	–	–	–	–	–	–
Leith Walk	–	–	–	–	–	–	–	–	–	–
London	32	41	43	50	49	52	52	55	54	52
Longport	19	19	20	23	23	24	20	20	20	21
Manchester	171	202	251	268	276	310	308	312	320	325
Newcastle	113	103	83	70	80	85	82	68	82	76
Newton	–	–	–	–	–	–	–	6	17	–
Rotherham	58	71	69	56	62	66	62	67	68	70
Shelton	26	31	28	27	24	25	27	27	22	24
South Shields	–	–	–	–	–	–	–	–	–	–
St. Helens	41	53	46	54	37	48	56	56	58	51
Stourbridge	275	281	284	279	280	288	286	295	298	323
Swinton	–	–	–	–	–	–	–	–	–	–
Tutbury	24	24	24	36	52	55	31	45	26	43
Warrington	49	61	74	87	92	71	58	60	92	102
Wordsbrodale	13	12	12	11	11	11	11	12	12	14
York	51	43	51	54	56	57	53	59	59	61
Totals	1,364	1,452	1,545	1,612	1,640	1,719	1,667	1,721	1,762	1,799

District	1872	1873	1874	1875	1876	1877	1878	1879	1880	1881
Barnsley	–	–	–	17	29	35	36	36	38	42
Bathgate	22	23	23	23	23	24	19	18	19	21
Belfast	–	–	–	–	–	–	–	–	–	–
Birmingham	321	340	354	362	346	343	351	346	345	351
Bolton	13	19	26	27	27	26	25	15	11	23
Bristol	4	2	3	3	5	5	5	5	6	4
Castleford	–	–	15	22	18	33	36	25	23	25
Catcliff	10	10	9	10	10	10	10	9	9	8
Dublin	19	16	16	16	16	14	17	18	10	22
Dudley	30	23	26	25	23	24	24	26	29	25
Edinburgh	67	63	61	60	65	81	71	54	74	77
Glasgow	82	72	80	76	68	90	83	82	80	80
Haverton Hill	–	–	–	–	–	–	–	–	–	–
Hunslet	53	64	53	74	78	65	54	61	52	44
Kilnhurst	20	16	15	13	15	14	12	14	15	15
Knottingley	–	9	10	9	11	12	14	14	15	15
Leith Walk	–	–	–	–	–	–	–	–	–	–
London	52	49	50	72	81	89	82	79	66	61
Longport	22	21	20	20	21	20	21	21	20	19
Manchester	333	317	315	341	360	379	355	350	344	305
Newcastle	74	100	113	100	97	105	104	104	99	98
Newton	19	21	20	–	–	–	15	15	17	24
Rotherham	60	63	65	58	54	54	55	48	46	44
Shelton	30	32	31	29	27	29	21	27	4	2
South Shields	–	–	–	–	–	–	–	–	–	–
St. Helens	59	64	54	53	51	35	33	31	41	39
Stourbridge	325	329	332	353	371	330	388	403	399	389
Swinton	–	–	–	–	–	–	–	–	–	–
Tutbury	53	47	54	59	53	56	52	54	50	45
Warrington	96	100	109	95	89	81	80	85	81	81
Wordsbrodale	14	15	15	–	–	–	–	–	–	–
York	62	60	64	77	92	84	80	86	84	78
Totals	1,840	1,875	1,933	1,994	2,030	2,088	2,043	2,026	1,977	1,937

Select bibliography

Primary sources

I. *The Flint Glass Makers' Magazine* and Rules and Regulations of the F.G.M.F.S.

1. *Magazine.* A complete set from 1851 to 1897, bound in twenty-one volumes, is held by Mr J. R. Price, 4 Prospect Hill, Stourbridge, Worcestershire. This set was microfilmed and is in the possession of the library of the University of Warwick. The volumes which are concerned with my research are as follows: I, 1851–53; II, 1853–57; III, 1857–60; IV, 1860–63; V, 1863–67; VI, 1867–71; VII, 1871–74 (new series, vol. 1); VIII, 1874–77 (new series, vol. 2); IX, 1877–79 (new series, vol. 3); X, 1879–80 (new series, vol. 4); XI, 1880–81 (new series, vol. 5). The Stourbridge Reference Library possesses vols. I and II (1851–57), vol. VIII (November 1876 only) and vol. IX (May 1877 only.) The Howell Collection in the Bishopsgate Institute, London, holds vol. VI (September 1869 – Special issue for the second T.U.C. – only) and vol. VII (August and October 1874 only). The Webb Trade Union Collection at the British Library of Political and Economic Science, London School of Economics, London, holds vol. IX (August 1879 only), six issues between August 1887 and February 1893, and ten continuous issues from January 1895 to April 1897. The archive of the Beatson & Clark Glass Company of Rotherham holds vol. IX (May 1878 only).

2. *Rules and Regulations*

Articles, Laws, and Rules of the Glass-Makers' Friendly Society, held at the House of Mr. William Wilson, Newcastle upon Tyne, 1800, (British Library).

Rules and Regulations of the Flint Glass Makers' Friendly Society of Great Britain and Ireland, revised at the Conference, held in London, June 15th, 16th, 17th, 18th, and 19th, 1858 (Brierley Hill Public Library).

Rules and Regulations of the Flint Glass Makers' Friendly Society of Great Britain and Ireland, revised and corrected April, 1859 (Birmingham Reference Library).

Rules and Regulations of the National Flint Glass Makers' Sick and

Friendly Society of Great Britain and Ireland, revised and corrected June 1867; in R.C. on Trade Unions, 11th and Final Report, 1868–69 (P.P.XXXI), vol. II, appendix, pp. 259–62.

Rules and Regulations of the National Flint Glass Makers' Sick and Friendly Society of Great Britain and Ireland, revised and corrected at Trades Conference, held at Manchester, July 16th, 17th, 18th and 20th, 1874, third edition, 1879. (Webb Coll., Section C, vol. 42, X, at the British Library of Political and Economic Science, London School of Economics.)

Rules of the London Glass Blowers' Trade Society, 1875 (Webb Coll., Section , vol. 42, IV).

Rules of the United Flint Glass Cutters' Mutual Assistance and Protective Society, 1887 (Webb Coll., Section C, vol. 42, VIII).

Rules and Regulations of the Pressed Glass Makers' Friendly Society of the North of England, February 17, 1872, revised in April 1874 (Webb Coll., Section C, vol. 42, XVI, XVII).

II. *Manuscript sources*

1. *Notebooks in the Webb Trade Union Collection at the British Library of Political and Economic Science, London School of Economics* (Section A, vol. XLIV): (a) Flint Glass Makers, pp. 1–256; (b) Glass Blowers, pp. 257–60; (c) Glass Bottle Makers, pp. 261–332; (d) Plate Glass Bevellers, pp. 333–50; (e) Flint Glass Cutters, pp. 351–97; (f) Window Glass Workers, Pressed Glass Makers, Glass Founders, Glass Painters, etc., pp. 398–408.

2. *Wages books*
   (a) Stevens & Williams of Stourbridge, in the archive of the Brierley Hill Crystal Company, Brierley Hill.
   (b) Beatson & Clark of Rotherham, in the archive of Beatson Clark & Co. Ltd, Rotherham.
   (c) Wood Bros of Barnsley, in Sheffield Central Library.

3. *Census records at the Public Record Office*
   Census Enumerators' Books of 1861, Stourbridge
   Census Enumerators' Books of 1851, and 1871, Stourbridge (Amblecote).

4. *Marriage registers*
   (a) *Parish Registers and Records of Old Swinford, Stourbridge, Worcestershire*, in Worcestershire County Record Office (microfilm, vols. 31–46.)
   (b) *Register of Marriages, St. Mary's Church in the Parish of Kingswinford, Staffordshire*, in Dudley Reference Library (3 vols.)
   (c) *Register of Marriages, St. James' Church in the Parish of Wollaston, Worcestershire*, in St. James's Church (1 vol.)
   (d) *Register of Marriages, Trinity Church in the Parish of Amblecote, Staffordshire*, in Trinity Church (3 vols.)

5. *Other manuscript sources*
   (a) *Birmingham Reference Library*
   Birmingham Trades Council Minutes Book, vol. I (1869–73).
   Dealey, R. M., Reminiscences, n.d.
   Letters, Accounts, Documents, etc., relating to the Union Glass
   Works, Dartmouth Street, Birmingham, 1817–82.
   (b) *Bishopsgate Institute, Howell Collection*
   Howell's Letter Book, vol. I and vol. II.
   Reform League Cash Book.
   (c) *Brierley Hill Public Library*
   Letters in the Trade Union file; in the Special Collection on
   Glass.
   (d) *Staffordshire County Record Office*
   Rates Book of Amblecote in 1861.
   Log Book of Wordsley School, vol. I (1863–73)
   (e) *Worcestershire County Record Office*
   Log Book of 3t Thomas Boys School, Stourbridge, vol. I.

III. *Official reports*

Children's Employment Commission, 2nd Report, 1843 [430] XIII;
   Appendix to 2nd Report, Part I, 1843 [431] XIV; Appendix to 2nd
   Report, Part II, 1843 [432] XV.
Children's Employment Commission, 4th Report, 1865 [3548] XX.
Select Committee, Contracts for Service of Master, Servants and Work-
   men, 1866 [449] XIII.
Royal Commission on Trade Unions, 10th Report, 1867–68 [3980–VI]
   XXXIX. 11th and Final Report, 1868–69 [4123] XXXI.
Royal Commission on Factory and Workshop Acts, vol. 1, Report and
   Appendix, 1876 [C. 1443] XXIX; vol. V, Minutes of Evidence, 1876
   [C. 1443–7] XXX.
Factory Inspectors' Reports, 1880 [C. 2489] XIV; 1881 [C. 2825] XXIII.
Labour Statistics – Return of Rates of Wages, 1887 [C. 5172] LXXXIX.

IV. *Newspapers and periodicals*

*Alliance News, Bee-Hive, Birmingham and General Advertiser,
Birmingham Daily Post, Birmingham Journal, Birmingham Mercury,
Brierley Hill Advertiser, Brierley Hill and Stourbridge Gazette, Capital
and Labour, Commonwealth, Gateshead Observer, Glasgow Sentinel,
Globe, Manchester Guardian, Midland Advertiser and Birmingham
Times, Morning Chronicle, Newcastle Daily Chronicle, Newcastle
Daily Journal, Northern Star, Operative* (1851–52, British Library), *Pottery Gazette, Reynolds's Newspaper, Saturday Evening Post*
(Birmingham), *Scotsman, Stourbridge Observer.*

V. *Other sources*

An Account of the Receipts and Expenditure of the Glass Makers'

Friendly Society. From December 30 1835 to July 28 1837, 1837. (Brierley Hill Public Library.)

A Circular from the Brierley Hill Glass Works to Glass Manufacturers, October 26 1858. (Archive of the Brierley Hill Crystal Company.)

The Glass Washers' Lockout, An Appeal to the Servant Girls of the United Kingdom on Behalf of the Flint Glass Washers' Friendly Society Fellow Working Girls, Sturbrig [sic], January 13 1859. (Brierley Hill Public Library and Birmingham Reference Library.)

London Trades' Council to the Trades' Societies Generally, 1866. (Howell Collection).

Mr. Potter and the London Trades' Council, 1865. (Howell Collection.)

National Reform League Midland Department, 2nd Annual Report, July 1867. (Howell Collection.)

Reform League – List of Departments and Branches, 1867. (Howell Collection.)

Reform League Notes (Howell Collection)

Register of Apprentices, Bound or Assigned by the Board of Guardians of the Stourbridge Union (Staffordshire County Record Office).

Report of Conference on the Laws of Masters and Workmen under their Contracts of Service, held in London on 30th, 31st May and 1st and 2nd June 1864. Glasgow, 1864. (Webb Coll. Section B. vol. II, 3.)

Report of a Meeting of Master Cutters in 1845. (Stourbridge Reference Library.)

To the Glass Masters of the Stourbridge and Wordsley District, March 30 1872. (Brierley Hill Library.)

Secondary sources

I. Books and pamphlets quoted

Armstrong, W. *et al.* (ed.), *The Industrial Resources of the District of the Three Northern Rivers*, 2nd edition, London, 1864.

Allen, G. C., *The Industrial Development of Birmingham and the Black Country, 1860–1927*, London, 1929.

Barker T. C., *Pilkington Brothers and the Glass Industry*, London, 1960.

—, *The Glassmakers. Pilkington: the Rise of an International Company, 1826–1976*, London, 1977.

Barnsby, G., *The Working Class Movement in the Black Country, 1750 to 1976*, Wolverhampton, 1977.

—, *Social Conditions in the Black Country, 1800–1900*, Wolverhampton, 1980.

Baxter, D., *The National Income*, London, 1868.

Beatson, Clark & Co. Ltd, *The Glass Works, Rotherham, 1751–1951*, Rotherham, 1952.

Bienefeld, M. A., *Working Hours in British Industry: An Economic History*, London, 1972.

Booth, C., *Life and Labour of the People in London*, 2nd ser.: Industry, vol. II, London, 1902–04.

Bremner, D., *The Industries of Scotland. Their Rise, Progress, and Present Condition*, Edinburgh, 1869.

Briggs, A. (with Saville, J.) (ed.), *Essays in Labour History*, vol. I, London, 1960.

___, *History of Birmingham*, vol. II, London, 1952.

___, *Victorian People*, London, 1954.

Burritt, E., *Walks in the Black Country and its Grey Border-land*, London, 1868.

Chart, D. A., *An Economic History of Ireland*, Dublin, 1920.

Cole, G. D. H. (with Filson, A. W.) (ed.), *A History of British Trade Unions since 1889*, London, 1964.

___, *The Payment of Wages*, London, 1918.

___, *Studies in Class Structure*, London, 1955.

Corbett, J., *The Birmingham Trades Council, 1866–1966*, London 1966.

Court, W. H. B., *The Rise of the Midland Industries, 1600–1838*, Oxford, 1938.

Crossick, G., *An Artisan Elite in Victorian Society. Kentish London, 1840–1880*, London, 1978.

Dent, R. K., *Old and New Birmingham*, Birmingham 1879.

Dobbs, S. P., *The Clothing Workers of Great Britain*, London, 1928.

Engels, F., *The Condition of the Working Class in England*, 1845, trans. and ed. W. O. Henderson and W. H. Chaloner, 2nd edition, Oxford, 1971.

Enville, E. M., *English and Irish Cut Glass, 1750–1950*, London, 1953.

Foster, J., *Class Struggle and the Industrial Revolution. Early Industrial Capitalism in three English Towns*, London, 1974.

Fraser, L., *Pressed Glass. A Short History of Geo. Davidson & Co. Ltd., 1867–1948*, Newcastle 1948.

Fraser, W. H., *Trade Unions and Society. The Struggle for Acceptance, 1850–1880*, London, 1974.

Fyrth, H. J., and Collins, H., *The Foundry Workers*, Manchester, 1959.

Gammage, R.G., *History of the Chartist Movement, 1837–1854*, 1894 edition, Newcastle upon Tyne.

Gillespie, F. E., *Labour and Politics in England, 1850–1867*, Durham, N.C., 1927.

Gillinder, W., *A Treatise on the Art of Glassmaking*, Birmingham, 1851.

Glass Bottle Makers of Yorkshire United Trade Protection Society, *The Quarterly Report*, No. XLVIII.

Glossary of Terms used in the Glass Industry, British Standards Institution, n.d.

Godfrey, E. S., _The Development of English Glassmaking, 1560–1640_, Oxford, 1976.

Gosling, H., _Up and Down Stream_, London, 1927.

Gray, R. Q., _The Labour Aristocracy in Victorian Edinburgh_, Oxford, 1976.

Guttery, D. R., _From Broad-glass to Cut Crystal. A History of the Stourbridge Glass Industry_, London, 1956.

Haden, H. J., _The Stourbridge Glass Industry in the 19th Century_, Black Country Society, 1971.

Harrison, B., _Dictionary of British Temperance Biography_, Society for the Study of Labour History, 1973.

—, _Drink and the Victorians_, London, 1971.

Harrison, R. J., _Before the Socialists. Studies in Labour and Politics, 1861–1881_, London, 1965.

Hartshorne, A., _Old English Glasses_, London and New York, 1897.

—, _A Historical Sketch of the Birmingham Trades Council, 1860–1926_, Birmingham, 1927.

Hobsbawm, E. J., _Labouring Men. Studies in the History of Labour_, London, 1964.

—, _Revolutionaries. Contemporary Essays_, London. 1973.

Hodgson, G. B., _The Borough of South Shields_, Newcastle, 1903.

Howell, G., _The Conflicts of Capital and Labour_, 2nd edition, London, 1890.

—, _Labour Legislation, Labour Movement and Labour Leaders_, London, 1902.

Humphrey, A. W., _Robert Applegarth. Trade Unionist, Educationist, Reformer_, Manchester and London, 1913.

Jefferys, J. B., _The Story of the Engineers, 1880–1945_, London, 1946.

—, _Labour's Formative Years, 1849–1879_, London, 1948.

Johnston, T., _The History of the Working Classes in Scotland_, Glasgow, 1929.

Joyce, P., _Work, Society and Politics. The Culture of the Factory in late Victorian England_, Brighton, 1980.

Kenyon, G. H., _The Glass Industry of the Weald_, Leicester, 1967.

Lauderdale, J. B., 'History of Sowerby's Ellison Glass Works, Limited, (typescript), n.d.

Lenin V. I., _Imperialism and the Split in Socialism_, 1916; Collected Works, Moscow, 1964, vol. XXIII, pp. 105–20.

Leventhal, F. M., _Respectable Radical. George Howell and Victorian Working Class Politics_, London, 1971.

Lohri, A. (ed.), _Household Words_, Toronto, 1973.

Macdougall, I. (ed.), _The Minutes of Edinburgh Trades Council 1859–1873_, Edinburgh, 1968.

Mackearin, G. S. and H., _American Glass_, New York, 1941.

Marwick, W. H., _Alexander Campbell_, Glasgow, 1963.

Marx, K., _Capital_, vol. I, English edition, London, 1889.

Middlebrook, S., _Newcastle upon Tyne. Its Growth and Achievement_, Newcastle upon Tyne, 1950.

More, C., *Skill and the English Working Class, 1870–1914*, London, 1980.

Musson, A. E., *British Trade Unions, 1800–1875*, London, 1972.

—, *Trade Union and Social History*, London, 1974.

National Association for the Promotion of Social Science, *Trades' Societies and Strikes*, London, 1860.

—, *The Report of the Social Science Association, 1863*, 1863.

Newcastle and District. An Epitome of Results and Manual of Commerce, Newcastle upon Tyne, 1889.

Pelling, H., *Popular Politics and Society in Late Victorian Britain*, London, 1968.

Perlman, S., *A Theory of the Labor Movement*, New York, 1928.

Phillips, R., *A Dictionary of the Arts of Life and Civilization*, London, 1833.

Postgate, R. W., *The Builders' History*, London, 1923.

Powell, H. J., *Glass-making in England*, Cambridge, 1923.

—, *et al.*, *The Principles of Glass-making*, London, 1883.

Pratt, E. A., *Trade Unionism and British Industry*, London, 1904.

Reports of Artisans, selected by a Committee appointed by the Council of the Society of Arts to visit the Paris Universal Exhibition, 1867, London, 1867.

Price, R., *Masters, Unions and Men. Work Control in Building and the Price of Labour, 1830–1914*, Cambridge, 1880.

Revi, A. C., *American Pressed Glass and Figure Bottles*, New York, 1964.

Ridley, U., 'The History of Glass Making on the Tyne and Wear' (typescript), n.d.

Rothstein, T., *From Chartism to Labourism*, London, 1929.

Salmon, T., *South Shields. Past, Present and Future*, South Shields, 1856.

Saville, J. (ed.), *Democracy and the Labour Movement*, London, 1954.

—, *Ernest Jones: Chartist*, London, 1952.

Schloss, D. F., *Methods of Industrial Remuneration*, London, 1892.

Simms, R., *Contributions towards a History of Glass Making and Glass Makers in Staffordshire*, Wolverhampton, 1894.

Spender J. A., *The State and Pensions in Old Age*, London, 1892.

Stedman Jones, G., *Outcast London. A Study in the Relationship between Classes in Victorian Society*, Oxford, 1971.

Tate, G. K., and Jacobs, J., *London Trades Council, 1860–1950*, London, 1950.

Tholfsen T. R., *Working Class Radicalism in Mid-Victorian England*, London, 1977.

Timmins, S. (ed.), *Birmingham and the Midland Hardware District*, London, 1866.

United Kingdom First Annual Trades' Directory, 1861.

Ure, A., *Dictionary of Arts, Manufactures and Mines*, vol. I, London, 1853.

Victoria History of the County of Durham, vol. II, 1907; *Stafford*, vol. II, 1967; *Warwick*, vol. II, 1908; *Worcester*, vol. II, 1906.

Wakefield, H. G., *Nineteenth Century British Glass*, London, 1961.

Ward, J., *The World in its Workshops*, London, 1851.

Watkins, L. W., *American Glass and Glass Making*, London, 1950.

Webb, S. and B., *The History of Trade Unionism*, London, 1894 and 1920 editions.

—, *Industrial Democracy*, London, 1901 and 1920 editions.

Welbourne, E., *The Miners' Unions of Northumberland and Durham*, Cambridge, 1923.

West, J., *A History of the Chartist Movement*, London, 1920.

Westropp, M. S. D., *Irish Glass*, London, 1920.

Winskill, P. T., *The Temperance Movement and its Workers*, vol. II, London, 1891.

Worshipful Company of Glass Sellers of London, *Essays on the Glass Trade in England*, London, 1883.

II. *Articles quoted*

Allen, V. L., 'Abstract of "a methodological criticism of the Webbs as trade union historians"', *Bulletin of the Society for the Study of Labour History*, No. IV, spring 1962, pp. 4–6.

—, 'Valuations and historical interpretation', *British Journal of Sociology*, XIV, 1963, pp. 48–58.

Barnsby, G., 'The standard of living in the Black Country during the nineteenth century', *Economic History Review*, 2nd ser., XXIV, 1971, pp. 220–39.

Buckly, F., 'The early glasshouses of Bristol', *Journal of the Society of Glass Technology*, IX, 1925, pp. 36–61.

Clements, R. V., 'Trade unions and emigration, 1840–80', *Population Studies*, IX, 1955, pp. 167–80.

Clephan, J., 'Manufacture of glass in England: rise of the art on the Tyne', *Archaeologia Aeliana*, new ser. VIII, 1880, pp. 180–226.

Cole, G. D. H., 'Some note on British trade unionism in the third quarter of the nineteenth century', *International Review of Social History*, II, Leiden, 1937, pp. 1–25. Reprinted in Carus-Wilson, E. M. (ed.), *Essays in Economic History*, vol. III, London, 1962, pp. 202–20.

Coltham, S., 'The *Bee-Hive* Newspaper: its origin and early struggles', in Briggs, A., and Saville J. (ed.), *Essays in Labour History*, vol. I, London, 1960, pp. 174–204.

—, 'George Potter, the Junta, and the *Bee-Hive*', *International Review of Social History*, 2nd ser., IX, 1964, pp. 391–432, and X, 1965, pp. 23–65.

Cookson Glass Works, Newcastle, 'A day at a glass factory', *Penny Magazine*, XIII, No. 786, June 1844, supplement, pp. 249–56.

Erickson, C., 'The encouragement of emigration by British trade unions, 1850–1900', *Population Studies*, III, 1949–50, pp. 248–73.

Field, J., 'British historians and the concept of the labour aristocracy', *Radical History Review*, XIX, winter 1978–79, pp. 61–85.

Hanson, C. G., 'Craft unions, welfare benefits, and the case for trade union law reform, 1867–75', *Economic History Review*, 2nd ser., XXVIII, 1975, pp. 243–59.

Harrison, G., 'Stourbridge fireclay', in Timmins (ed.), *Birmingham and the Midland Hardware District*, London, 1866.

Harrison, R. J., review of Pelling's *Popular Politics and Society in Late Victorian Britain*, *Victorian Studies*, XIII, 1970, pp. 364–66.

Hobsbawm, E. J., 'The labour aristocracy in nineteenth-century Britain', in *Labouring Men. Studies in the History of Labour*, London, 1964, pp. 272–315.

—, 'Lenin and the aristocracy of labour', in *Revolutionaries. Contemporary Essays*, London, 1973, pp. 121–9.

—, review of Pelling's *Popular Politics and Society in Late Victorian Britain*, *Bulletin of the Society for the Study of Labour History*, No. XVIII, spring 1969, p. 52.

Hopkins, E., 'An anatomy of strikes in the Stourbridge glass industry, 1850–1914', *Midland History*, II, 1973–74, pp. 21–31.

—, 'Changes in the scale of the industrial unit in Stourbridge and district, 1815–1914', *West Midland Studies*, VIII, 1976, pp. 30–5.

—, 'Small town aristocrats of labour and their standard of living, 1840–1914', *Economic History Review*, 2nd ser., XXVIII, 1975, pp. 222–42.

—, 'Working conditions in Victorian Stourbridge', *International Review of Social History*, new ser., XIX, 1974, pp. 401–25.

Lushington, G., 'An account of the strike of the Flint Glass Makers in 1858–59', in National Association for the Promotion of Social Science, *Trades' Societies and Strikes*, London, 1860.

[Martineau, H.], 'Birmingham Glass Works', *Household Words*, V, No. 105, 1852, pp. 32–8.

—, 'Secret organisation of trades', *Edinburgh Review*, CX, 1859, pp. 525–63.

Marwick, W. H., 'Scottish social pioneers, VI: Alexander Campbell', *Scottish Education Journal*, 26 February 1932, pp. 260–61.

Musson, A. E., 'The Webbs and their phasing of trade-union development between the 1830s and the 1860s', *Bulletin of the Society for the Study of Labour History*, No. IV, spring 1962, pp. 6–8.

Neal, R. S., 'The standard of living, 1780–1844: a regional and class study', *Economic History Review*, 2nd ser., XIX, 1966, pp. 590–606.

Osler, F. and C., 'British industries: III, Glass', *Tinsley's Magazine*, August 1889, pp. 343–53.

Pellatt Glass Works, London, 'A Day at a flint glass factory', *Penny Magazine*, X, No. 572, February 1841, supplement, pp. 81–8.

Pelling H., 'The concept of the labour aristocracy', in *Popular Politics and Society in late Victorian Britain*, London, 1968.

Potter, G., 'Strikes and lock-outs, from the workman's point of view', *Contemporary Review*, XV, August 1870, pp. 543–66.

Reid, D. A., 'The decline of Saint Monday, 1766–1876', *Past and Present*, LXXI, 1976, pp. 76–101.

Sandilands, D. N., 'The early history of glass-making in the Stourbridge district', *Journal of the Society of Glass Technology*, XV, 1931, pp. 219–27.

—, 'The last fifty years of the excise duty on glass', *Journal of the Society of Glass Technology*, XV, 1931, pp. 231–45.

Simon, D., 'Master and servant', in Saville (ed.), *Democracy and the Labour Movement*, London, 1954, pp. 160–200.

Swinburne, R., 'The manufacture of glass', in Armstrong *et al.* (ed.), *The Industrial Resources of the District of the Three Northern Rivers*, 2nd edition, London, 1864.

Turner, W. E. S., 'The British glass industry: its development and outlook', *Journal of the Society of Glass Technology*, VI, 1922, pp. 108–46.

Waley, J., 'On strikes and combinations, with reference to wages and the conditions of labour', *Journal of the Statistical Society*, XXX, March 1867, pp. 1–20.

Woodward, H. W., 'The glass industry of the Stourbridge district', *West Midland Studies*, VIII, 1976, pp. 36–42.

III. *Theses*

Barnsby, G. J., 'Social Conditions in the Black Country in the Nineteenth century', Ph.D., University of Birmingham, 1969.

—, 'The Working-class Movement in the Black Country, 1815 to 1867', M.A., University of Birmingham, 1965.

Bell, A. D., 'The Reform League from its Origins to 1867', D.Phil., University of Oxford, 1961.

Brown, C. M., 'Changes in the Location of the British Glass Industry since about 1833', Ph.D., University of London, 1970.

Brundage, D., 'The Glass Bottle Makers of Yorkshire and the Lock-out of 1893', M.A., University of Warwick, 1976.

Coltham, S., 'George Potter and the *Bee-Hive* Newspaper', D.Phil., University of Oxford, 1956.

Crossick, G., 'Social Structure and Working-class Behaviour: Kentish London, 1840–1880', Ph.D., University of London, 1976.

Fraser, W. H., 'Trades Councils in England and Scotland, 1818–1897', Ph.D., University of Sussex, 1967.

Gray, R. Q., 'Class Structure and the Class Formation of Skilled Workers in Edinburgh, *c.* 1850 – *c.* 1900', Ph.D., University of Edinburgh 1971.

Hopkins, E., 'The Working Classes of Stourbridge and District, 1815–1914', Ph.D., University of London, 1972.

Matsumura T., 'The Flint Glass Makers in the Classic Age of the Labour Aristocracy, 1850–1880, with Special Reference to Stourbridge', Ph.D., University of Warwick, 1976.

Moberg, D. R., 'George Odger and the English Working Class Movement: 1860–1877, Ph.D., University of London, 1953.

Sandilands, D. N., 'The History of the Midland Glass Industry, with Special Reference to the Flint Glass Section', M.Com., University of Birmingham, 1929.

Taylor, E., 'The Working Class Movement in the Black Country, 1863–1914', Ph.D., University of Keele, 1973.

Index